DATE DUE

MY 20 '02			
JE 10 '02			

Demco, Inc. 38-293

My Baseball Diary

My
Baseball
Diary

JAMES T. FARRELL

New Foreword by Joseph Durso

Southern Illinois University Press
Carbondale and Edwardsville

Library of Congress Cataloging-in-Publishing Data

Farrell, James T. (James Thomas), 1904–1979.

My baseball diary / James T. Farrell : new foreword by Joseph Durso.

p.   cm. — (Writing baseball)

Originally published: New York : A. S. Barnes, 1957.

1. Baseball. I. Title. II. Series

GV873.F32   1998

796.357—dc21

ISBN 0-8093-2189-0 (paper : alk. paper)

97-43794

CIP

The paper used in this publication meets the minimum requirements of American National Standard

for Information Sciences—Permanence of Paper for Printed Library Materials, ANSI Z39.48-1984.♾

Writing Baseball Series Editor: Richard Peterson

To my nephews

Jimmy Dillon, Bill Farrell, and Sean Holland

and to my son

Kevin Farrell

Contents

Foreword

Joseph Durso

One day in the summer of 1978, a wiry little seventy-five-year-old man wearing eyeglasses and a black beret walked into Central Park in New York carrying his Louisville Slugger baseball bat. He was James T. Farrell, and he wanted to get in a little batting practice.

When a man writes fifty-three books in less than fifty summers, he tends to get a bit rusty swinging the bat, especially if he is a switch-hitter with some power. So, Jim Farrell approached that problem the way any red-blooded American boy would: by grabbing his bat and heading for Central Park.

In Jim's case, the struggle between the athletic arts and the literary arts was decided early in his life. Although he won nine varsity letters in high school on the South Side of Chicago, he hit a kind of grand slam in his first turn at bat as an author by creating Studs Lonigan. And after that, though his baseball career suffered, the novels flowed from the pen of this gifted and wise person until a heart attack ended his life and both careers in his Manhattan apartment in 1979.

One of his circle of friends in baseball was Ralph Kiner, the home run king of the Pittsburgh Pirates for several years and a television broadcaster for the New York Mets for most of his life afterwards. Kiner, reflecting on Farrell's dual personality, said, "I'll tell you why James T. Farrell wrote books. He couldn't make it as a second baseman for the Chicago White Sox."

Jim Farrell, who saw his first major league game in 1911 in Comiskey Park and remembered that the White Sox lost it when Ty Cobb hit a home run through the slats of the picket fence in right

field for the Detroit Tigers, conceded Kiner's point: "It wasn't altogether a joke," he said.

Wherever he went, whatever he wrote, James T. Farrell always
kept this hankering for baseball. He saw maybe forty games each
season. He became a familiar figure on the field, in the dugout, and
in the press box. He could tell Johnny Bench how the old pitcher
Red Faber used to throw the spitball at five different speeds. He
also could remember when scorecards cost a nickel, only two
umpires officiated at a game, and the lineups were announced on
the field by a man with a megaphone. Yes, he also could remember
when the man with the megaphone at Wrigley Field in Chicago was
Pat Piper, who sat during games on a folding chair nestled against
the low brick facing of the box seats behind home plate, where he
frequently ducked foul balls, and who went to work after games at
his "other" job as a waiter in a downtown restaurant.

In his later years, Jim Farrell even attended spring training in
Florida. He would usually stay in St. Petersburg on the Gulf coast
with his sister Helen Dillon and would prowl around the nearby
camps, starting with the Mets. Or, he would hitch a ride down to
Sarasota to see the White Sox and sit in the sunshine with Bill
Veeck, swapping tales of old Chicago. Once, he spent some time
visiting the Yankees on Florida's east coast, back when they were
world champions again, and later he wrote this scouting report to
me: "The Yankees don't look good in Fort Lauderdale. It could be
that, as a team, they are collectively too old."

After one training game in Sarasota, he drove across the cause-
way and glided gracefully into his other life: the intellectual life.
Fresh from three hours of bantering with Veeck, the master show-
man, he spent the evening with an old friend, Meyer Schapiro, the
distinguished art historian of Columbia University. And Jim Farrell,
rocking on his heels with his arms clasped and his eyes flashing,
switched his mind from shortstops and pitchers to the great issues
of literature, art, and politics.

He was a fierce letter writer: anything from one sentence to
three pages, whenever he had a flash. Once, he wrote a flurry of
ideas to me on things like the Los Angeles Dodgers, the business
of books, and a Franklin Library edition of *Young Lonigan*, when he

suddenly added, "Meyer Schapiro remarked that one thing he liked about Lou Gehrig as a student is that, while Gehrig was so outstanding an athlete at Columbia, he didn't try to cut any corners on his school work and did his home work, conscientiously and carefully."

Then, realizing that I had written a book about the Gehrigs with Lou's wife, Eleanor, he added, "You might tell this to Eleanor Gehrig. After all, Meyer Schapiro is one of the most brilliant men of our times."

Another time, he opened a letter, without warning, with these words: "Baseball was very popular by the time of the Civil War. But it was not until 1876 that we got the organization of the National League. There is a reason why some time was needed: Besides the development of more skill in playing, the railroad system of the nation had to become fairly well organized, with lines connecting many towns and cities. By 1876, the railroad system in America made baseball feasible."

He was big for postscripts. After Reggie Jackson hit three home runs in the final game of the 1977 World Series, he wrote a letter on many literary topics, then added this note: "P.S. It all goes to show. You have to pitch him very fast and in spots where he'll swing and lose sight of the ball. Or else, he'll lose the ball."

Another time, at the end of a baseball letter, he wrote with a kind of shy pride: "P.S. I was nominated for the Nobel Prize."

In the final year of his life, television revived public interest in Studs Lonigan, and a torrent of honors deluged him. That amused him because he had written the book forty-five years earlier. But his obsession with baseball stayed. In an essay for *The American Scholar*, he wrote, "Some adults think that to watch baseball is to waste one's time in a childish way. But for some of us, there is a peculiar attraction to baseball. It has its own drama. I have always loved the game. I don't care whether or not it is childish."

That's why, in his seventy-fifth year, James T. Farrell walked over to Central Park for some batting practice.

"The Young People's Socialist League team had a game," he explained, "and I thought they might let me hit a few." They did. And then the old switch-hitter from Chicago quickly realized something: the speed was gone.

"I was hitting right-handed to right field and left-handed to left field," he said. "So, I knew it was time to retire." With that, he handed his Roberto Clemente model bat to one of the kids and headed back to the books.

He leaves us *My Baseball Diary*, plus all those wise letters with their postscripts on Reggie Jackson, Bill Veeck, and Meyer Schapiro. He leaves us this rich legacy. He leaves us the unforgettable memory of Studs at second base.

Preface

It was inevitable that I write a book about baseball. I have been threatening to for something like twenty-five years. Now I have carried out my threat. Any attempt to explain this book would be over-gilding the lily. I offer it to fans with the hope that they might find some interest and enjoyment in it.

Many persons have aided me in the preparation of this book, and I wish to make grateful acknowledgment to them. Lowell Pratt, of A. S. Barnes & Company, gave me the encouragement to publish this work. Don Schiffer, editor of A. S. Barnes, has aided me almost invaluably in the editing of this book. My secretary, Luna Wolf, also assisted me in the editing. Knowing nothing of baseball, she collaborated with me most assiduously and intelligently. Mrs. Louise Richmond typed the manuscripts, laboring through my virtually illegible handwriting. Dick Johnston, of *Sports Illustrated*, gave me several assignments which resulted in some of these essays, and through him I was able to learn more of the baseball world. Ray Schalk not only consented to my request for an interview, but was most kind in helping me to get some of the other stories I have included here. He and Marty Bleeker, Buck Weaver's best friend, were instrumental in my meeting Buck. James Henle, of the Vanguard Press and my friend of over two decades, encouraged me as he has always done. Lee Scott, traveling secretary of the Brooklyn Dodgers, was of great assistance to me in my getting to know that club. Tommy Holmes, veteran baseball writer of the *New York Herald Tribune*, patiently talked baseball to me. He and my old friend, Hugh Bradley, of the *New York Journal American* read some of the manuscripts and offered me valuable suggestions. I learned much from other baseball writers, among them John Carmichael of the *Chicago Daily News*, and of them I say—may their tribe increase.

I regret certain omissions in this volume. Especially, I am sorry that I did not write about Rogers Hornsby, who besides having been a great ball player, is a man of character.

Finally, this book is a family affair. Part of it recounts the happy baseball days my older brother Earl and I knew as boys. And some years ago, at a family reunion, I said that I wanted to write a book on baseball which would be dedicated to my nephews and my son, Kevin. It is done, and it is for them, more than anyone else.

I believe that my own baseball diary is like that of many of my generation. A younger generation never saw some of the players mentioned, Cobb, Speaker, Collins, Schalk, Weaver, Cicotte, Walter Johnson, Lajoie, Babe Ruth. I hope that I will at least convey some sense of these and other players and of baseball as it was to interested fans of the newer generation. I have told something of what baseball meant to me. I am glad I grew up as a fan. And here is the record and memory of one who has been a fan since 1911.

Acknowledgments

The following excerpts from novels by James T. Farrell are re-printed by permission of the publishers, Vanguard Press Inc.:

"A Back Yard Ball Game," pages 19–22, from No Star is Lost, copyright, 1938, by Vanguard Press Inc.

"A Letter to Connie Mack," pages 23–25, from Father and Son, copyright, 1941, by James T. Farrell.

"Ed Walsh Pitches a No-Hit Game," pages 45–55, from A World I Never Made, copyright, 1936, by Vanguard Press Inc.

"A Workout in the Park," pages 67–74, from No Star is Lost, copyright, 1938, by Vanguard Press Inc.

"A Player Loses Confidence," pages 83–85, from Father and Son, copyright, 1941, by James T. Farrell.

"A Game in the Park," pages 87–92, from Judgment Day, copyright, 1935, by Vanguard Press Inc.

Baseball: A Fan's Notes

James T. Farrell

Baseball was part of my growing up. As a matter of fact, I understood the game and could follow the plays before I could read or
write. My memories of baseball go back to the season of 1911. At
the time, there were relatively few automobiles. Movies had not yet
come out of the nickelodeon stage. Tennis and golf were looked
upon as sports of the upperclasses—sometimes scorned as "sissy
games"—and football was a college game, and interest in it did not
extend much beyond college alumni circles. As entertainment,
baseball had practically no competition.

Major league baseball parks were located near public transportation. Comiskey Park, home of the White Sox, was located at
Thirty-fifth Street and Shields, on the nearer southwest side of
Chicago. Thirty-fifth Street was a through street with a trolley line
that ran from Lake Michigan for a number of miles west—at least
to Western Avenue. Comiskey Park could also be reached easily by
the el, which stopped a few blocks away on Thirty-fifth Street.

Public transportation was cheap—a nickel for adults, three
cents for a kid under twelve. Often the conductors (mostly
Irishmen) wouldn't question a kid's age even if he looked a little big.
The prices of admission to the ball park were inexpensive, too: one
dollar for a box seat; seventy-five cents for the grandstand; fifty
cents for a pavilion seat, which ran from back of first and third
bases to both right and left fields; and twenty-five cents for bleachers. The bleachers extended all around the outfield. Occasionally,
when there was an overflow crowd, fans would be admitted and allowed to watch the game from behind ropes in the outfield. Whenever this happened, any ball hit into the crowd in fair territory was

a ground-rule double. I saw this happen during the City Series of
1911 between the White Sox and the Cubs. I saw it again in September 1920 in a game between the White Sox and the Yankees. This
was the game in which, for the last time, Babe Ruth batted against
the White Sox star pitcher Eddie Cicotte, who was one of the disbarred and so-called Black Sox.

Scorecards cost a nickel. So did cold drinks. Root beer was the
most popular soft drink in those days. No alcoholic beverages were
sold at the ball parks—not even beer. Popcorn and Cracker Jacks
were five cents. The most expensive item sold was a hot dog; it cost
ten cents. A workingman could see a major league game for a dollar or less. And for just a little bit more he could take one of his kids.

The game itself was essentially the same. The cork-centered
baseball, which had been introduced in 1909 to replace the rubber-
centered ball, was not as lively as it is today. Home runs were rare.
Pitchers were not as quickly relieved; if one got into a jam with men
on bases, it was up to him to try to pitch himself out of his predica-
ment. If he failed, he might be relieved. But there weren't regular
relief pitchers in the sense that there are today. Usually, a pitcher
who went in to relieve was a second stringer rather than a starter.
(And, of course, the rule permitting the designated hitter, which is
followed in the American League and some minor leagues, was not
in effect.) Some pitches which have since been ruled illegal were
then allowed. The most common of these was the spitball. There
were many spitball pitchers. Usually, a spitball pitcher chewed slip-
pery elm to give the pitch a good wetting. One of the greatest spitball pitchers of the time was Big Ed Walsh. Another one, who joined
the White Sox later, in 1914, was Urban "Red" Faber. Faber once told
me that he could throw a spitball at five different speeds.

Pitchers would sometimes rough up the surface of the ball. A
new pitch, called the shineball, was first described in the newspapers in 1915 but it had been invented earlier. A southpaw named
Doc Dave Danforth (the Doc was for dentist), who pitched for the
White Sox, used the shineball. He would rub the ball on his pants
until it had a shine on it. The ball thus shined could be made to take
breaks that could fool the hitter. Eddie Cicotte learned the
shineball from Danforth and added it to his repertoire. Cicotte was

a great pitcher. According to his catcher, Ray Schalk, Cicotte could still throw a fastball when he was thirty-five. He had a curve. And he could throw a spitball and a knuckleball. No one seems to know how many other pitches he had, but his record is proof that he had enough to pitch winning ball consistently.

There was no radio and no microphone in those days. Announcements were made by a man with a megaphone. He would walk out on the field after huddling with the umpires and give his information to the crowd through his megaphone. "Ladies and gentlemen, the batteries for today's game are: for Chicago, Walsh and Block; for Boston, Collins and Carrigan." These were the actual batteries of a game played between the Chicago White Sox and the Boston Red Sox one Sunday afternoon, August 27, 1911. My older brother, Earl, and I saw this game. The White Sox won 5–0. Big Ed Walsh pitched a no-hit, no-run game. I described it in my novel *A World I Never Made*.

Two umpires officiated at the game, one behind the plate and the other on the bases. If there were plays at two bases which had to be covered simultaneously, the home plate umpire would run to one of the bases. If an umpire was sick or injured, the other umpire would handle the entire game. Originally, of course, there was only one umpire calling plays at major league games. There is a famous legend about those days. It concerns King Kelly, an early star who played with Chicago and with Boston. The song "Slide, Kelly, Slide" was written about him. According to the story, Kelly was on first base. The batter hit the ball to the outfield and the sole umpire followed the course of the batted ball. Kelly cut across the diamond, running from first to third base right through the pitcher's box, thereby eliminating second base from his itinerary. The legend is that Kelly got away with it. I don't know how true this story is but I used to hear it a lot as a boy.

But back to facts. Even though baseball is essentially the same, the strategy of play then and now is different. This is familiar knowledge. As I mentioned earlier, in 1911 the starting pitcher could expect to finish the game. Today, at the first sign of weakness he is relieved by a pitcher whose specialty is relief pitching. There are even short, middle, and long relievers. Today every batter, particularly those in the American League where the designated hitter rule applies, is a threat to the pitcher, especially if there are men on bases. Now a hitter averaging .250, .220, or .200 is liable to swing from his heels and knock the ball out of the stadium, ruining what may have been—up until the moment of that wallop—a well-pitched game. This was much less likely to happen then.

Another difference in the game is the size of the gloves. Today's are much bigger than the gloves of the past. Then, a one-handed catch was considered a sensational play. Nowadays it is often regarded as a routine play. Aside from being smaller, the old gloves had less padding and it took more time to break them in. In fact, it took such a long time to get a good pocket in a glove that, once you did, you were inclined to keep it, even after the leather covering your palm cracked—or developed a hole. I know this from personal experience, playing as a boy. But I have seen big leaguers play with gloves that had a hole in the pocket.

In 1911, none of the three White Sox catchers, Billy Sullivan, Freddie Payne, or Bruno Block, wore shin guards. The first White Sox catcher I saw wearing them was Red Kuhn. Red Kuhn came closest to being the Sox's first-string catcher in 1912. It was unusual for a catcher to catch a hundred or more games during a season. Relatively few catchers did. Kuhn, wearing shin guards, caught in seventy-five games. He hit .202. He might have had a regular job, at least for a year or two, had it not been for a teenager who looked more like a batboy than a major league ball player and who showed up as a rookie catcher at Comiskey Park one day in August. He weighed less than 150 pounds. One of the first acts of Charles Comiskey, then owner of the Sox, was to make arrangements for the kid to be fed into more weight.

This preposterously young busher was named Ray Schalk. He had been purchased from the Milwaukee club of the American Association, then in the triple A league. Baseball legend has it that on his first day with the White Sox, Schalk, not even knowing the signals, was put into the lineup to catch Big Ed Walsh and showed his mettle by not only catching Walsh but talking back to the handsome Chicago idol. But this is not true. Schalk was assigned to catch the game that was played against the Philadelphia Athletics (managed by Connie Mack) but the pitcher was Doc White.

Ray Schalk not only replaced Red Kuhn before the 1913 season had been played out but he also quickly gained the reputation as baseball's "greatest living catcher." Before Schalk, most catchers were big fellows. Roger Breshnahan, inventor of the shin guard, was small but there were few others who weren't large men. Ray Schalk looked too young and too light to be a great catcher but year after year he caught in more than a hundred games. The other catcher on the White Sox team had little to do but catch during batting practice or warm up possible relief pitchers.

Schalk was innovative as a catcher. Before him, catchers didn't move around the field much. Schalk did. He would run down to first base, following the batter on an infield ground ball. I believe that he was the first catcher to do this. Today it is standard procedure for a catcher. Schalk threw well, too, and he could catch the toughest of pitchers. He caught Red Faber, who threw a heavy ball and was unafraid of any and all batters. He, Faber, had contempt for Ty Cobb even after they both were long retired. The reason was that Cobb's lifetime batting average against Faber was .226. Cobb's overall batting average was .367.

In one of his early games, Schalk threw a man out at second base. It made the sports pages. Today it probably wouldn't. Schalk once told me that when he was a young catcher he learned from two players: Hal Chase, the sensational first baseman who played with the White Sox for part of the 1913 and 1914 seasons, and Eddie Collins, the great second baseman.

In his day, Schalk was called "the perfect catcher." He was. But I have watched Bill Dickey of the New York Yankees catch, too. And I have watched the great center fielder and hitter, Tris Speaker. Like Eddie Collins and Joe Jackson, Tris Speaker played in the shadow of Ty Cobb. It is hard to forget Tris Speaker as a player. But after watching Joe DiMaggio, I could. DiMaggio was as close to being a perfect ball player as I have ever watched. But there are so many players whom I have watched in the course of a life-time, so many players that I will never forget.

✳   ✳   ✳

A couple of years ago, while waiting in the clubhouse for a game to start here in New York City, I started talking about some of these old-time ball players. Most of the sportswriters present were very interested and remarked, in effect, that it was almost as though I were speaking of ancient Greece. They had never talked to someone who had seen Hal Chase, Ty Cobb, Eddie Collins, Nap Lajoie, Stuffy McInnis, Joe Jackson—I could go on.

I was reminded of an incident that had happened earlier. I had gone to Shea Stadium with my late friend, Tommy Holmes, the great baseball writer. We had met at Grand Central Station and taken the subway out to Shea. Once inside the stadium, we went into the Mets clubhouse to say hello to Yogi Berra and Rube Walker. It was early and the room wasn't crowded so it was easy to spot Yogi. We walked over to him.

"Hi, Yogi," Tommy said. "Jim and I have been having a swell time talking about baseball all the way out here from Grand Central. We didn't mention a single player who played after the year 1930."

On another night—a bitter cold one in October of 1973—I went to a party after a Mets-Oakland World Series game. I started talking to Casey Stengel. He told me about breaking in the game during the 1912 season with the Brooklyn club. Old names came up— Fred Mollwitz, Vic Saier, Johnny Evers, Heinie Zimmerman, Jimmy Archer, Jack Coombs, and many others. We talked, with Casey doing most of the talking, until past three o'clock in the morning. He told me about the first time he played against the Chicago Cubs with Johnny Evers at second base. Casey singled. On the first or second pitch, he legged it to second base in an attempted steal. Evers covered the base. Both he and the ball were there ahead of Casey. Johnny Evers caught the ball, slammed it into Casey's face, and said, "There, busher, that'll teach you to come sliding into me."

Stengel talked about playing against Jimmy Archer. Casey was on first base; whether he got there with a hit or by a walk, he didn't say. Archer was catching. Casey took a short lead off first base, just a few inches. Archer, remaining in a squatting position, and without even looking toward first base, snapped the ball down to the Cubs' first-base player—I believe it was Vic Saier—who picked

Casey off. Casey said that even then, in 1973, more than fifty years later, he couldn't figure out how Jimmy Archer had done this, considering the short lead that he, Casey, had taken.

He spoke of Heinie Zimmerman. Casey said that most of the young ball players admired Zimmerman. In those days, men wore collars, mostly stiff, that were attached to their shirts with buttons. These needed to be laundered often. Casey and some of the other young players couldn't afford to wear a fresh collar every day. But Heinie Zimmerman could. The younger players thought this was elegant.

Baseball is frequently characterized as a boy's game played by men in short pants. It is a boy's game. Many boys love it. More recently, it has become a girl's game. But baseball is also a game for adults. The development of the game, the relative perfection of the rules of play, the geometrical layout of the diamond—the distances between the bases and from the pitching mound to home plate— these are all wonderfully well-thought-out plans. The assumption that an interest in baseball is not worthy of a serious adult with presumably more serious interests is both true and false. Some adults think that to watch baseball is to waste one's time in a childish way.

But for some of us, there is a peculiar attraction to baseball. It has its own drama. I have always loved the game. I don't care whether or not it is childish. Long before I possessed any capacity to examine myself or the reasons for the game's appeal to me, I loved it.

✳   ✳   ✳

Not long ago, someone asked me why I had chosen to become a novelist. Ralph Kiner was standing next to me and laughed.

"I'll tell you why James T. Farrell wrote books. He wanted to play second base for the Chicago White Sox, and couldn't."

We all laughed. But everyone in the crowd knew, as I did, that for those of us who love the game the way we do, it wasn't altogether a joke.

Memories of a Baseball Boyhood

*These are some of the happiest memories of my
life. They will, I hope, explain why I have loved
baseball and remained interested in it. As I wrote
this piece, I thought of the boys I played with, of
the long days when the world was baseball.*

I REMEMBER a gray day in 1910. I was six years old. My
grandfather was ill, and usually, he would be on a small
cot in the dining room of our apartment on Indiana Avenue.
I was dreamily playing with my baseball pictures. In those
days, pictures of ball players were inserted in packages of
cigarettes. I recall one brand in particular—Sweet Caporals.
My brother Earl had a large collection of these pictures and
I, following his example, had managed to get a sizeable one
of my own. Earl gave me pictures of which he had dupli-
cates. My aunt and uncle got others for me. I was not able to
read, but I knew the name of every player on my pictures.
Some of these names still stand out significantly in my mind,
among them, Topsy Hartsel and Joe Tinker. The picture of
Tinker showed him with bat in hand, against a dull, purplish-

1

red background. In some way, the picture of Joe Tinker was associated with my older brother. Also, I often had an optical illusion when I looked at it. It seemed to me that the handle of the bat was curved, shaped like a cane, and while I knew that this was not correct, I would often see the curved handle of the bat when I looked at this picture. At times I was unable to erase this illusion from my mind. It disturbed me. But on this particular day, I was playing with my pictures, imagining and absorbed.

Suddenly, I heard that Father Dondaville had come to see my grandfather. He was my grandfather's friend, and also mine. This sick call of Father Dondaville is one of my important early baseball memories. He was a big, jolly, rather plump, and understanding priest. I liked the friendliness of his voice. I believed that he liked me. He paid attention to me, and flattered me in the way he asked questions about baseball and my pictures. He also asked me to show him how the various players batted, and talked to me about the game. I had not then, of course, learned to imitate the stances of the players accurately, but I did it nonetheless. He held the cards in his hands and asked me who each player was, and I identified the players correctly, and according to the teams on which they played. I told him what players batted and threw right or left-handed. All of this was knowledge that I had absorbed and heard, mainly from my older brother. The priest was amazed, and his compliments pleased me very much. He gave me the nickname of Young Ty Cobb.

Later, in 1911–12 during my first-grade year, and subsequently until he was sent to a new parish about 1913, he used to visit our classroom at Corpus Christi School at Forty-ninth and Grand Boulevard (now South Parkway). He called me by my first name, and I would stand up, and then answer baseball questions in class, and would again imitate big-league players at bat before the entire class. I always was thrilled; these visits of Father Dondaville's were some of the brightest occurrences of my early school days.

In 1912, my Uncle Tom bought me a blue baseball suit. I liked it that the suit was blue. During those days, the White Sox wore blue suits on the road. Father Dondaville arranged to take a picture of me in my suit, which he did in front of the parish house on Grand Boulevard. He had me squat like a catcher, with my hat turned around. I had a boy's catcher's mitt which cost about twenty-five cents. The picture is now lost, but I have frequently wished that I still had it. At home, the grownups laughed about the picture. But I believed that it gave me great importance. In the picture, my expression was so serious as to be funny.

My love of baseball originally goes back to those days. The pictures of players which came with packages of cigarettes, pictures of Topsy Hartsel in an Athletic uniform, of Joe Tinker after swinging, of Ty Cobb in a gray suit and against a yellow background, of Nap Lajoie, of Cy Young and others were my introduction to our national game, and the beginning of my lifelong interest in the game.

A Dollar to Spend

*Unfortunately in 1911 I could not read and,
therefore, I had not yet discovered the world of
Horatio Alger. In consequence, I am somewhat
ashamed to admit that I do not still possess the
first dollar I ever got. With taxes, prices, the value
of the dollar today, no one will be likely to be able
to keep or to save the last dollar they get or earn.*

Do you remember the first time in your life when you
had a dollar all your own and how you spent it? This
experience came to me in the summer of 1911. One of my
aunt's beaus was rich and jolly. He came to our home to
take her out to dinner on a date. While he waited for her
to get ready, I entertained him, hogging what attention I
could. I talked to him about Ty Cobb. He slipped me a
dollar. I told no one of my abundance. The next morning I
went two blocks away to a drugstore at Fifty-first Street and
Grand Boulevard and bought a big bat which I had looked
at in the window more than once. I bought that bat with my
first dollar and went proudly home.

"What in the name of God has he got there?" my grand-mother asked, flabbergasted.

She called my aunt.

"It's a Ty Cobb Louisville slugger," I said.

"God have mercy on me old soul, it's bigger than he is," my grandmother exclaimed.

"Where did you get it, Little Brother?" my aunt asked; she often called me "Little Brother."

"I bought it."

"You bought it." My grandmother blessed herself, and en-voked the Holy Family. "And what did it cost?"

"A dollar."

"Where did you get the money for it?"

I told them how I had got the dollar.

"Why, he can hardly lift it," my grandmother said.

There was a shaking of heads.

"El, bring him back and get the man that sold him that arrested. I'll get me cousin Willie O'Toole (a Chicago alder-man) to get him arrested. Making game of me little grand-son. Where's he at? Where's me hat? Let me put me hat on and let me see the man that sold it to him. I'll tear him limb from limb. I'll show him who's cheating me little grand-son."

"But I bought it. I want it," I said stubbornly but I was frightened as all Hell, and I clutched the bat closely to my chest.

Persuasion failed to move me and they both laughed. They didn't go gunning for the man in the drugstore. But my grandmother exclaimed:

"What in the name of God possessed him?"

I had a second round to win. That was my Uncle Tom. When he came home for supper that evening, the story was told him. He said that the bat was too heavy for me to swing. I almost cried and all seemed lost. But they allowed me to keep the bat.

I couldn't swing it, and, in fact, I never did get one decent swing out of it. Sometimes the older boys of ten and eleven would allow me to play in their games. Possibly the Ty Cobb Louisville Slugger bat was a reason. They would roll the ball on the ground to me and I would swing my bat over the dirt, hit the ball and run, gleefully and frantically to first base.

The next spring, an older boy named Johnny, who batted cross-handed, used my bat in a scrub game of sides in the vacant lot at Fifty-first and Grand Boulevard. He broke my Ty Cobb Louisville Slugger.

There is one more detail to the history of my bat. I used to leave it on the back porch. Sometimes I'd be careless and would lay it parallel to the floor. Several times it rolled away, under the railing, and dropped three flights into the yard. The neighbors were terrified and angry, and they complained to the owner about me and my baseball bat.

Another event in the life of an American boy entranced with baseball is the acquisition of his first regulation baseball. Nineteen-eleven, my first baseball year, is the time I got it. My Uncle Tom was a traveling salesman. While he was on the road in Minneapolis, he got a baseball from Rube Waddell who had gone down from the majors to the American Association and was pitching for Minneapolis. I do not actually remember if it was autographed but I believe that it was. I had heard that Rube Waddell had been a great pitcher and it was a feather in my cap to have this ball.

There was the side wall of an apartment building facing the alley between Calumet Avenue and Grand Boulevard at Fiftieth Street. I liked to play catch with myself by throwing the ball against that wall. With my older brother Earl, we invented a game to play against the wall. A ball caught on the rebound was an out. Or if we decided on a ball hit on the ground, we threw it low, fielded it, threw the ball and on catching the rebound, we called that an out. When the ball got by us or went over our heads, it was a base hit and we had areas for a single or for extra base hits.

I used Rube Waddell's ball to play this game. One chilly day after school in early September, I had no one to play with and I went out with my ball and played a game against the wall. My teams were the White Sox and the Athletics. I made up the batting order and I kept the score and the batters in my head. The game absorbed me completely. I'd fling the ball at that wall, sometimes low, sometimes high. There would be the cracking sound, and then the rebound. I'd try to catch it. I fielded grounders off the wall, trying to imitate big-league infielders, make a quick throw, try to set myself as a first baseman stretching to catch the throw as my Rube Waddell ball came back to me. Now and then a horse and wagon would force me to wait impatiently for a few moments. Then I went on with my game.

I was entranced and lost in it. I visualized Comiskey Park, with roaring and cheering fans, the players swinging, running to the bases. I imagined myself as a player and also a spectator seeing all of the action. My state of mind was almost describable as one of a waking coma. The sounds around me, of traffic on Grand Boulevard, an occasional horse and wagon, electric car or automobile on Fiftieth Street, of the elevated train, passing one block to the west, these all came to me as though muffled. They might have been the roar of the crowd at Comiskey Park. I continued playing, happy as if under a hypnotic spell.

The crashing sound of breaking glass broke the spell. In the center of the wall was a narrow window. I'd thrown the ball through the window. For a moment I was stunned. Then, in fright, I ran upstairs and bolted into the kitchen, pale and frightened. It was not only that I had lost the Rube Waddell ball which I valued, I also thought I'd done something wrong, something for which I could be punished and might even get in trouble with the police. My grandmother noticed me, "white as a sheet." At first I wouldn't tell her and my aunt what had happened. When I did they laughed in relief.

The window was paid for and I regained my ball. It didn't last long. It was thrown against the wall in the alley, and used for scrub games in the vacant lot. But I always told the other kids that it was the ball Rube Waddell gave me. They didn't know who Rube Waddell was.

When the seams were ripped and the cover came off, it was covered with black tape and used some more.

Rube Waddell was one of my favorite ball players all during boyhood. I found out all I could about him and told the funny stories of his escapades many times. When he died it was very sad for me to think that he was dead. I hoped that he was in Heaven and sometimes I even said a prayer for the repose of his soul. Naturally I saw only the comedy in his antics, and not the fact that he was emotionally disturbed and had helped to destroy himself. He was one of the players who, for me as for many others, took on the proportions of legend. And also there were times when I almost might have convinced myself that I'd seen him pitch.

Playing Ball as a Boy

Today, baseball is different for boys. We organized our own games. Sometimes the boy who owned the bat would become angry and take his bat home, ending the game. But this is the way we played ball.

I WAS walking in the Bois de Boulogne one Sunday afternoon two years ago and I saw a small group gathered about a muddy softball diamond. The diamond was not laid out carefully and there was no backstop. A few fellows were playing catch. I asked if I might join them, and I played catch, participated in a pepper game, caught and hit out flies. They were scheduled to play the team from the American Embassy. However, the weather was bad and the game wasn't played.

Throwing, catching and hitting a softball is not a particularly interesting thing to do, at least not for me. But fooling around this way on a gray Sunday afternoon brought back memories to me.

The Bois de Boulogne is many miles and years of memories

11

away from Washington Park in Chicago, but while hitting
out flies and catching them, my thoughts constantly went
back to Washington Park and to my boyhood. The ball field
of Washington Park is large. During my childhood, there
were ten regular diamonds there, and now there are more.
On a Saturday or Sunday afternoon, all diamonds would be
in use, and the field would be a spectacle of crowds, and of
men and boys playing. There would be the sight of white
shirts, and of men, small because of distance suddenly moving, running, throwing, sometimes sliding. You would hear
shouts and the crack of the bat as a ball was hit.

I began going to Washington Park when I was eight years
old. I would go with my brother, my uncle or alone, and I
would play with anyone who was willing. Near the Fifty-
first Street end of the ball field, there was a big clubhouse.
Every morning in summer, a group of men would be out,
fooling around, and sometimes they would play a scrub
game. Some of them worked nights. One was a race track man
and there was a glamour about him. Several were salesmen.
I used to play catch with some of them, watch them hit out
and catch flies, and listen in wonderment when they talked
of baseball. Often around twelve o'clock, and after a workout, they would sit around in a circle and talk. The race track
man, Jack Hogan, would sometimes speak of horses, and of
the races. And baseball talk. Ty Cobb, Honus Wagner,
Christy Mathewson, Nap Lajoie, these magic names falling
from their lips. Another was Willie Keeler who had then
finished his big-league playing days. And not only was there
wonder in me. There was also ambition. I wanted to grow up
fast, so that I could play with men, and become a big-leaguer.
I would sit and listen and dream of myself as a man, a big-
league star. I would imagine men sitting around in a circle in
Washington Park in years to come and talking of me and of
my exploits on the diamond. I would hear one of them saying:

"He used to play as a kid out here in Washington Park."

We played all kinds of games in my boyhood. My folks lived at Fifty-first Street and Prairie Avenue. There was a long, rectangular back yard. It was bordered by greenhouses, and one end of it was fenced to divide it from the garden of the man who owned the greenhouses. In those days, ten-cent indoor or softballs were on the market. They were more or less the size of baseballs. We used to play ball in the back yard with these ten-cent indoor balls. Regularly, a ball would be hit over the fence and into the garden. The attendant of the greenhouses was a grouch, and would not return our balls. He was our natural enemy and we plagued his life. For not only would we hit balls into his garden, but now and then, a foul ball would break one of the windows of the glass houses. Whenever a ball was hit over the fence into the garden, the game would stop and there would be a debate as to who would climb the fence and retrieve our ball. It was an adventure to do this. The man never did more than growl and shout at us, but we were afraid of him. We feared that he would keep us prisoner. When we were flush and had several balls, we would not try to retrieve the ball.

Earl and I collected a group of neighborhood kids, and every night after dinner we would choose up sides and have a game. We played overhand, swift pitching, and worked out an elaborate set of ground rules. No base stealing was allowed. There were porches behind third base and in our short left field. If a ball was hit on the first floor, it was a single; a double on the second-story porch; a triple on the third floor. There was a back fence, and a ball hit over it was a home run. When anyone knocked a pitch over the fence into the garden, it was a double.

A man who lived in our building began to play with us. He would catch for both sides and shout, and was full of pep. He not only made our games more interesting, but he was protection. He was bigger than the greenhouse attendant, and we knew that he could beat him up in a fight. When he was with us, we did not fear to climb the fence to retrieve our balls.

When there were no others around for a game, Earl and I devised a game to play by ourselves. We marked off every part of the yard and established rules as to what was the value of a hit ball going to any part of the yard. We each represented ourselves as a big-league team, and made out line-ups. We played, imagining ourselves big-leaguers. If the player batting was left-handed, we batted left-handed. For right-handers, we swung from the right side of the plate. We had seen most of the players of the day and we tried to imitate the batting stance of each player when his turn to bat came. Earl was bigger and older than I. He usually won. Most of the time he was the Boston Red Sox and I was the White Sox.

There was little grass in our back yard. After supper until dark, there was no peace for the neighbors. The yard would be full of yelling, shouting kids. And life was not easy for the man who tended the plants and flowers in the greenhouses. But we had lots of fun.

When I was nine and ten, there were two teams of older boys and I used to watch their games, root for them and think of the boys in these teams almost as I did of big-leaguers. One of these teams, called the Sterns, played indoor ball. Softball has taken the place of indoor ball now. The indoor ball, as many will remember, was bigger than the contemporary softball. The Sterns played most of their games in a vacant lot at Fifty-second Street and Calumet Avenue. They were a good team and I used to dream of some day playing on a team like it. One of their players was Johnny Kleutch.

The other team played hard ball in Washington Park and was called the Old Roses. They had gray uniforms trimmed

in red, and some of the same boys played on the Sterns as
well as the Old Roses. I remember watching their games, and
growing excited with each pitch, cheering, yelling, having
my moments of excitement, hope and anxiety as the games
proceeded. And it was a matter of pride to me that I knew
the boys on their teams and that they called me by my first
name.

In 1915 and 1916, there was a playground team organized in the newly built Washington Park playground. When
the playground was constructed, little thought was given to
ball playing. The space for our diamond was small and surrounded on two sides by iron picket fences. There were
women playground directors instead of men. But they used
to play with us. One of them would slide and there was much
talk of her sliding. The older boys especially used to talk of
her sliding and the bloomers she wore. One year the older
boys played in a playground tournament, held at Fuller
Park. My parents and brothers and sisters lived near Fuller
Park and I sometimes played there. Earl and a boy named
Gowdy, who had a reputation in Washington Park because
he was related to Hank Gowdy of the Boston Braves, had
a quarrel with the Washington Park boys. They deserted
the team and played with Fuller Park. The Fuller Park
neighborhood was a tougher and poorer one than the old
Fifty-eighth Street neighborhood. The Washington Park
older boys wanted to beat up my brother and Gowdy but
didn't because the Fuller Park boys protected them. I became a deserting fan and rooted for Fuller Park. Washington Park lost their first game. And that day, my grandmother
had made me a big lunch. In the morning, I left it in the park
locker room and watched the tournament game. When I
went to get my lunch it had been stolen.

The rules of playground ball were equivalent to indoor
ball. There was one important difference. A hitter could run
either to first or third base, as he chose. We, in Washington

Park, never played according to these rules, and in the tournament games, the other teams confused us. Frequently, the batters would run to third base, rather than first. That was how we would lose.

One of the boys who played with us was George Lott, later destined to become a doubles champion and an internationally famous tennis player. George was nicknamed Junior. His folks were or seemed to be richer than those of most of the other boys and this did not help George's popularity. However, he was a natural born athlete, and in any game when sides were chosen, he was always one of the first to be picked. As a boy, he was almost as good at baseball as he was at tennis. Concerning his tennis playing, it was so sensational that when he was still in short pants, and before he had entered tournament play, crowds would gather to watch him when he played in one of the Washington Park tennis courts.

I played in playground tournaments. I had not been confident of my ability to make the teams but I was chosen. One year we played in a tournament at Armour Square Playground, near Comiskey Park. I was at second base. There were ten men on a playground team, three outfielders, a first, second and third baseman, and two shortstops, one of whom played up close to the batter, and, of course, the pitcher and catcher. In our first game, we were matched with Sherman Park. Heretofore, the Sherman Park boys had always beaten us. When we went to their park to play, there was always the danger of a fight. Once, one of our boys had to bribe the Sherman Park boys with a gift of a baseball bat so as not to be beaten up.

But in this tournament game, we beat Sherman Park convincingly. I came up early in the game with the bases full. I swung. The ball soared and I was surprised by my own wallop. I circled the bases, but in my excitement I didn't touch second base. When I reached home, the boys shouted at me, telling me that I hadn't touched second. I turned, ran back, touched third base, and second base and ran back to third and was thrown out at home plate. It was almost a six-base hit. The ball had traveled the entire length of the playground. I was both a hero and a goat.

After licking Sherman Park we played Ogden Park in the second round of the tournament. We never had a chance. The Ogden Park boys would bunt and chop their hits and run to third base instead of first. We were dizzy and bewildered, and lost. We won no medals.

For two summers, we played indoor ball almost every day in the Washington Park playground. We would have one to two games in the morning, and then one or two more in the afternoon. Sometimes we chose sides. Then for a period we formed two teams and played a world series. We counted the number of home runs we hit over the back fence. The summers passed. Going home at the end of the day, there were lemonade and sandwiches waiting for me. And there were thoughts of the games played, and hopes and expectations of the games to be played the next day. The biggest of worries was the threat of rain. Running, hitting, diving for balls, hitting one over the short picket fence, quarreling, throwing oneself fully into each play—this was all part of some very good boyhood days.

Secretly, some of us imagined ourselves as big-leaguers with the world watching us. Disappointment and despair hung on a hit or an out. Nothing was more important than what we did on that small, rectangular ball field of ours. Far away in Europe, armies were fighting in the trenches. America was moving forward to war. Woodrow Wilson campaigned for his second term as President of the United States. The White Sox fought it out with the Boston Red Sox for the pennant. And we played and yelled and slid and scratched ourselves and tore our black stockings and trousers or bruised our knees and elbows and we loved it. The summers passed. The misery of a new school year and the melancholy approach of autumn wrote finis to the happy vacation time of summer when you could play ball from morning to supper time.

A Back Yard Ball Game

This is a small section from my novel, NO STAR
IS LOST. *It is one of my earlier efforts to express
and describe playing ball as a boy.*

DANNY liked playing different kinds of ball games with
Bill and pretending that these were big-league games.
When they played them, each of them would represent a
team and they'd talk about the players they supposed in the
game. Sometimes, they'd pitch balls and strikes for nine
innings this way. Sometimes, one of them would be a first
baseman and the other an infielder or outfielder. The first
baseman would throw flies and grounders to the other one,
and these had to be fielded cleanly to be outs. They'd go on
that way for nine innings, too. But the game Danny liked
best, except Steel's, was the one they played in the back yard
with a ten-cent soft ball. They each represented a big-league
team and batted according to that team's lineup, hitting
right-handed or left-handed just as the real players in the
lineup did. They played swift pitching and called balls and
strikes. The home base was near the back fence so they didn't

19

have to chase pitched balls that weren't batted at. The whole yard was plotted out and the game was played according to a complicated set of rules devised to make hits hard to get and to keep the score tight. Foul balls that went over the back fence or up on the greenhouses to the right were outs. Over the whole yard, there were only certain places where batted balls were scored as base hits. Over the back fence was a home run.

But Danny wasn't good enough to beat Bill at this game because Bill was bigger and could hit harder, and he could hit better left-handed. Danny wasn't so good yet batting left-handed. But he gave Bill good games and he was getting better all the time, so that their games were getting tighter. Now he warmed up before starting, and this time he wanted to win. He was going to play carefully, wait out Bill's pitches, place his hits carefully. He wanted to win one of these games.

In the last of the eighth inning, the score was four to four, and this was his chance. He was on edge to win, and he had right-handed batters coming up in his lineup. He caught Bill's warm-up pitches, nervous, anxious to get going and score some runs this inning. He had a good chance of holding Bill down for one inning because there were many innings in these games when Bill couldn't score.

"Who's up, Dan?" Bill called.

"Schalk, Tom Daly, my third baseman in this game, and Jim Scott," Danny said.

Danny stood waiting, batting in Ray Schalk's stance and prepared to imitate that player's choppy swing at the plate. He waited Bill out to the count of two and three. Then Bill tried to fool him with a slow ball. Danny caught it squarely and slammed it onto the first porch below his. That was a two-base hit. Here was his chance. He stood ready to bat again, his face determined, his lips clenched, his eyes alert.

"You outguessed me that time. This time you won't," Bill

said confidently; he wound up and pitched one in swift, cutting the heart of the plate.

"Strike," Danny said.

He picked up the ball and flung it back to Bill.

He bunted the next pitch for a sacrifice hit. That made one out and a runner on third. He had two chances, and Scott and Buck Weaver, his batters, were right-handed.

"Letting Scott, your pitcher, bat, or putting in a pinch hitter?" Bill asked.

"He's batting," Danny said grimly.

He waited. Instead of using the stance and swing of the players he was representing, he was going to swing as hard as he could to get a run in.

"Come on, pitch," Danny said while Bill dallied, pulling at his belt, looking at the ball.

"My catcher's coming out to have a conference with me," Bill said.

Danny liked going through all these pretendings, as if there were talks of players on the field and all that. But Bill was doing it now to get his goat. Bill always took a lot of time if Danny looked as if he might start a hitting rally.

"Come on, pitch!" Danny said impatiently while Bill continued to stall.

Bill walked away from the pitching box.

"I'm talking about what I'm gonna do with my infield," Bill yelled, grinning at Danny, knowing that he was making Danny nervous.

Danny stood swinging his bat, stamping his feet, asking himself if he could slam a couple of hits out now, anxious to have the game go on, losing his nerve and his confidence with every second Bill delayed.

Bill went back to the pitching box. He started winding up slowly. Now he had to hit.

"Come on, hurrish! Come up here!"

Bill pitched a wide one.

"Ball," Danny called, as he bent down to pick the ball up.

"Come upstairs, Son!" Mrs. O'Flaherty called.

"Mother, I'll be right up as soon as we finish our game," Danny called to her.

She took the whistle out of her apron pocket and blew it loudly.

"We better go, Dan, and we can come down and finish the game afterward," Bill said when they both realized that she wouldn't stop blowing that whistle until they went upstairs.

Danny dropped the bat, and Bill left the ball in the pitcher's box. Danny followed Bill upstairs, disappointed and sulky. He had just that kind of luck. Darn it! Now, maybe when they came down again to finish the game he'd be jinxed. Darn it! Just his luck!

A Letter to Connie Mack

This is a section from my novel FATHER AND SON. *However, the mood of truth is upon me, the White Sox are, at least temporarily, in contention, and I did write a letter similar to this one when I was in my teens. I kept no copy of the original letter and recomposed one when I decided to use such an incident in fiction.*

But with permissible originality, let me say that times and baseball have changed. Today the ball club would write to the boy.

DANNY sat at his desk with his bedroom door closed. He was elated. Just after he had made up his mind that he didn't have the call, the idea had come to him like an inspiration. And now he had gotten the letter finished, written carefully and legibly so that it looked as if a man had written it. It ought to work, too. Connie Mack was known above all other managers as the man to pick promising players off the sand lots and develop them into stars. Well, after receiving this letter, why shouldn't Connie send a scout out to Washington

Park to look him over? And maybe the scout would see him
on a good day and sign him up for a tryout with the Athletics
a couple of years from now when he was old enough. Players
had been signed up at fifteen before. There was the case of
that pitcher, Hoyt. Proud of himself, he read the letter he'd
just composed.

> Mr. Connie Mack
> Shibe Park
> The Philadelphia Athletics
> Philadelphia, Pennsylvania.
>
> Dear Mr. Mack:
>
> I am writing you this letter to tip you off about a
> kid named O'Neill who is to be seen playing ball in
> Washington Park in Chicago all of the time. He isn't
> ripe just yet because he is only fifteen or sixteen,

That was a smart idea, to make out that the man who was
supposed to be writing this letter didn't know too much about
him, so it was best not to give his exact age.

> but he is coming along fast for his age, and he will
> be ripe soon enough and he looks like a real comer.
> If you look him over you can pick up a promising
> youngster now for nothing and he seems destined
> for the big show. I am a baseball fan and like to see
> kids get a chance, and take pride in picking them.
> I picked some before and was a good picker.
> Years ago when George Moriarity was playing on
> the sand lots of Chicago I picked him, and I think
> you must admit I picked a big leaguer then because
> Moriarity is a big leaguer. You can pick this kid up
> now for nothing and you will never regret it. He
> plays out in Washington Park all of the time, and

you can send a scout out there to look at him and easily find out who he is.

I know you will not be sorry for this tip.

A baseball fan, a real one

T. J. Walker

He was pleased and satisfied with his letter. All year he'd really felt that 1919 was going to be an important year for him. Maybe this letter might begin to prove that it was. He was smart to have thought up this idea.

I See Some Games

*Today, when I go to Comiskey Park or Wrigley
Field, I do not merely see the game in progress.
I remember the games I saw decades ago. Here
are some of them.*

Most of the ball games I saw in 1911 and 1912, and even
in 1913, have melted together in my memory. I recall how greatly excited I would get. I would cheer loudly,
shouting to the players as though I knew them, as though my
cries could be heard and could actually encourage and help
them. I would be taken by my Uncle Tom, or else he or my
grandmother would give my older brother and me the money
to go to a game. The two of us could get in the grandstand
for the price of one seventy-five-cent ticket, and usually we
sat in the grandstand, although occasionally we sat in the
fifty-cent pavilion which ran along left and right field, or
else in the bleachers. Bleacher tickets were then twenty-
five cents. In 1912, my grandmother started going to ball
games on Ladies Day and she would take me. By 1913, when
I was nine years old, I sometimes went to games alone.

One of my first White Sox heroes was Ping Bodie, the burly center fielder from the same area of San Francisco which later was to give baseball the Di Maggio brothers and other Italian-American stars. Bodie was nicknamed "The Fence Buster," and he was a long-ball hitter for the dead-ball era, but he never did become quite the star I hoped he would. He lasted with the White Sox from 1911 to 1914. His real name was Francesco Stephano Pezzolo. His best years with the Sox were 1911 and 1912, when he hit, respectively, .288 and .294. In 1914, he played in only 107 games and batted .229. He went back to the minors. Connie Mack brought him to play with the last place Athletics in 1917, and in 1918, he played with the New York Yankees. Bodie, along with Meusel, Wallie Pipp and Home Run Baker, formed the original Yankees Murderer's Row when Babe Ruth played his first year in a New York uniform.

Ping Bodie was a burly, barrel-built player and he took a good cut at the ball. Why he became one of my first heroes is something I do not understand. In that first, sudden and total enthusiasm for and absorption in baseball which we feel in early boyhood, a name, a nickname, some accident of feature, of a stance at the plate, is sufficient to make a player a boy's hero. At all events, I talked of Ping Bodie more than I did of any other player, and in my neighborhood I acquired the nickname of "Young Ping." This stuck with me until 1915, when Bodie was back in the minors.

I understood baseball in 1911, but could not read and had not, as yet, started going to school. I entered school in September of 1911. Every day, I pestered my aunt until she read me the accounts of the games in the newspapers, usually the *Chicago Daily Tribune.* One of its baseball writers was Ring Lardner and thus I actually grew up in baseball on Lardner. I managed to know and keep up with the game, the records and standings, even though I was unable to read. Earl, of course, also supplied me with data. And when my other

Uncle Bill, who then lived in Madison, Wisconsin, came to town and had dinner with us, he and my Uncle Tom would sit at the table over their tea and talk about baseball nostalgically. They'd remember Spike Shannon who had played with the New York Giants, Mike Donlin, Wee Willie Keeler, Rube Waddell, and many others. Listening avidly to their every word, I filled in on the history of baseball and the players before my day. I heard much of the Hitless Wonders, the Chicago White Sox of 1906, who had pulled a big upset and defeated the famous Chicago Cubs of Tinker-to-Evers-to-Chance fame. In Chicago, at least, that World Series had gone into baseball legend and was much remembered. And in 1911, five members of the Hitless Wonders were still with the White Sox, Big Ed Walsh, Doc White, the left-handed pitcher who was usually difficult for Ty Cobb to hit, and who was the boyhood baseball hero of Sid Keener, present director of the Cooperstown Hall of Fame and Baseball Museum, Billy Sullivan, the catcher, Lee Tannehill, shortstop, and Pat Dougherty, left fielder.

Obviously, because I was born on the South Side of Chicago, I became a White Sox fan. Since baseball took such a strong hold upon me, it permeated my boyish thoughts and dreams. It became a consuming enthusiasm, a part of my dream or fantasy world. The conversation about baseball which I sometimes heard at home, the nostalgic recollections of players who had passed out of active play, the talk of players and games in an almost legendary way, all this was part of an oral tradition of baseball passed on to me, mainly in the home, during the early years of this century. It was a big treat to a little boy to be taken to the ball game and also to sit listening while his elders talked of the game. Along with this, my elders approved of my interest in baseball and encouraged me. When I was taken to a game by my uncle or my two uncles, they seemed to approve and like it when I cheered and shouted, and they were quite proud of my rapidly developing and precocious knowledge of players, line-ups, teams and averages. Baseball was a means of an awakening into life for me, an emergence from babyhood into the period of being a little boy. It corresponded with a natural period of development. Probably this has been true for many Americans, and for this reason, it retains its hold upon us through our long years of maturity and adulthood.

When I was a boy, I do not ever recall a kid asking a ball player for an autograph. Before a game, kids would be hanging out in front of the ball park to watch the players report, but none of them would crowd upon the players and ask for autographs; few would ever speak to the players. One day when Earl and I got to the ball park quite early, we stood outside and watched some of the players enter.

"Jim," Earl said, "there goes Pat Dougherty."

"Get the hell out of here," Pat Dougherty sneered at me; as I recall him, he was lean and rather lantern-jawed and he wore a brown suit.

I was not, of course, approaching him. I was too shy to have done that. Dougherty, at the time, was finishing his career. He had played with the Boston Red Sox and the New York Highlanders. In the second game of the 1903 World Series, Dougherty became the first player to hit two home runs in a World Series game.

Now and then on a street car, a player would recognize a kid, or say hello to you when they were leaving the park. Doc White, the southpaw pitcher, got to recognize my brother and me, and after one game against the Detroit Tigers in 1911, we happened to climb onto a crowded Thirty-fifth Street trolley car with him.

"The two kids," he told the conductor, paying our carfare.

When I arrived home, I burst into our apartment, and loudly announced:

"Doc White paid my carfare."

"And who is he, Son?" my grandmother asked.
I told her that he was a baseball player.
"He must be a nice man."

Roy Corhan, the rookie shortstop whose career was wrecked by a bean ball, once paid our carfare also, and a couple of years later, Death Valley Jim Scott did likewise. Scott, for a few years, was a crack spit-ball pitcher and to this day Ray Schalk will speak admiringly of how much stuff Scott had on the ball.

Also I got a few balls through my uncle. He had come to know a second-string Cleveland catcher, Grover Cleveland Land, and Land had given him a ball for me. Once in a while, I would see Land catch and would hope for him to make a hit when a blow wouldn't affect the outcome of the game. I doubt that anyone else in the stands cared if Land made a hit or even whether or not he was catching. It was almost the same for a young substitute outfielder on the Cleveland Naps, Heinie Butcher. Butcher was not interesting to me as a ball player, but rather because his old man was my father's landlord. But we never did see Heinie Butcher get a base hit. I saw him strike out and foul out, but never get a base hit. In fact, I don't recall ever seeing Grover Cleveland Land make a base hit either, although he did make some.

In July 1915, I saw the Chicago Cubs play the Cincinnati Reds at the old West Side ball park. One reason why Uncle Tom took me was so that I might shake hands with Wade Killefer, outfielder and brother of Bill Killefer, battery mate of Grover Cleveland Alexander, and a ranking catcher of his day. Between games, I shook hands with Wade Killefer, and received a shiny white National League official baseball. I boldly asked Killefer to take me on the bench.

"Oh, I couldn't, Jimmy. Buck Herzog wouldn't allow it. No, he wouldn't let me do it."

In those first years, 1911, 1912 and 1913, I would guess that I must easily have seen forty to fifty big-league ball games. During those years, the White Sox shaved into fifth place with a 77-74 record, fifth again with a 78-76, and sixth 78-74. I could only dream of the far-off day when they would win the pennant and the World Series. But each day was unto itself, and if the White Sox won, I was happy. This was especially so when I was at the ball park.

There were three games in 1911 which were most exciting. One was a seventeen-inning contest between the Detroit Tigers and the Sox. The extra innings produced the tenseness which is familiar to fans, but in the last of the seventeenth, Ping Bodie came up with a man on base and lined one low out to left-center between the fielders and the runner romped in with the winning run. Since Bodie had broken up the ball game, victory was singularly sweet to me.

I remember a second game played on a raw day in August. The White Sox beat the St. Louis Browns. I was chilled and all of my hollering couldn't keep me warm. I do not know how he managed it, but my Uncle Tom got me onto the Browns players' bench. I don't believe that the word dugout was in use then. At least, I do not recall it. Jimmy Austin, St. Louis third baseman, put his sweater on me. I swam in it, and sat huddled on the bench, shy but impressed and wanting very much to be noticed. Austin asked me several times if I was warm enough. The other players scarcely noticed me. I recall one player in particular, Molly Meloan, right fielder. He had come up with the White Sox but they had passed him on to St. Louis. He would get up, talking about how he was going to get a hit but he didn't. I felt a conflict of loyalties. The Browns were more than kind to me, allowing me to sit on the bench. But in my heart I couldn't want them to win. The only compromise I made was not to cheer for the White Sox from the Brown's bench.

The third game I recall was Ed Walsh's no-hitter, pitched

on August 27, 1911. To this day, Walsh's game remains as one of the most satisfying and exciting of all the many big-league ball games I have watched.

In the Boston Red Sox line-up that day were two of the three fielders who gave Boston one of the most famous out-fields in modern baseball history. Duffy Lewis was in left field, and Tris Speaker, now a Hall of Famer, played center field. But in right field, the Danish-born Olaf Henricksen was in place of Harry Hooper, the third of the Red Sox trio of pickets. Henricksen was one of the most dangerous pinch-hitters of his day, and in this game he was the lead-off man.

When the day began, the weather was sunny but muggy. Walsh struck out Henricksen and I was one of the fans who cheered the big, handsome man on the mound. Then Clyde Engle, an infielder, grounded out, second to first. Speaker took his turn at the plate. He had already won recognition as one of the stars of the period. He was very relaxed at the plate and met the ball with an easy, level swing. Walsh struck Speaker out, and walked into the dugout with more cheers ringing.

In their first time at bat, the White Sox jumped ahead. This was the way I liked it. Ed Walsh setting the opposition down in order, and the Sox pounding out a lead at the start of the game. I could, in those days, always enjoy a one-sided game if my side was winning.

Matty McIntyre, right fielder, led off for the White Sox. Stepping into a pitch by Ray Collins, a southpaw and one of Boston's most effective pitchers, he sent the ball sailing to-wards the right-field bleacher fence, and I was standing on my seat, screaming. It was a triple. Harry Lord, the third baseman and, like McIntyre, a left-handed batter, popped out. But Jimmy Callahan bunted in a run. Two more hits produced a second White Sox run.

Walsh struck out two more batters while retiring the Red Sox one-two-three in the second inning. My team was in the lead; my favorite pitcher was in peak form. I was delighted. But the ball game was delayed by rain. I waited, hoping, wanting to pray for the sun to come out so that four-and-a-half innings might be played. And the sun did reappear. I joined in the cheers when the players again took the field.

In the third inning, Lee Tannehill, the rangy White Sox shortstop who was then near the close of his career, poled a long fly between right and center field. Speaker and Henricksen, racing for the ball, collided; they were both stretched out on the field, and Tannehill reached third. It seemed that they were both seriously injured, but Speaker was able to walk off the field; Henricksen was carried off.

By the fourth inning, fans began to realize that Walsh was holding Boston hitless, and from then on, tension mounted. With each successive inning, Walsh was cheered. By the seventh inning, I was close to breathlessness. I watched and prayed with many pitched balls. The eighth inning was a torture of worry and release with each batter going out. And then the ninth inning came up. Walsh took the mound and threw his warm-up pitches to Jim Block. I couldn't talk and sat with my eyes riveted on the big pitcher. I was especially hopeful because the tag end of the batting order was up. But I was in fear. One hit and it would be spoiled. One hit could seem more terrible than the end of the world.

Yerkes, the second baseman, stepped into the batting box. Out. Then, as the next hitter went to the plate, the announcer came out with his megaphone, informing us that Nunamaker, a substitute catcher, was pinch-hitting for the pitcher. I anguished with each pitch, but Nunamaker struck out. The game was now narrowed down to one batter. The crowd watched, silent, gripped and held as I was. There was the crack of the bat. I was about to groan. But Amby McConnell, the Chicago second baseman, went to his left, grabbed the ball and the batter was thrown out. Chicago won, 5 to 0. There was a roar as the players quickly scuttled off the ball field.

And I felt as though I were one of the important persons in the whole world. I had not only seen a no-hit game pitched; I had seen it hurled by my favorite baseball hero.

Some of the most exciting early games I saw were in 1912, when the Boston Red Sox came to town. They won the pennant that year, and they always beat the White Sox when Earl and I went to the games. Smoky Joe Wood, who belongs in the Hall of Fame, won 34 and lost 5 that year. In memory, it seems as though he hurled all those games against Chicago. With the shadows pushing over the ball park, he would stand out there on the mound in his red-trimmed gray uniform, hitch up his pants and throw. To this day, I have a recollection of a strange sensation as if my head had emptied while he fired the ball in the shadowy park. The White Sox couldn't touch him. Once or twice I tried to play a dirty trick on him.

"Take him out!" I yelled.

This was a common cry of the fans, but my uncle had advised me never to shout this. He'd said that to do so was unsportsmanlike, and that it really hurt a pitcher's feelings. I didn't at all want to be unsportsmanlike, but somebody had to do something about Smoky Joe Wood. To keep seeing the White Sox lose was not at all as bad as going to Hell when you would die, but it was Hell enough. So I cast sportsmanship to Hell-and-gone.

"Take him out!" I yelled again.

Today this would be described as putting the whammy on a pitcher. However, it was Smoky Joe Wood who did the whammying.

Up came the White Sox. And the fans yelled and commented. For Wood on the mound jerked up his pants, and wound up. Perhaps Walter Johnson was faster than Wood. Perhaps Grove and Feller were. But Wood threw smoke and in 1912, if there was a better pitcher than Wood in baseball, even Walter Johnson or Christy Mathewson, the difference was merely academic. No pitcher ever depressed a little boy in the stands more than Joe Wood did me. Why did the Boston manager, Jake Stahl, have to pitch him against the White Sox?

"Pull 'em up, Joe!" a fan would yell.

And Joe Wood jerked at his pants. But that did the White Sox no good. A semipro team could have done as badly against Wood as the White Sox.

But after 1912, Joe Wood was never the same again. His arm went dead. He came back as a good outfielder with Cleveland and played in the 1920 World Series.

Of course Tris Speaker was a Red Sox player, and so were Duffy Lewis, and Harry Hooper, as well as Larry Gardner who, for years, stood out as a hard-hitting and superior third baseman. He was one of the near-great players of his time.

There were many frustrations for me. I saw the White Sox lose too much. One of my principal consolations was that they could beat the Cubs every year in the City Series. I was not rabidly anti-Cub, but I liked to see or read about the White Sox beating them.

Ed Walsh was the only great player on the White Sox roster in 1911. Ray Schalk came in 1912, and by the end of 1913, he was regarded as a great catcher. It was exciting when Hal Chase was traded from New York to Chicago in 1913. Once, while he was with New York, I saw him single twice in a row and each time, he immediately stole second and third. For the short time he was with the White Sox, the games were more interesting. Chase, coming in on a bunt, was almost as exciting as Ty Cobb or Jackie Robinson on the bases. He was fast and graceful. He played farther away from the base than the other first baseman of his day, and he initiated the double play from first to second just about as perfectly as it has ever been done. While good fielders are greatly admired, not many of them are thought of as exciting fielders, except when they make spectacular catches. Joe Di Maggio was such a player because of his grace and sure judgment of fly balls. Chase was. He could be called a dramatic fielder. A left-hander, he could pivot like a ballet dancer; in fact, it is not at all inappropriate to speak of his movements, his footwork and his throwing and fielding as though it were a dance. I might add that Hal Chase was the only left-handed player I ever saw play second base. In 1916, when he was with the Cincinnati Reds and led the National League in batting, he played some games at second. Late in the season, Christy Mathewson, manager of the Reds, pitched for the last time. Opposed to him at the Cubs Park, now known as Wrigley Park, was Three-Fingered Brown. Both of the great pitchers and old rivals were finished, and just about all that Mathewson had left was his wonderful ease of motion. He was the winning pitcher that day in the most sentimental ball game I have ever attended. In Chicago, the memories of the old Giants-Cubs rivalry were strong and legendary. A remembrance of past baseball drama was felt among the fans even though the game was sloppy. Added to this was the fact that Joe Tinker was then the Cubs' manager. And Chase was the second sacker that day when Three-Fingered Brown lost his last one to Matty and left the pitcher's box in tears. There were few right-handed second basemen whom a manager would have preferred to Chase.

Hal Chase's brief career with the White Sox left an impression on me. I was sorry to read that he and Harry Lord had jumped to the Buffalo Federals in 1914. When the Federal League disbanded after the 1915 season, I remember how I hoped that Chase would be back in Chicago. I believe that the White Sox owner, Charles A. Comiskey, Sr., didn't want him back even though in 1916 the White Sox needed a first baseman. If the White Sox had had Chase in 1916, and he had played honestly, they might have won the pennant.

In 1920, the news broke that Chase had been quietly dropped from organized baseball for crookedness. This, coming on top of the expulsion of the eight "Black Sox," was a

shock. By then, I was a freshman in high school. We had a
weekly assignment of a composition in English. I filled almost
half a composition book sentimentally lamenting over the fall
of "Prince Hal," as he was called. My teacher, Father Albert
O. Dolan, O. Carm., who is now dead, got ten to fifteen times
more than he had asked for, at least in volume. This was one
of my first high-school compositions, and perhaps it might
suggest that it's no accident for me to be writing how I feel
about baseball.

Even now, when I see a game, I will occasionally recap-
ture a fleeting and fragmentary sense of those long forgotten
games, and of men, many of them almost lost in baseball
memory, going through the pre-game practice motions, and
then, after the pre-game formalities at the plate, and the
megaphoning of the batteries by an announcer, dashing out
on the field to take their position. Their achievements and
failures are now practically devoid of meaning. What does
it mean that the rookie outfielder, Ray Demitt, came to bat
as a White Sox pinch-hitter late in a losing game and in his
first official time at bat whammed out a triple to right? I
thought a star had been born. Or in 1913, a burly left-hander
in a White Sox uniform strode to the mound as a relief
pitcher. Before many of the fans had gotten his name, Reb
Russell had struck out Joe Jackson and Nap Lajoie. Or that
Red Kuhn was the first White Sox catcher to wear shin
guards. In 1911, Billy Sullivan and the other White Sox
catchers didn't wear shin guards. These are memories of dead
hopes and successes and of dead failures. There was Larry
Chappell, the $10,000 lemon who came to the White Sox in
1913 and didn't make it. But once, this was all vividly and
dramatically important and thrilling. Those were good and
happy moments, whether the White Sox won or lost. I am
glad to have known them.

My Grandmother Goes to Comiskey Park

My grandmother is no more. She passed away in her sleep in 1931. I was raised by her and probably she wanted to see a baseball game because I was so full of baseball in my boyhood, and she most likely wondered what it was which interested her grandson, her son, Tom, and so many of the men.

She was born in County Westmeath, Ireland, and emigrated to America during the Civil War. Working as a domestic in Brooklyn, her lady one day sent her to a nearby bakery. She heard tell that Mr. Lincoln was dead, shot. She always retained much of her Irish peasant girlhood in her speech and way of seeing life. She never quite understood all the change that was going on in this country. Baseball was part of the excitement and strangeness of her new country. But once she saw a game, she wanted to see more, and as a little old woman, in her Sunday black dress, she went to ladies day games alone in the early 1920's.

*Not telling anyone where she was going, she
would dress up of a Friday afternoon and go to
Comiskey Park on the street car. She came home
excited. She liked to see the way the men would
"lep" and run.*

*Baseball to her was part of the new world of
America, but she saw it with the wonder of an
unlettered peasant woman who had run the fields
of Ireland as a girl in bare feet.*

M Y grandmother knew absolutely nothing about baseball. At home, we talked of it incessantly, and whenever my brother and I, or my uncle and I went to a game, she
always questioned us about it. She seemed keenly interested
in who won, even though she knew nothing of the rules of the
game. Hearing that Friday was Ladies Day at Comiskey
Park and that women were admitted free, she decided to
see a game. She dressed up in her Sunday black silk dress,
put on the new hat which she wore to Sunday Mass, and off
we went to Comiskey Park.

This was in 1912, and the first Ladies Day game we saw
was a contest between the New York Highlanders and the
White Sox.

That year, as I've already indicated in one of these essays,
Ping Bodie was one of my favorites. Late in this particular
Ladies Day game, Ping was on third base. With a pitch, he
lit out to steal home. There was the slide and the cloud of
dust. I thought that he had been called out. In disappointment, I let out a shrill cry:

"Hard luck, Ping."

But my disappointment was needless. Ping Bodie safely
stole home. It so happened that Earl was at the game that
day, seated at another end of the park. He told me that night
that he had heard my shout when Ping Bodie stole home.

My grandmother plied me with questions, root-beer, hot

dogs and Cracker-Jack. She was intensely excited and bewildered. She watched everything and understood nothing.

"Son, why is the man leppin' for the ball?"

"Son, why do they make him out?"

"Why don't they let him run?"

I tried to answer her questions, and all about me there were genially amused men watching and listening to the talk between the little boy with glasses and curly hair and the little old Irish woman in her Sunday black clothes.

A man tried to explain a point of the game to her and she told him:

"Don't be making free with me. Sure and I know all about the baseball."

A few moments later she was leaning forward and asking the man:

"Mister, are you married?"

He told her no.

"Sure and a fine man like you, you should have a wife. Me oldest son isn't married. He supports me."

My grandmother went often to the Ladies Day games, and became a familiar figure in the grandstand back of the White Sox dugout near third base. She would, of course, take me and she would always wear her Sunday best clothes. And I never was able to explain to her what the game was about. She loved it even though until her dying day she didn't know what the plays meant.

Her favorite team was the Boston Red Sox. She was convinced that the best of all baseball teams was Boston because many of her relatives from the old country had settled in that city. They were fine people and if Boston was their home, then the Boston baseball team had to be the best of all, just as Westmeath was the best county in Ireland.

Several times, she took me to see the Boston Red Sox play the White Sox and whenever we saw these two teams play, the Red Sox won. This made her proud and happy. At supper

on those nights, she would tell my uncle with great enthusiasm:

"Tom, the Bostons won. Tom, you should see the way the
Bostons lep for the ball."

"Mother, did you understand the game?"

"Indeed I did, and you should see the men play. Ah, the
Bostons are fine men. Me mother's cousin settled in Boston
town . . ."

She would then be off on her relatives.

She never learned to read or write and was always asking
someone to read the newspaper to her. She would ask one of
us to do this and would invariably give the command:

"Read me the death notices."

Then she would say: "Read me about the Bostons."

When I came in at night with the box score edition of the
evening paper, she would ask:

"Son, did the Bostons win?"

If the Red Sox had won, she would brag and crow. Sometimes at supper she would tell my uncle:

"Tom, the Bostons won again."

In 1914, I was ten years old. One Friday afternoon we
went to the Ladies Day game as usual. I used to be let in
without charge at the turnstile where women were admitted.
But this time, the man at the turnstile refused to admit me
and told my grandmother that she would have to pay for me.
At first she was surprised and she said:

"The little boy is me grandson."

This didn't move the man. I stood there disappointed and
a little ashamed. I wanted to ask my grandmother to pay
for me and didn't want her to argue with the man.

But argue she did, until she had attracted a small crowd.

"If you don't let me grandson in with me, I'll never darken
this place as long as I live," she said in anger.

And she said more.

" 'Tis the last time I come here!

"I'll tell me cousin, Alderman Willie O'Toole, and he'll fix you. He'll fix you for insultin' me and me little grandson."

I was quite embarrassed. I pulled at her skirt and weakly said:

"Mother . . ."

"Be still Son," she said, and looking up at the man:

"I'll tell the man that owns the ball park."

The man at the turnstile tried to explain to her that only ladies were admitted without the price of admission. This meant nothing to my grandmother. She gave him one of her best tongue-lashings. Then in a gesture of pride and with her head raised in dignity, she took my hand and said:

"Come on, Son, we'll never be seen here again."

My hopes were gone. But just as she started to lead me away, the man at the turnstile relented:

"All right, Lady, come on in and the boy too."

She proudly passed through the turnstile, her head held high. Then she said to the man:

" 'Tis well for you you let me grandson in."

"That's all right, Lady . . ."

"Aw, you're a fine man. Tell me, are you married?"

"Yes, Lady."

"Well, God will bless you and your wife."

After 1914, I didn't go often to the games with her. But then, she would go alone. When she came home she would always say:

"I hied meself down to the baseball. It would do your heart good to see the men and the way they ran and lep for the ball."

She kept going to Ladies Day games on into the middle 1920's, and invariably, she came home excited and happy. And she never deserted the Bostons. They always remained her favorites.

She loved baseball and understood absolutely nothing about the game.

Ed Walsh Pitches a No-Hit Game

I waited over twenty years to write of Ed Walsh's no-hit game. And my account of it is part of my novel, A WORLD I NEVER MADE. *Walsh pitched this game on August 27th, 1911, and I never forgot it. Down the years, I did not see another no-hit game pitched until Don Larsen hurled his perfect game in the 1956 World Series. Perhaps because I was a boy in 1911, Walsh's game excited me more than Larsen's.*

"I HOPE Ed Walsh pitches today. If he does, he'll skunk them, because he's the greatest pitcher there is," Danny said as they walked toward Fifty-first Street.

"How about Three-fingered Brown?" Bill said.

"Wait till you see Walsh pitch if he does today."

They paid the fare at the Fifty-first Street elevated station and waited in the center of the long boarded platform. Near them was a young fellow wearing a blue suit, high stiff collar and a plaid tie, and a girl in organdie with puffs of chestnut hair.

"Darling, it won't always be hard times," the fellow said. "When things are better, we'll announce our engagement," she answered.

"They're in love," Bill said, smirking at Danny.

Danny wondered what it meant to be in love and thought of how swell it was to be going to a ball game. He jumped about, twisted himself around, wished that he were already at the ball park.

"Jimmy Callahan is back in the game, Dan," Bill said.

"I like Pat Daugherty," Dan said.

"But Pat ain't the man he used to be. Pa was telling me something about how he helped win the world series of 1903 by hitting a home run with the bases full. Pa doesn't think, either, that Pat is the man he used to be. He's getting old," Bill said.

"I guess so," Danny said thoughtfully.

The train stopped alongside the platform. They got in and Bill took a seat next to the window. Danny wished he had it. But the bigger guy always got what he wanted over a littler guy. At home they could tell him what to do, and they could tell Bill, too. And Bill, because he was four years older and bigger, could take what he wanted and give Danny the pickings. Just wait until he was a big man!

"If we were getting down earlier, we could stand by the players' gate and watch them come in their clothes, but it's too late now," Bill said, and Danny was even more disappointed than Bill. "Remember the game we saw with the Athletics, and we stood before it by the players' gate and when I said to you that there was Pat Daugherty, he cursed us?"

"Uh huh!" said Danny.

"Doc White and Roy Corhan are nicer. They paid our carfare on the car after games this year. I guess Doc White, the pitching dentist, is a favorite of both of us, huh, Dan?" Bill said, and Danny nodded agreement.

They got off at the Indiana station. A kid of about ten

kept staring at Danny and looking at his white stockings, and Danny would have been afraid if Bill wasn't along to stick up for him.

"Uncle Al makes you wear sissy stockings, doesn't he?" Bill said, noticing the kid staring at Danny's stockings.

"I don't want to. I got to. He makes me," Danny gloomily said.

"Papa calls Uncle Al the dude. Pa said to Ma that her two goddamn brothers were dudes, and Ma got sore, and they had a fight, yelling at each other, until Pa took a sock at Ma. Then he got sorry and sent me out for ice cream, and we had ice cream, and Pa started kissing Ma, and petting her, the same way she pets us kids."

They boarded another train, and stood on the platform where men were smoking. Danny overheard a fat man saying that the White Sox were no good, so he guessed that the fat man must be a Cub fan, just like Bill was. They got off with the crowd at Thirty-fifth Street. Crossing State Street, the sight of so many groups of Negroes lolling and talking on the corner made Danny afraid, because at home they always said that niggers would do things to him, and you never could trust a nigger because if you gave him an inch he always took a mile.

Bill took such long steps that Danny almost had to run to keep up with him as they pressed along Thirty-fifth Street in the steady parade of people who were hastening to the ball park a few blocks west. Suddenly, Bill pulled out a box of Melachrino cigarettes, paused to light one, proudly puffed and inhaled, letting the smoke come out of his nostrils.

"I copped these on Aunt Margaret the other night. But if you snitch on me, I'll lam your ears in," Bill said, placing his closed fist under Danny's nose.

"I won't. Honest!" Danny said, cowering.

They passed under the viaduct, and still Bill was walking too fast for his brother. A popcorn machine zizzed in front of the Greek ice-cream parlor at Thirty-fifth and Wentworth. Danny kind of thought he wanted a soda, but Comiskey Park, Home of the White Sox, was just ahead, and they had to hurry. They could spend their money on popcorn and pop and red-hots inside the ball park. Drawing near the grandstand entrance at Shields Avenue, they heard clapping and cheering from inside the stadium. Bill ran, and Danny tore after him on his little legs. Both of them were admitted through the turnstile on the single ticket. Bill galloped up the runway to the grandstand, and Danny, out of breath, tried courageously to keep pace with him.

Outfitted in gray uniforms with red trimmings, the Boston Red Sox went through their batting practice. One player after another took cuts at pitched balls while substitutes and pitchers trotted about the outfield catching and retrieving balls which traveled that distance.

"That's Tris Speaker batting, Dan," Bill said, pointing, both of them eating red-hots and sipping pop through straws.

They both watched the well-built left-handed batter take an even, graceful swing which seemed to have little force behind it, and yet the ball he hit bounced off the right-field bleachers' fence, several hundred feet from the home plate.

"An easy double, may be a triple in the game," Bill said, pleased with the blow Speaker had cracked.

"It's only practice and doesn't count," Danny said.

"Tris hits 'em the same in the game," Bill said.

"Gee, I wish it would start," Danny said, and he smiled, for just as he spoke he heard the bell signaling the end of the Boston team's period of batting practice.

He watched the White Sox, wearing white uniforms and white stockings, as they trotted out on the field. Hugh Duffy, the manager, slapped grounders to the infielders and they scooped them up and tossed the ball around. The outfielders shagged fly balls that were fungoed to them.

"Ed Walsh is pitching today, Dan," Bill said, and as he spoke he pointed to a pitcher warming up near the White Sox bench by third base, a husky man with a long-sleeved red flannel undershirt under his uniform shirt.

"The Sox are going to win," Danny said, eagerly clapping his hands together, watching Ed Walsh toss pitches to a catcher.

"Don't count your chickens before they're hatched," Bill said.

Bill puffed on a cigarette. Danny watched the White Sox infielders practicing.

"Only fifteen more minutes and the game starts," Bill said after the bell had jingled again and the Boston Red Sox took the place of the White Sox on the field and went through their period of fielding practice in the same fashion as had the White Sox.

"A southpaw's warming up for the Red Sox, Bill," Danny said, pointing over toward the Boston bench, where a left-handed pitcher was throwing to a catcher.

"Dan, see that fellow on the third-base foul line hitting fungo flies out to right field?" Bill said, pointing.

"Who is it?"

"Buck O'Brien. He's one of the best fungo hitters in the big leagues," Bill said.

They watched Buck O'Brien toss a soiled ball into the air, grip the long light willow bat he held, swing, lift the ball, and it sailed out and out. Danny lost sight of it until he saw the bleachers' fans way out in right field scrambling.

"Knocked it clean out of the park," Bill said with admiration.

"They ought to hurry up and start the game," Danny said.

"Hold your horses," Bill said.

There was applause. Two blue-shirted workmen appeared, carrying a white-boarded wooden rectangle. They laid it on each side of home plate, whitewashing in the batters' boxes, and at the same time another workman traced in the foul lines with a little whitewash cart.

A popcorn man came by, shouting in a peppy manner, selling freshly buttered Blue Ribbon popcorn, and they bought sacks. Eating it, they watched the captains gather by the home plate with the umpire, saw the White Sox trot into position, saw the announcer go with his megaphone directly behind the home plate, and call up the lineups to the press box. Then the announcer turned and began calling the batteries into the grandstands at various angles.

"THE BATTERIES FOR TODAY'S GAME! FOR CHICAGO, WALSH AND BLOCK! FOR BOSTON, W. COLLINS AND CARRIGAN!"

"It's good luck for a pitcher to strike out the first batter that faces him," Danny said to Bill with joyous hope, while the crowd still cheered, and Henricksen, the Boston lead-off man, took a trip back to the bench with his bat in his hand.

"There's twenty-six more to get out before the ball game is over. But let's watch the game instead of jawing. There's Clyde Engle at bat now," Bill said, pointing, and just as he did the right-handed hitter at the plate swung, hitting a ground ball to second base and being retired at first.

Scattered handclapping greeted Tris Speaker as he stepped into the batter's box and stood waiting, measuring off his swings while Walsh cupped his hands over the ball and held it before his mouth.

"Put a lot of saliva on it for this boy, Ed!" a fan near Danny yelled in a booming voice.

"Come on, you Bull Moose! Oh, you Ed Walsh, strike him out!" Danny shrieked in a high-pitched voice, causing men around them to watch him with amusement.

"What do you think of that?" Danny breathlessly said to Bill amid his shrieks and cheers after Ed Walsh had retired the side by striking out Tris Speaker.

"It's just luck when any pitcher whiffs Tris," Bill said, but Danny did not listen to him, because he eyed Ed Walsh striding off the diamond, dropping his glove on the foul side of the third-base line, walking with lowered head to the White Sox bench.

"Come on, you White Sox, skunk them green!" he piped, while the White Sox lead-off man, Matty McIntyre, a left-handed hitter, faced the pitcher. He stepped into a pitch, the crack of the bat echoing, the ball sailing out into right field. The crowd was on its feet, cheering. Danny jumped up to his feet and clapped his hands with joy. Henricksen was throwing the ball in, and Matty was rounding second and coming on. Safe on third!

A contagious animation permeated the spectators, and they sat cheering, calling, clapping, whistling, hoping that Harry Lord, another left-handed batter, would drive home the first run. There were groans. A pop-up, smothered easily by Yerkes, the Red Sox second baseman. Jimmy Callahan stepped into the right-hand batter's box, and he was applauded, entreated to bring in that run. And again Danny was on his feet. A bunt. The run in. A cheer. Calahan beat the throw to first base.

"The game's young yet. Lots can happen in eight more innings," Bill said, unheard by Danny.

The crowd broke loose as a burly ballplayer stepped into the right-hand batter's box, nervously pounded his bat on the white rubber home plate, half swung it in the air, faced the pitcher.

"Come on, Ping Bodie! Come on, Ping Bodie!" Danny cried.

"We'll see what the dago from the Pacific Coast League can do," Bill said.

"Give it the spaghet, Ping!" a mighty-voiced fan roared, drawing laughter from those who heard him.

"Oh, you fence-buster!" Danny shrilled as Ping Bodie stepped into a pitch, the ball traveling out into left field like a rifle shot.

Before the crowd had recovered its breath, Amby Mc-

Connell, the second baseman, had rifled a one-base hit to right field, and the second run was home. Danny clapped his hands, squirmed on his seat. The White Sox were winning. Ed Walsh was pitching, and he was seeing it all. The inning ended with a pop-up, and a foul fly which the catcher caught, and the teams changed positions. But he knew the White Sox were going to win. And he was again cheering, and clapping when the White Sox trotted off the field a second time, and Ed Walsh was again greeted like a hero for having retired the side in order, chalking up two more strike-outs.

The Sox up again. Block the catcher. Out. Walsh. Out. "Come on. Matty, sock it green!" Danny called.

His expression dropped. McIntyre hit a slow bounder to Clyde Engle, the first baseman, and streaked it down the base line. A cheer went up, and Danny clapped his hands because he was safe. And now Harry Lord was up, and he ought to hit one because he was the captain of the team. The pitch, the swing, the crack of the bat, a sizzler over first base, both men running, McIntyre on third base, Lord on second, and everybody yelling. The White Sox were winning, and Ed Walsh was pitching. Wait till he got home to tell Uncle Al about it. Callahan batting amid cheers, swinging, the rising roar, Danny jumping on his feet, a groan of disappointment when the ball was caught way out against the bleachers.

"Nothing ever gets by Duffy Lewis in left field," Bill said proudly.

"Wait till next time, you wait!" Danny said.

"That boy Lewis isn't an outfielder, he's a well," a fan behind them said.

"It's raining, Dan. If the game doesn't go to four and a half innings, it doesn't go in the record," Bill said.

"Gosh darn the luck," Danny said broken-heartedly.

They had pop and red-hots and Danny fretted while the game was delayed. He looked out with a pouting face on the green outfield and on the infield, which workmen covered with canvas. The rain continued. Gee, it was awful, the old rain cheating him and Ed Walsh. He asked God please to stop it from raining so the game could go on, and Ed Walsh not be cheated. Please, God, stop that rain!

He yelled when, after ten minutes, the canvas was drawn off the infield and the game went on. And with two men out in the third inning, Lee Tannehill, the rangy White Sox shortstop, swung a trifle late, and the ball soared out into right center field. He jumped on his seat, and saw Tannehill on third. Two Red Sox outfielders were lying on the ground, and players ran to them. There was a buzz of anxious conversation all around them, and Bill stood up, watching, and he wouldn't tell Danny what had happened. One of the players was walking in, helped by teammates. The other was not as badly hurt. The crowd cheered.

"Henricksen is hurt worse than Speaker. I'm glad that Tris isn't too badly hurt," Bill said.

"What happened, Bill?" Danny asked.

"They ran into each other," said Bill.

"Gee, poor Speaker," said Danny, his voice sad.

Substitutes were sent in, a first baseman named Williams taking Engle's place, Engle going out to center field and Riggert to right field. The announcer called out these changes, and the game continued.

The fourth inning. Engle getting a base on balls. Williams in Speaker's place on the batting order, out. Duffy Lewis, lofting a fly to right field, caught without effort. The Sox coming in, and Danny heard a man beside him saying that they hadn't gotten a hit off Walsh yet, and that was the first man to reach base.

"Bill! Bill! Maybe Walsh will pitch a no-hit game," Danny said.

"The game's young yet," Bill said.

In the fifth and sixth innings, both teams were set down in one-two-three order. Danny was clapping, twisting again.

The White Sox were winning. And nobody was even getting a hit off the Bull Moose. He watched the big pitcher stride onto the field for the start of the seventh inning. God, please don't let it be the lucky seventh for Boston. Only three more innings to hold them. If Big Ed could do it. He would! God wasn't going to let Boston get any hits.

"I hope that he goes on and doesn't give them any hits. It would be tough luck to go this far and then get nicked," Bill said, making Danny so glad, because now Bill was for Ed Walsh, and not against him.

Two out already in this inning. God was helping Ed Walsh. Riggert up. Out. Oh, you Ed Walsh. God wouldn't let him hit Walsh now. He stood on his seat, yelled himself hoarse, clapped his small hands, and Walsh walked in to the bench receiving a thunderous ovation. And it increased when he walked out, bat in hand to start the White Sox half of the inning. He laced out a single, and the bat boy ran around to first base carrying a blue sweater for him to wear on the bases so that his arm didn't get cold. Danny watched Ed Walsh, his foot on first base, putting on his sweater. With eyes of adoration, he followed Walsh's fingers while the big fellow buttoned his sweater. And he clapped his hands when Ping Bodie, with two men out, smaked a single, and Walsh scored.

And the eighth inning. He couldn't stand it. Each time Walsh pitched, the ball might be hit safely. When he drew his hands to his mouth to spit on the ball, all the fans were quiet. They waited, just as Danny did, holding their breath, while Walsh pitched. They were so glad, as he was, when it wasn't hit. Three out. Another ear-splitting ovation. When he grew up, maybe the fans would cheer him like this. He wanted the White Sox to hurry up and get out. He couldn't wait. He wanted Walsh to strike them out, one, two, three, in the last inning. They were out now. The last inning. God was going to help Walsh. God was! God, please!

Yerkes, the second baseman up, come on, Ed, you got the end of the batting order, please, God, help him, and out, one gone. Now a pinch hitter for the pitcher. Who was it? Would he ruin things? The announcer. Nunamaker, the third-string catcher, a right-handed hitter. He couldn't be so hard. Strike one! Strike out. Danny cheered as loud as he could, his voice now feeble from hoarseness, his hands sore from clapping. Bill glanced up and down his score card, and said that that made eight strike-outs today for Walsh, and Danny was glad, but he couldn't talk. The last man. If God helped Ed Walsh get him out, he would never again try to miss Mass, or not do what he was told at home. He would try every way he could to be as good as his guardian angel, and never hurt God's feelings. A bounder. He held his breath. Amby Mc-Connell had it, the throw to first base. Out! Whee! He stood up on his seat and gave all of himself in a last yell, as the applause and cheering boomed. The players hurriedly scuttled off the field, Walsh chased by fans who wanted to get near him.

Just think of it, he had seen Ed Walsh pitch a no-hit game. And some day he was going to be like him.

"Come on, Dan, we'll go under the stands by the clubhouse and watch the players come out. We'll be able to see Ed Walsh."

My First World Series Game

In Chicago of 1917, it was, perhaps, a bigger event to see a world series game than it is today. Almost any boy in America can see such games now on television.

Eddie Cicotte pitched one of his masterful games. Today's generation is not usually aware of how great a pitcher Cicotte was. They did not see him, and, further, he was one of "the Black Sox" and confessed to having helped throw a world series for money. But for his pathetic mistake, Cicotte would today be in the Hall of Fame. When he confessed to a grand jury, he is reported to have said:

"I have cried aplenty over this case. I didn't weep and wail as some say, but I guess there were plenty of tears in my eyes and the crying I have done inwardly is much greater than the tears which actually came out."

But in 1917, Cicotte had no cause for tears and he hurled one of his masterful and artistic games. But for 1919, not only Cicotte, but also Weaver, Jackson and, perhaps, Felsch would be memo-

*rialized in Cooperstown, along with Ray Schalk
and Eddie Collins.*
*This game is one which I have remembered
down the years.*

I HAD heard the World Series talked of before I understood
anything about baseball. In fact, I had grown up on the
feats of the 1906 Chicago White Sox, known as the Hitless
Wonders. My uncles, Earl, and my father had spoken of how
this team had beaten the famous Chicago Cubs, managed
by Frank Chance. The names of White Sox players of that
year had acquired an almost legendary significance—Jiggs
Donohue, George Davis, Fielder Jones, Nick Altrock, and
the substitute infielder, George Rohe, who had smashed out
a triple and become the Series hero. And there were Pat
Dougherty, Lee Tannehill, Ed Walsh, Billy Sullivan and Doc
White, all of whom I had seen play.

My first opportunity to see a World Series game was in
1917 when my team, the White Sox, and New York Giants,
managed by Muggsy McGraw, were to play. My Uncle Tom
was on the road selling, but he sent me a money order for
five dollars so that Earl and I could see a couple of games.
The opening game was on a Saturday morning. Earl slept
with me at my grandmother's the night before, and we arose
at about 4 A.M. I had read newspaper stories of how lines
of fans waited all night to buy bleacher seats. I wanted to do
this. I was thirteen that year. Like many fans, I saw baseball as an historic sport. I hoped to see an historic World
Series. I could talk of this in the years to come, just as I had
heard my father and my uncles, and other men, talk of the
1906 Series. And since 1911, I had waited for the White Sox
to win a pennant. Now it had happened. I was inwardly excited, and filled with a sense of the dramatic.

Outside it was dark. There had been some rain the night
before and I was anxious about the weather. We were very

quiet in the kitchen, which was off of my grandmother's bedroom in the flat on South Park Avenue where we lived. She
had prepared sandwiches for us to take along to the game,
but we made our own breakfast. During all my boyhood
years coffee and sweet rolls never tasted better than they did
on that October morning of 1917.

And there, against the radiator, was my shaggy airedale
dog, Gerry. I loved her. My uncle had found her on a street
in Boston and had shipped her home to us. With her black
tip of a nose, she stared at us mutely pleading for food. We
gave her breakfast. We tried to get her to drink coffee, but
she wouldn't touch it.

Finally, and well before 5 A.M., we were off, leaving by
the back door, going down the back stairs, and along the
alley to Fifty-eighth Street in the chilly pre-dawn. We took
the elevated train to Thirty-fifth Street, the Thirty-fifth Street
trolley to Wentworth Avenue and found the line-up of men
waiting before the bleacher ticket office. It was still dark
when we took our places in this line. There were about three
hundred men ahead of us in one of the waiting lines. My
anxiety disappeared. I had feared that there might be thousands waiting when I arrived. I had attributed to others, and
to grown men, my own feelings about baseball. I was a boy
still in short pants. The men about us in line greeted our
coming with friendliness. They liked seeing such a young
and devoted fan waiting as they were.

It was a bit raw, and here and there, men had built fires.
Venders were out with hot coffee and we bought and drank
quite a quantity of it. About every hour, we ate. I felt important and I was very happy. All the cares I had in my mind
were those of my own impatience for time to pass, so that I
would get inside of the ball park—so that it would be time
for the players to come out on the field for practice—so that
it would be time for the game to begin. And of course, there
was the greater care or worry—would the White Sox win? I

had impatiently looked forward to all of this. I was flattered and pleased with myself when one of the men in line said he thought I was a brave little fellow, to come out so early to see the game. And there was much baseball talk. I spoke up with the authority of an old-time fan. Earl and I talked of how many games we'd seen together—of Babe Ruth pitching, Smoky Joe Wood in the box, Tris Speaker, Ed Walsh's no-hit game in 1911, Rabbit Maranville and his singular way of suddenly jerking out his hands at the level of his belt line to catch pop-ups. And we discussed the White Sox and Giant players. Now, we would have more to talk about.

The dawn came, gray and still chilly. My sense of excitement grew. This long wait was an adventure rather than a boring experience. These strange men standing in line, sitting on boxes, squatting by a fire, playing poker, chatting intermittently about baseball, showing the same concern as I did about the weather, shivering a bit as I did—they and I were bound together by a common passion. And those around me were kind and friendly. I felt secure and unafraid and I was like them. And then, too, I was here in line and would actually see something which I believed that almost all of the men and boys in America were interested in and wished they could see. Then also, I was a boy. Someday I would grow to be a man, and—I hoped—a big-league star who would play in a world series game . . . while other men and boys would stand in line to see me as I was standing in line to see Eddie Collins, Joe Jackson, Ray Schalk and all of the other players who would be out on the diamond of Comiskey Park.

The hours passed. Behind us, the line swelled rapidly. Looking behind me, the men stretched out of sight, and I was told that the line was over two blocks long. A cold sun was coming up. Twice men approached Earl and me and offered us money for our place. The men about us told us to let these men in and for us to stay in line. We made about a dollar that way, but the third time we were asked, the men behind us said that was enough. We held our places this time rather than sell them.

At ten o'clock, the line began to move. The gates were open. We got inside and took seats high up in the right-center field bleachers. Fans poured in after us and the gates were quickly closed. The big bleachers at Comiskey Park were jammed with fans.

I controlled my impatience as best I could, waiting through the morning, looking out at the large empty playing field, and at the empty grandstand and box seats. The crowd kept pouring into the bleachers, and into the pavilion.

There was the diversion of a band. And Earl and I ate more than we should. And there was the constant sense of expectancy. Finally, after the slow wait, there was a cheer. The White Sox were coming out. Far away in their dugout, a few players could now be seen. Then more, and the players appeared on the field to engage in warm-up catching practice. And then, very soon, the White Sox engaged in their batting practice.

The White Sox wore new red, white and blue uniforms instead of their regular season all white uniforms. These latter were white with a black S on the left side of the shirt. The stockings were pure white. The new World Series uniforms, occasioned by the War, were trimmed with red and blue. The S on the shirt was red and blue against a white background and the white stockings were banded with blue and red stripes. I liked these new uniforms very much and hoped that they would be worn in the 1918 season. They weren't.

We sat through the long practice session, alternately interested, impatient and bored. The air of tension, expectancy and excitement slowly grew through the periods of fielding and batting practice. The grandstand and box seats began to fill up. There were sporadic cheers for players, as one or an-

other hit a long ball in the batting practice. There were the
Giants to watch when they took their turn at batting practice. Two of the Giant players in whom Earl and I were most
interested were Benny Kauff, the center fielder, and Heinie
Zimmerman, the third baseman. Heinie Zimmerman, several
years earlier, had been one of Earl's favorites. He had then
played on the Cubs and in 1912 he had led the National
League in hitting. During the 1913 and 1914 seasons in particular, Zimmerman had received much publicity because of
his run-ins with umpires. He had acquired the reputation of
being hot-headed, had been put out of some games, and had
almost become engaged in a serious fight with Rabbit Maranville, and one or two other players of the Boston Braves. He
was a natural hitter, and I feared that he would be dangerous to the White Sox. Benny Kauff had led the Federal
League in batting and had been heralded as a new Ty Cobb.
When the Federal League had broken up, Kauff had been one
of the most sought after of the players. McGraw had gotten
him for the Giants. He hadn't fulfilled the expectations, but
in 1917, he had hit over .300. Kauff batted and threw left-
handed, and we took him at the value which sports writers
had placed on him. Still, I insisted and believed that Happy
Felsch, the White Sox center fielder, was a much better
player. We'd both read that Kauff was a very fancy dresser
and that he was supposed to carry twenty-six suits around
with him and we talked of this, watching him catch flies
during the fielding practice.

Finally the practice and the opening ceremonies were
over with, and the White Sox ran out onto the field, full of
pep, and hailed by cheers. I was confident. For there was
Eddie Cicotte in the box. When he was right, he was almost
unbeatable. McGraw had been expected to pitch his ace,
Schupp, but he pulled a surprise and sent in Slim Sallee.

On the fifth pitch, George Burns, the New York left fielder,
stung a single over second base. A bad beginning. But the

game was young. Earl said that now Buck Herzog, the Giant second baseman, would try to sacrifice. Instead Herzog hit an easy fly to Joe Jackson in left field. McGraw was going to keep trying to cross up the·White Sox. Well, this time it hadn't worked. Then Benny Kauff hit an easy fly to Joe Jackson. And on the second ball pitched to Heinie Zimmerman, Burns went down to second. There was a tense moment. Schalk would get him. But Burns slid around Eddie Collins for a stolen base. It was Cicotte versus Heinie. But Zimmerman flew out to Happy Felsch in center field. I always enjoyed watching Felsch snag fly balls and considered him to be the equal of Tris Speaker as a fielder.

One Giant inning was safely gone. Now if the White Sox would go out and give Cicotte a lead, he would hold it. And the White Sox lead-off man and right fielder, Shano Collins, lined a one-base hit to right field. Then McMullin, the third baseman, sacrificed Collins to second. It looked good and there was drama in the very first inning. With a man on second and one out, the two White Sox stars, Eddie Collins and Joe Jackson, were coming up. And Eddie Collins was a good money player. But the Giant shortstop, Art Fletcher, threw Eddie Collins out at first by a step and Buck Herzog killed our hopes when he went back at top speed and snagged a low fly off Joe Jackson's bat. Sallee looked as though he would be hard to beat.

The game turned into a pitcher's battle. The play was almost air-tight. But in those days, a pitcher's battle was as interesting as a slugging match is today. In the second inning, the Giant first baseman, Holke, got an infield hit, but Cicotte neatly picked him off first base. In the third inning, the Giants put two men on base, but Benny Kauff ended the inning by fouling out to Chick Gandil off of first base.

The White Sox scored in the third inning. Heinie Zimmerman was booed because Cicotte handcuffed him at the plate, and the fans liked to razz Zim. But he made a fine play at

third base in the third inning, robbing Ray Schalk of a hit.
Then Eddie Cicotte, a switch hitter, and a good batsman,
lined a single to center. A moment later, the crowd was yelling when John Shano Collins shot a line single to right field.
Cicotte was running the bases as pitchers do not in the
modern game. Robertson, the Giant right fielder, recovered
the ball fast. He had a powerful left arm. I watched him
throw, eager but confident. Far away in the infield there was
the slide and the play and then, disappointment and dis-
gruntlement. Cicotte was out. What was the matter with
Pants Rowland, the White Sox manager, and Kid Gleason,
the coach? All around me, they were condemned. I sat back
glum. A chance to score had been killed. However, Collins
had gone to second on the play. Fred McMullin was at bat.
He hit the ball on a line to center field. Benny Kauff played
one of the roles for which he, like Heinie Zimmerman, was
destined. He played the goat. Kauff dashed in for the ball,
took a foolish dive, trying to make a shoestring catch. He
failed. John Collins scored. McMullin was on second base.
My hero, Eddie Collins, was at bat and I was happy. Eddie
Collins popped out to Art Fletcher. But our White Sox were
winning one to nothing, and with Cicotte in top form, this
might be all that was needed.

Heinie Zimmerman opened the fourth inning by delight-
ing many of the fans. He walked up on a pitch and lunged.
Ray Schalk, the catcher, caught the foul ball which he hit.
In the White Sox half of the fourth inning, Happy Felsch
became a World Series hero. He swung. The ball traveled.
The crowd shouted. It knew what had happened. So did
George Burns over in left field. He started to run and then he
stopped to watch Felsch's powerful drive sail through the
sunny afternoon. The ball landed in the bleachers. Home
Run Baker in his heyday couldn't have done better. Happy
Felsch trotted around the bases. In those days, such home
runs were achievements.

In four innings, the White Sox had given me in the right-center field bleachers and Eddie Cicotte on the mound all that we needed—two runs.

But in the fifth some of my smug confidence was cracked like smashed china. Lew McCarty, the New York catcher, insulted Eddie Cicotte. Babe Ruth never was able to hit a home run off him. McCarty would have done this if he didn't have to run on a game leg which had been broken earlier in the season. McCarty unleashed a tremendous drive to right-center field. Because of his bad leg he was slow in turning this into a triple. Then Slim Sallee sent McCarty home with a single and the Sox only led two to one.

In the sixth inning Benny Kauff did as well at bat as he'd done in the field on McMullin's low liner. He fanned on three pitched balls. In the Giant seventh, Shoeless Joe Jackson took the same kind of a dive as had Benny Kauff. But where Benny became a goat, Joe flung himself into the role of hero. With Holke on first base, Lew McCarty smashed a low liner to left. Jackson came in and went for the ball head first. He caught the ball inches off the ground in one of the most spectacular catches I have ever seen. The umpires rushed out to left field as Jackson lay sprawled with the ball safe in his hands and thumbed an out signal amidst many cheers. Then Slim Sallee ended the inning with an easy fly to Happy Felsch.

In the eighth inning, Benny Kauff didn't fan. He hit a slow easy roller to Buck Weaver who made a wild throw for the only White Sox error of the day. With Zimmerman at bat, Kauff took a lead off first. This was a mistake. Cicotte threw quickly to Chick Gandil. Kauff was trapped and thrown out on a relay to second. The Ty Cobb of the Federal League was no Ty Cobb against the White Sox and the fans liked this.

Heinie Zimmerman was first up in the Giant ninth. Zim had made no hits all day, but he had offended the South

Side of Chicago by making two fine fielding plays. Now what would he do? He tapped to Cicotte in the pitcher's box and didn't even run. Art Fletcher and Davy Robertson were also easy outs and Cicotte walked off the field after pitching one of his masterpieces in his first World Series game. In 1919, it was different.

I went home thrilled and happy. The White Sox had won the first World Series game I ever saw. They would become World's Champions.

But the glorious afternoon didn't end happily. When I got home, my airedale dog, Gerry, was gone. She had run away during the day. She was never found and her loss hurt me more than even a New York Giant victory would have. It took from me the happiness and sense of thrill that I had carried home from Comiskey Park at Thirty-fifth and Shields.

A Workout in the Park

Here is another section from NO STAR IS LOST. *In fiction, I attempted to convey some sense of a boyhood memory which endured in my mind for years.*

"HELLO, Al," a lanky fellow said as Danny and Al came upon the group of men who were sitting on the grass, while others were catching flies which a fellow was fungoing out to them. The lanky fellow was standing up watching the ball as it was batted out, caught, thrown back to the hitter. He had a cigarette between his lips, and his shirt was off, showing the top of his B.V.D.'s and a sun-tanned pair of arms and shoulders.

"Hello, Joe," Al said.

"Glad to see you again, Al," said Joe.

"Ditto, Joe, old man," Al said.

"How was business this trip?" Joe asked.

"I was away on a vacation this time. But I'll know about business soon, because I'll start on the road for my fall trip after Labor Day," Al said.

"Think it's going to be good?" asked Joe.

"I don't know. This war in Europe makes everything uncertain," said Al.

"Say, wasn't that a damn crazy stunt for them Europeans to pull off, starting that war? It looks like the Germans are going to bounce the French around, too, and maybe take Belgium and France like Jack Johnson took Jim Jeffries," said Joe.

"The Germans like to dominate, that's the trouble with them," said Al.

"You know, that's a fact, Al. Now, down in my office there's a German. Do you know, he doesn't like to run his own department. He likes to run the whole office. He comes in to see me and says that I ain't attended to some damn thing or other, and that I ought to do everything more orderly. That's a fact. They want to dominate," said Joe.

"Of course, this war can't go on a very long time. Wilson and the Pope will probably stop it the way Teddy Roosevelt stopped that war between Japan and Russia," Al said.

"I guess so, but you know what I'm more interested in than this war on the other side of the ocean? I'm more interested in who's going to win that World Series," said Joe.

"Who do you think will win the National League pennant first?" Al asked.

"I don't know. Those Braves have spurted into second place, but then I think Muggsy McGraw is going to bring the Giants down the home stretch," said Joe.

"I think so. Boston hasn't much of a team. They have Johnny Evers, but Evers can't win it alone, smart as he is," Al said.

"Looks like Connie Mack's just about cleaned up his league again with that hundred-thousand-dollar infield of his," Joe said.

* * *

"Out for a workout, huh, O'Flaherty," the man hitting out flies yelled.

"Yes," Al called over to him.

"Well, go on out and I'll give you some to shag," he called.

"I want to warm the old soupbone up first," Al called back.

"Going to warm up first, huh, Al?" Joe said.

"Yes. You always have to do that or else you're liable to throw your arm out," Al said.

"We're all getting old and got to watch out for our wings now, don't we?" a stout fellow on the grass said.

Danny watched the man with the bat lift one way out, watched a fellow out there judge it, draw the ball down with both hands. He wished he could catch long flies now like that man did.

"Let's warm up, Dan," Al said.

They played catch in a corner by the gravel walk which ran through the park at this edge of the athletic field. There were two old men on a bench near them, talking Yiddish. Danny thought that it was funny, old men talking Yiddish. They were Abie Kabbibles, that's what they were. Al threw the ball with an easy and unstrained overhanded motion. He was a southpaw, and after tossing the ball he spit into the glove on his right hand. Danny caught the throw, returned it. Al continued tossing them easy. Danny wished that he was a little bigger and that Uncle Al was a pitcher on a team, and that when Uncle Al pitched, he would catch him. He wished that he could catch everything Uncle Al threw just as Bill did. Uncle Al could pitch pretty good. He had a fast ball, and a curve. Bill thought so, too, and Bill often caught Uncle Al, warming him up in the back yard. He guessed that when Uncle Al was younger and played ball a lot, he must have been a pretty good pitcher.

"I'm going to throw them faster now, Dan," Uncle Al said.

"All right. I can catch them," Danny called back; he spat into his glove, wished that he had a catcher's glove on. But then, by catching hard ones with a fielder's glove, he would toughen his hands, and it would be good for him to learn how to catch them fast with a fielder's glove.

Uncle Al wound up like a pitcher, swinging his left arm around in a circle twice, raising his right foot, and then he zoomed the ball at Danny straight and fast. His windup and motion were graceful. Danny caught the ball, returned it to him.

"Good work, Dan," Uncle Al said.

Danny set himself as Uncle Al wound up. He hoped that Uncle Al wouldn't toss them in too fast, and he hoped that he would. He hoped that he'd catch everything that Uncle Al threw at him, and he hoped that Uncle Al would burn them in, and he was a little bit worried because he only had a fielder's glove on, and he was worried anyway because maybe Uncle Al would pitch them too fast. He tried to imagine himself a big-league catcher warming up somebody like Red Russell or Eddie Plank just before a game. He missed a pitch.

"You didn't watch. I signaled to you that I would pitch a drop that time," Uncle Al said.

"I missed it," Danny said; he turned and trotted to retrieve the ball.

He tried to wing it all the way on the fly to Uncle Al, but he didn't have enough power in his arm. The ball rolled to Uncle Al. Danny trotted back to where he had been standing, to continue warming up his uncle.

✳ ✳ ✳

Uncle Al was out farther with the men, catching long flies that were being fungoed out there. Danny wished that he could go out farther and catch flies with them, but Uncle Al had told him to stay in closer, and to catch the throws as they came in and then to relay them to the fungo hitter. He had to stand in close, and every so often the man hitting out the flies and using the fungo bat Uncle Al had brought with them would bat him an easy fly or grounder. That wasn't so much fun. He was hardly able to wait until he could hurry up and get bigger so that he could play ball with bigger guys and men and catch flies with the men instead of being made to stay in here close. The man with the fungo bat was signaling to him that he was going to hit an easy one now. Danny set himself, his hands on his knees, waiting, watching the man with the fungo bat. The man slapped an easy grounder to Danny. Danny moved in on the ball to field it as if he were an infielder who was going to get off a quick throw and nail a man on a slow infield roller. The ball came bobbling along the grass. Danny grasped it. It dropped out of his hands. Just as if he'd made an error. Danny threw it underhanded along the ground. He was disappointed in himself. He stood now, hands on hips, and watched the man hit out a long fly, watched the ball sail outward in a curving arc, a small-white pellet outlined against the enormous blue sky.

"I have it," he heard Uncle Al cry.

He watched his uncle back up a few feet, wait, make an easy cupped catch. Uncle Al caught flies nicely. Uncle Al threw the ball to him, rolling it along the ground, his throw overhanded and without strain. The ball just rolled to Danny. He picked it up and flung it side-arm to the man batting them out.

But this wasn't any fun for him.

✳   ✳   ✳

Danny and Uncle Al sat with some of the men on the grass near the gravel path. He liked this. He might have liked it even better if he was with these men and Uncle Al wasn't around, because then he wouldn't have to watch what he said as he had to do now. And if his uncle wasn't one of the men, the others would let go in their talk, even if he was with them and was only a kid. But even so, he still liked it.

"Well, O'Flaherty, it wasn't a bad workout this morning, was it?" Joe said.

"It was good, good exercise," Al said.

"The kid here looks to me like he ought to be a ballplayer some day," Joe said, pointing at Danny. Danny beamed; he liked this fellow Joe, and he hoped that Joe was right in what he said.

"He has to learn a little yet," Al said.

"Sure he does. Everybody's got to learn. But he looks like he's got the makings of a ballplayer," Joe said.

"Want to be a ballplayer, Son?" a fellow named Jake asked Danny.

Danny nodded his head in the affirmative.

"Answer the gentleman, Sport," Al said, glancing proudly at his nephew.

"Yes, yes sir," Danny said.

"That's the Sport," Al said.

"Well, we won't have many more of these days," a fellow named Guy said.

"Nope, we won't," said Joe.

"Another summer come and gone. Pretty soon, you know, I'm going to be giving up this sort of thing. I was forty-three years old last week," Guy said.

"You want to say forty-three years young, not forty-three years old," Al said.

"It's all right to say that. But many a time I feel like it's old, not young," Guy said.

"Guy remember this. Tuck it away in your bonnet and keep it there. A man is as old as he feels, or as young as he feels. You know this thing in the air that they call psychology. Well, a man ought to use that. It'll work wonders for him, personally and in his business," Joe explained.

"That's the ticket, Joe," Al said.

"Psychology won't do a damn thing for an old soupbone. Ask Ed Walsh about that if you don't believe me," said Guy.

"Well, I don't know, now," Joe said, puffing on a pipe.

"If you have the right slant on something, that doesn't do you any harm or impede your progress. And psychology now, I have gone into it and studied it some in the last couple of years. Psychology amounts pretty much to having the right slant on something," Al said.

"Well, that much might be true, come to think of it," Guy said.

"Who's playing out to the Federal League ball game today?" a fellow named Jack asked.

"The Buffeds," Danny answered promptly.

"Rankin Johnson pitching?"

"He ain't due today. But he's started off good with the Chifeds," Danny said.

"That kid knows his game. Well, it's a good thing to keep a growing boy's mind occupied. Keeps them from asking too many questions," a fellow named Mike said, getting his words in before Al could speak. Al had opened his mouth to say something, and Danny knew what it was going to be. Uncle Al was going to call him down for using the word *ain't*.

"The kid is up on the game," Joe said.

"Yes, he is," Uncle Al said, and Danny was grateful for the men talking just then because they had saved him from a calldown on that use of *ain't* which he hadn't intended at all.

"Well, it's a great game, for men as well as kids. You know, I was thinking, if those Europeans that are at each other's throats now in this war had a national sport like baseball, they wouldn't be having this war. You got to have something that lets the steam off, and baseball does that. Yes, sir, if they had baseball, the French would be playing a series in Berlin now, and the Germans would be yelling kill the ump instead of trying to kill the Frog-eaters," Guy said.

"There's something to what you say there," said Jake.

"Why did we have a war with Spain and why have we got trouble with the greasers in Mexico if that's so?" asked Mike.

"That was different. They sunk the *Maine* on us. And anyway, we had our rights to protect in Cuba, we had to make the Cubans free," Guy said.

"Well, I tell you fellows, it's pretty hard to say what's what these days," Joe said reflectively, tossing a ball up and catching it.

Joe tossed the ball in the air again but missed the catch. The ball glanced off a bat and popped away. Danny got up to retrieve it. . . .

Danny came back and dropped the ball beside Joe.

"Anyway, you guys can go ahead and jaw. I got to get home, see what the missus has put on the table and then hop down to work. See you boys tomorrow," Jack said, rising.

"I have to be going, too. Come on, Sport," Al said.

Danny jumped up, and after saying so long, he and his uncle left.

My First Uniformed Team

Today, it seems natural for boys to play on teams with uniforms. The Little League not only provides uniforms, but also closed parks with stands, and Little League games simulate the atmosphere of the big leagues. In my day, it was quite different and boys were thrilled to play on a uniformed team.

Today, likewise, boys teams and leagues are directed and there are probably fewer situations like the one described in the next few pages. We ran our own team completely with results which will become apparent to the reader.

I have lost touch with the boys who played on this team, but some have passed on into the shadows, among them Paul O'Dea who is mentioned in "From Washington Park to the Big Leagues." Clarence Rowland, Jr., who is mentioned also in this article, is now with a brokerage house on La Salle Street in Chicago.

Here at all events is a story of us, boys, when we organized a team and had uniforms.

IT was finally in 1918, after many years of hoping and dreaming, that I played on a team with uniforms. A grocery store owner named Mr. Hirsch on Fifty-eighth Street put up fifty dollars, five dollars each for ten uniforms, and we boys on the team each paid three dollars and fifty cents. Our uniforms were gray and trimmed in green with the name HIRSCHES sewn diagonally across our shirts. Our stockings were gray with green stripes. It was needless to say that I was proud to wear this uniform and also was able to wear my first pair of spiked shoes. Mr. Hirsch lived next door to us on South Park Avenue and he had two sons with whom I often played. These boys convinced their father to put up the money for the uniforms.

We used to play two or three games a week, mostly with boys' teams in Washington Park. Several of the boys were very good players, especially one to whom I have referred elsewhere in this book named Paul. He played third. I was the second baseman and lead-off man. My brother Earl was appointed our manager and one of the many sources of friction on our team resulted from this. He was accused of favoring me.

Having a penchant for averages, I proposed that the scores of all our games be kept, and that we figure out our batting and fielding averages.

This became the source of endless wrangling among us. Earl and I took on the task of figuring out the averages and making listings of them in a big black-covered old ledger book. We did this weekly, but every time that we showed the boys the results, there were complaints and accusations. Soon, a good average became more important than a game won. We turned into a crowd of noisy individualists. Most of us were either of Irish-American or Jewish parentage, and the friction over averages and records as well as other frictions led to a split between the Irish and Jewish boys. We ended up saying nasty and prejudiced things to one another.

But before this happened we were a proud bunch of boys. Just like the older fellows, we would walk to the Park ball field, clad in full uniform, and carrying our gloves, balls, bats and spiked shoes. We were not merely a bunch of kids going out to play a scrub game. We were a team. With our uniforms we looked serious. We looked like little ball players, and possible stars to be. I knew how to roll my baseball pants and stockings together the same way that big-leaguers did. I was quite vain about this modest accomplishment.

We advertised for games in the sporting page of the *Chicago Daily Journal* and in that way booked a few games in Washington Park or elsewhere. Sometimes we would make up a pot of from two and a half to five dollars and play for the pot. We won more games than we lost, but every time we lost a game we rowed like hell.

We destroyed our chance to have fun by quarreling. There were few fist fights on the team, but the danger of them was always present.

By July, our team was on the verge of breaking up. We talked to one another only to be challenging and insulting. And then, we did break up.

I joined another team, and our star player, Paul O'Dea, came with me. The new team had been organized by "Young Pants" Rowland, the son of the manager of the Chicago White Sox. He was also a White Sox mascot. Today, he is on the Chicago Stock Exchange. I played better with this team than I had on the Hirsches. We neither kept averages nor did we quarrel. There were Irish and Jewish boys on the team but this caused no friction. Towards the end of the summer we scheduled a game with the remnants of the Hirsches and played it on a Saturday afternoon. It so happened that few games were played on that afternoon and the crowd of men and boys who used to go to Washington Park to see a ball game, all watched us. I was as mad at my former teammates as they were at me. We were no longer on speaking terms. In addition, over five hundred people stood along the base lines and in the outfield watching the game. I had wanted nothing better than this chance. I began the game at third base. I fumbled the first ball hit to me. At bat, I struck out and hit weak grounders. I had a kind of psychological blackout and was in a somewhat dazed state. My play was so poor that I was taken off third base and put out in left field. I stood out there watching the game in this dazed state as though I were a spectator from far away instead of one of the players. Inning after inning passed, and I was unable to shake myself out of my panic. Each time I came to bat I swung and either missed or else hit a dribbling out. We won and Paul O'Dea's hitting helped us gain the victory. I contributed nothing. Revenge was un-sweet.

But that was the end of the Hirsches.

Day after day, between 1918 and 1922, I would go to the big ball field after breakfast and play in any game that I could get into. I'd go home for lunch, return, play again, catch flies, field grounders and be home for supper. By seven I'd be back again and could get in another game, thanks to daylight savings time.

I continued to dream of a future as a big-leaguer, and everything I did was with this in mind. I played in any game I could, with kids or men. Sometimes there were scrub games with easy pitching. Not being on any team, I would play with any team which needed a player. Sometimes, I'd get into a game with a team of boys from around Fifty-first Street. There was a second team from around Fifty-fifth and Ellis which usually needed a player, and a third one from among boys who lived in the area of Sixty-first and

Prairie Avenue. I also played and practiced with different groups of men.

Most of the boys and men I played with loved baseball. They played for the fun and joy they experienced in the game itself. Many of them came out day after day, night after night, on every Sunday from early March until late October or early November. We played as soon as the spring weather permitted, and as late into the autumn as we could.

I was still only a kid in short pants but the men in Washington Park treated me with noticeable kindness. They never played jokes on me, never made fun of me, and whenever I would do well in a game, they would praise me and talk of my play. Now, these men are old and many of them must be dead. One of them, Bill Fitzpatrick, was a bricklayer then in his forties. He hadn't played ball for a number of years. Suddenly, he began coming out to play ball every night and on week ends. He wore his working clothes and a pair of tennis shoes. At first, he would run swiftly and get charley horses. These passed and he got into condition and used to play hard in any game. He had a young son who sometimes came out to watch. His boy later became a priest in Chicago. I got to walking home with Bill almost every night. It would be dark and we would walk out of the park and along the edge of Washington Park by the tennis courts, talking of baseball, of how we had played that night, and now and then of some other subject. Whenever Bill had played well he would be pleased. Sometimes, he'd speak of his stiff muscles and say that he was too old to play; he'd declare that the current year was his last one of ball playing.

Some of the younger fellows had fought with the American Army in France, and I used to look on them with awe. Often of a night when it was too dark to continue our game, we would sit around in a circle and talk. The ex-soldiers spoke of France and the War, and of having been under fire. Listening to them, knowing them, was almost like knowing a big-league ball player. They had been in the trenches. They had gone over the top. They had been among the men who helped stem the German offensive tide in the summer of 1918.

There we were sitting around in a circle under the fine summer skies, with most of the men smoking and with my friend, Bill Fitzpatrick, chewing tobacco. We could hear the chirping grasshoppers, and the trees and shrubbery bordering the park had grown black. We talked. Bill Fitzpatrick spoke of George Moriarty who had grown up in Chicago to become a big-league third baseman. Bill had known him years ago. And I was growing up in Chicago and hoped desperately that I would make the big leagues. On such nights especially, my heart and soul were in this hope, this desire. I would listen and daydream about my future. And I would resolve to try all the harder to improve my playing ability.

There was almost no talk of girls or sex and if the subject came up, Bill Fitzpatrick or one of the other men would see that this subject was changed, mainly because of me, "the kid." Most of them were clean men and they thought of me as a boy. They were a very good influence on me morally.

A spirit of camaraderie grew among us. Sitting around in the grass and talking in the twilight and growing darkness became a nightly custom. Garner was a lonely man from a rural district in Iowa who lived in a boarding house. He was a quiet, very restrained man, but he warmed up and talked. In our group, he found escape from loneliness and a furnished room. Stories were told. Baseball was discussed as it had been by Jack Hogan and the men back in 1912. We spoke of players and games and the current season. Then we got up and parted, walking our different ways, pleasingly tired from playing ball. The group would separate into small moving shadows crossing the big park field in different directions. The nights were warm and clear and full of stars. Washington Park was a little island of baseball comradeship for us. Trouble, work and responsibility dropped from my mind. We knew little of the private lives of most of the group. And there was never any quarreling or serious friction. No rivalries developed. We gradually organized a team and played regular games on Saturday afternoons. Bill Fitzpatrick would pick the players and make out the batting order. His authority was never challenged.

In memory, this all seems somewhat idyllic. Strange men came together so easily and got on so well, and they were all so kind to me, "the kid."

There was a group of men from a Masonic Lodge which played a game every Sunday morning. One Sunday morning when I was fourteen, they needed an extra player and I got into the game, playing right field. I made a Texas league single off swift pitching and caught a fly ball in right field. After that they often let me play with them; finally, I played every Sunday, graduating from the outfield to the infield. I didn't get to know these men as well as our night group, but a couple of them became members of the group that played at night. Most of the Masons were Jewish and they were small-business men, merchants and salesmen. They took their ball playing very seriously. When one of them played badly, he went glumly home to his family's Sunday dinner. Two good hits the next Sunday, and the same man felt utterly different. One of this group was named Rodney. He and I often walked home from the ball field after a game, talking of the morning's play. He began coming out nights to our other group, and would sit with us in our talks. Whenever I played well, he praised me and he would insist on my getting into as many of the Sunday morning games as possible. Sometimes there would be a big crowd out to play—more than eighteen men—and they all wanted to play. They chipped in for the expenses and had a right to play, as I didn't. But even on such mornings Rodney sometimes got me into a number of games.

Once in a while, we would have a game with a big crowd watching. I would then become almost exhilarated. There I would be, a kid in short pants, playing with men and batting against swift pitching, and I was being watched. I used to daydream about and wait for such games. In one of these games on a late fall Sunday, I got a hit to center field. I felt almost as though I had proved that I could be a big-leaguer. But I was far from being a good enough player. I was a regular on my high-school team but played most unevenly. I outdid Casey at the bat by striking out three times with the bases full. This was below par because I could hit—sometimes.

These men also were, in a sense, comrades. I think of them often. Hitting, running, sliding, concentrating only on a ball game, dreaming of the future, and loving the feel of it all, the crack of the bat, the grip of the bat, the thrill of smacking a ball and knowing that it was a hit—all this, and the warm days and nights remain in my memory. And this is all part of the appeal of baseball; it touches us sometimes in an almost poetic sense. And, in addition, this is an aspect of life in America. Baseball and its memories are part of the river of our national life which flows on and on. Our own memories, comradeships and hopes have gone into the making of the current of the American river of memories. This is another reason why we love baseball.

A Player Loses Confidence

This is from my novel, FATHER AND SON. *The boy, Danny O'Neill, here outdoes Casey at the Bat. But in having written this piece, I fear that I have partly disqualified myself from writing about baseball. For I once, as a high school player, struck out three times with the bases full.*

WEARING his baseball suit, Danny crossed Stony Island at Sixty-fourth Street and walked toward school. His state of dejection showed in his slow and aimless gait. He scraped his spiked shoes on the sidewalk and twirled his fielder's glove.

Back on the Jackson Park baseball field, S.S. was losing to Saint Marks. And it was his doing. Although he usually hit southpaws, he had faced a left-hander three times this afternoon with the bases full. Now instead of talking about Casey at the bat, they could talk about Danny O'Neill up there. He was supposed to be a slugger, too, and he had struck out three times with the bags loaded. He remembered the taunts from the crowd.

"You swing like a rusty gate."

"Four-eyes couldn't hit the blind side of a barn!"

"Try hitting it with your head!"

And then, that ball that had come to him in left field. Why had he run in on it? There he had been in left field, waiting, confident that he would catch anything he got his hands on. The sacks were filled. A line drive was hit. With the crack of the bat, he'd come forward instead of running back. The ball had gone over his head for a home run.

Well, the baseball season was over at S.S. The team had had a disastrous season. He was ashamed to have played on it. They'd lost one game 26 to 0, and another, 18 to 2. And he hadn't been a star himself. Yes, he had made two long doubles against Augustine, one of them with the bases full. And yes, he had smacked out a triple in another game. But he had gone hitless in some games, and then today, look what he'd done. He remembered the last strike he'd missed. He'd swung so hard that he'd lost his balance and fallen down. Boy, if he had ever connected! But the simple fact was that he hadn't connected.

Some of the fellows had said that it was a dark day and that O'Neill had bad eyes and couldn't see the ball. Well, he did have bad eyes. But that was no excuse. If he wanted to be a big-league star, he had to make the grade with what eyesight he had. And he just wasn't developing as a ball player.

For three years he had daydreamed of how he would be a scintillating high-school baseball star and how he would hit a home run with the bases full. And look at the way he had folded up in a pinch. Yes, after kidding himself about his destiny, and having the nerve to think that he would be a star like Ty Cobb or Eddie Collins, he was a miserable failure. Whenever he was in a tight situation, he was a bust, a flat tire. He didn't have what it takes. He was eighteen years old, and he was no good. He lacked something—nerve, con-

fidence. In a pinch, it was always the same. He lost his confidence. When he didn't have time, a few seconds in which to
think, it was different. That was why he was better in football and basketball than he was in baseball. In baseball when
you batted, there were those few seconds and fractions of a
second between pitches, when your mind undid you. In football and basketball, you didn't have the time as you did in
baseball. That made the difference. And it was in just that
period of a few important seconds that he was no good. Yes,
even though he was considered one of the best athletes in
school, he was never really going to be any good.

Well he had another year. Next year was going to be his
big year in all sports. But there he was again, filling himself
full of crap.

He walked through the schoolyard and downstairs. He
stood alone under a shower, berating himself, telling himself
that he was never going to be any good.

A Game in the Park

Many games like this one were played in the parks of Chicago. I attempted to describe one fictionally and used it in the final volume of STUDS LONIGAN—JUDGMENT DAY. *Since I began writing, I always planned to include in my fiction various aspects of baseball.*

STUDS stood on the grass edge of the large, rectangular skin-dirt athletic field, hearing the crack of a baseball bat while a group of fellows snapped through infield practice, and a lad in a khaki shirt fungoed flies to five others in the outfield. About five yards from him a group of four sat watching.

The third baseman, a lank lad in a faded blue shirt, fozzled a ground ball, and, seeking hurriedly to pick it up, kicked it around in the dirt.

"The bush leagues for you, Spunk."

"Get off your can and come out here and do better."

"The bushes, boy. You're getting old."

"All right, Cal, get the lead out of your tail," one of the

fungo hitters called, lifting a long high fly which was easily caught by a swarthy left-handed fellow in a white shirt.

Studs watched the infield practice, the grounders slapped hard, cutting over the dirt, the ball snapped around from player to player. They were pretty good, and they worked fast. Even though he had never cared a hell of a lot for baseball, it was something to watch, neat, quick work. The shortstop ran low to his left, smeared a fast grounder with one hand, bobbed the ball, off balance, to the second base who caught it, wheeled around in the same motion and whipped the ball to first base.

"Spunk, how do you like that?" One of those on the grass called while the ball was pegged around.

"This is the million-dollar infield."

"Yes, if it had a third baseman."

Studs edged a bit closer to the group on the grass. Looked like a nice bunch of lads, and they had enough for a game. He'd like to play.

"That boy Spunk is good."

"He ought to get a try-out in the big shows."

"He's good around here, but he wouldn't make the grade. Can't hit a sharp-breaking curve ball. A pitcher like Jack Casey who was with me at the Braves' training camp last year could make him eat out of his hand. And Jack never made the grade."

"How about you, Artie?"

"Couldn't get myself lined up, so I'm playing semi-pro. Hell, this country is full of guys trying to get into the game, and plenty of them are good. With minor leagues folding up like tents, and with old-timers coming down from the big leagues and the Class A. A. outfits, and then with chainstore systems like the one the Cardinals run, it's damn hard getting lined up even in a dinky little X. Y. Z. league."

"Maybe you're right."

"Look at Jack. He thought he'd make a go of it in pro

athletics, and he did have one good season in the Three I
League but then he threw his arm out. He's up the creek, and
he doesn't make any too much peddling insurance. If I could
get a decent job, I'd throw the idea up, too, and stick to my
job, maybe just picking up a few pennies on Sunday playing semi-pro and having some fun playing basketball in the
Christopher League in winter."

A Christy. Studs looked at him, a light-haired, husky,
square-faced fellow in his early twenties, the kind of a mug
and build a ball player would have.

"Let's get going with the game," Spunk called, walking in.

Studs watched them choosing up, hoping, because there
were only seventeen.

"Hey, lad, want to play?"

"Sure, all right," he said, slowly taking off his coat.

"You're on my side," the fellow named Artie said.

"Say, I just heard you talking. You're a Christy, aren't you?
I just went through Kempis Council. My name's Lonigan."

"Mine's Pfeiffer, Timothy Murphy Council. Say, a young
kid named Lonigan went to Mary Our Mother when I was
there."

"Yeah, that was my kid brother."

"What ever happened to him? I know he left M. O. M. to
go to Tower Tech."

"He's working a little with my old man in the painting
business."

Studs put his left hand in the fielder's glove offered him
and walked nonchalantly out to right field. He stood with
hands on hips, waiting. Easy pitching and he'd get by, even
if he hadn't played in years. And it would keep him in the
sun. He bent forward with his hands on his knees, while the
pitcher lobbed the ball up to the right-handed batter, a short
fellow in a gray shirt. A high fly soared toward right center
and Studs, seeing the ball come somewhere near him, ran
forward to his right, confused, afraid of muffing the catch.

Seeing that he was misjudging it, he ran backward, still to his right, with his eye on the lowering ball.

"I got it," the center fielder called.

Studs stopped in his tracks, and watched the center fielder gracefully nab the ball on the run. Breathing quickly, but glad that his misjudgment hadn't been serious, he returned to his position. He waited, over-anxious. A line single was driven to left, the pitcher picked a pop out of the air, and a dumpy Texas leaguer over third base placed runners on first and second.

"You better go back and play in a grammar-school league," Spunk said, stepping to bat after Pfeiffer had dropped an easy toss at first base.

Spunk waited, swinging left-handed, and Pfeiffer motioned Studs backward. Spunk connected, and the ball traveled high out to Studs, who wavered around in circles, the ball landing three feet away from him.

" . . . what a Babe Hermann that was," the center fielder exclaimed more loudly than he had intended, while Studs clumsily retrieved the ball. A pain cut paralyzingly into his shoulder when he threw wildly to the infield.

"Take it easy, Lonigan. It's only a scrub game," Pfeiffer said when Studs came in abashed at the end of the inning.

"Hell, I haven't played in years. I used to be pretty good but I'm out of practice."

"Everybody muffs a few."

"Hey, Artie, bushel baskets are cheap these days," Spunk called from third base.

"I'm going to knock your hands off when I get up," Artie called.

Studs stood several feet away from the players on his side, who grouped themselves on the grass edge. When he came to bat he'd redeem himself.

Pfeiffer, a left-handed batter, stood at the plate after the first two batters had flied out and, swinging late, stung a line drive just beyond Spunk's gloved hand.

"What's that you say about bushel baskets?" he megaphoned through his hands, standing on second base.

"Save us a lick, Pete."

"I'm getting fed up with nothing to do but lay around this damn park."

"Write a letter to Hoover. Maybe he'll put you on some commission and you'll get a job to help keep other people out of jobs."

"No, Jack, I'm serious. I ask myself how long is this thing going to keep on."

"Well, do what I say. Write a letter to Hoover."

"The bathing beach is going to open soon and maybe we can all get on as life guards."

"I can't swim well enough."

"Hang around until 1933 and you can get a job at the World's Fair."

"Swell hit, Pete. Come on, Al, lean on it."

"All I can say is some damn thing has got to happen."

"Hire a hall, you ain't got no kick. Laying around in the sun, playing ball, looking at nursemaids, and hearing the birds sing."

"Swell catch, Spunk, you lucky bastard."

Studs waited anxiously in right field, but batter after batter came up without hitting him. He walked in at the end of the inning more confident. He'd get a rap this time and sock one.

"Save us a bat, lad," a fellow in a dirty gray sweatshirt called while Studs stepped up with two out. The bat seemed too heavy and, facing the pitcher, he lost confidence.

"Hey, which side am I on?"

"Wait till the inning's up."

He decided that this fellow could take his place. He swung late, fizzling a grounder to the pitcher, and didn't even run.

"Hey, Pfeiffer, he can take my place."

"No, it's only a scrub game, Lonigan."

"Well, I'm kind of tired anyway."

"Come around again and tell the kid brother I was askin' about him."

He crossed the driveway and walked along the gravel path flanking the lagoon, which lay below in shimmering sunlight. He should have gone on playing. He would have gotten into his stride, hit some solid ones, and nabbed fly balls, too. It would have been nice passing the time, and they seemed like a decent bunch. He imagined himself driving a home run over the center fielder's head and then making one-handed and shoe-string catches in the outfield. He shrugged his shoulders, laughed at his sudden interest in baseball.

The Debate

*My recollection of this experience has always
amused me. Since this debate occurred, I have
spoken all over the world and on many subjects.
But I never gave more in any public speech or
lecture than I did on this occasion during my
high school years. However, I still wish that I had
been assigned to praise the White Sox rather than
the Cubs. But for my fellow pupils and our
teacher, Brother Dionysius Lickling, it is probably better that I was given the other side in this
debate. Had I argued that the White Sox were the
better team, I might have talked for weeks.*

IN my freshman year, at high school, our English hour every
Friday afternoon was devoted to public speaking and
debates. At the very beginning of the term, our teacher, a
young brother named Frater Dionysius, proposed a debate
on baseball, and asked who was interested in the game and
wanted to be one of the debaters. My hand shot up. I couldn't
miss that. The question he posed was— "Resolved that the

Chicago Cubs are a better baseball team than the White Sox." He picked me as one of the four debaters but assigned me to the defense of the Cubs. There could not be any debate on such a proposition. The year was 1919. But there I was stuck with the Chicago Cubs.

As these papers more than indicate, I was a White Sox fan. I was not fanatically so; rather I was a pious fan. There is much to be written about the psychology of baseball, both from the standpoint of fans and that of players. In that complex psychology of and about the game, there is a pronounced element of fantasy and a very heavy dosage of sentimentality. I had both of these in my own attitude about baseball. And it all centered, of course, in the White Sox. More than that, theirs was a great ball team. If it means anything now, many fans, sports writers and even some baseball men claim that the 1919 White Sox were the greatest of all teams. Besides my personal feelings, I had to take the side of the debate which patently was not true. Furthermore, the Cubs did not interest me very much. I went out to the North Side fairly frequently to see them play and especially in 1918, when they won the National League pennant, I saw them a number of times. I liked to see Grover Cleveland Alexander pitch. He had an air of expertness and sureness on the mound, his control was excellent; and he hurled with little wind-up and an easy side-arm motion. Watching him, you quickly realized that he was a master at his profession. But the Cubs in 1919 finished third, and the White Sox were baseball's top dogs.

However I set to work and wrote out my debate, filling more than one composition book. I compared players, position by position, cited averages and records, invented, imagined, contrived, grabbed every advantage I could. Since I had no real case on my side, and since I wanted to shine and show off my baseball knowledge, I went at the debate with enough energy to crush my opponents. The other boys could not possibly know as much about baseball as I did. I had read box scores and sports pages since 1912 and had poured through the Reach and Spalding Official Baseball Guides. But the going was rough. How could I stack Leslie Mann against Joe Jackson, Dode Paskert against Happy Felsch, Charlie Deal against Buck Weaver at third base, and Buck Herzog and Eddie Collins. I could make out a case with Fred Merkle and Chick Gandil, and I could even believe I was right in comparing Charlie Hollocher at shortstop with Swede Risberg. Then I could argue that in pitching Alexander had it on Eddie Cicotte and Hippo Jim Vaughan was superior to Lefty Williams. Then I still had Lefty Tyler who had pitched with the 1914 Boston Braves. In 1919 with the Cubs, he had a record of 2-2, but I could talk about the 19 games he won in 1918 and the fact that he had been on a World Champion ball club in 1914. I dragged in the 1914 Miracle Braves in order to rout Dickie Kerr with Lefty Tyler. Then I could win some points on Max Flack, the Cub right fielder, as compared with Nemo Liebold or Shano Collins. In fact, if my word on Max Flack had been taken, he would long since have been rewarded with a plaque in the Cooperstown Hall of Fame. And then I dumped Ray Schalk for Bill Killefer, even arguing that Killefer was the better receiver because he caught Alexander.

I rolled on for pages. I did more work in one week preparing for that debate than I did in English for the entire remainder of the year. It was all bunk, plain and fancy. I even gave Buck Herzog more fighting spirit than Eddie Collins because Herzog had been reported in the sports pages as having had a fist fight with Ty Cobb. By the same token I should have made Gandil better than Merkle inasmuch as the former had had a rather mean fist fight with Tris Speaker at Comiskey Park. When I could not do anything with batting averages, a fist fight, the year 1914 or anything else, there were fielding averages. I combed Reach and Spalding to get any fielding average I could in order to knock over my favorite team.

Every day of that week, I found new arguments and reasons to establish my side of the resolution. I even pooh-poohed the fact that all through those years, the White Sox had an Indian sign on the Cubs and knocked them off with predictable regularity in City Series play. As I lathered things up, I kept wondering—but why did not Frater Dion assign me to defend the White Sox. Then I could have filled three composition books instead of one and a half if given the negative position in the debate. Why I could even have shown up the Chicago Cubs in such a light that they would have even been indistinguishable from the Philadelphia Athletics, a team which, in 1919, finished an undistinguished last with 36 games won and 104 lost.

The hour for the debate came. I was the first affirmative speaker and I was more than prepared to win my glory. I marched up to the front of the classroom, opened my notebook and began. One hour later I was still going and I was still quite far away from my major and most crushing argument—the presence of Grover Cleveland Alexander on the Cubs' pitching staff. The class was partly flabbergasted and considerably bored and exhausted. I am certain that some of the boys became convinced that I was crazy. Frater Dionysius merely shook his head and announced that the debate would have to be continued on the following Friday. It was. The judges decided that the debate was a draw. Statistics, words, fist fights, the 1914 Boston Braves, and sundry other facts, all true but mostly irrelevant, put the White Sox in their place.

"But of course," I said, "everybody knows that the White Sox are the better team."

Ever since that day I have waxed ironical whenever I have read any articles in sports pages which compare ball teams by matching the respective players according to position and their records.

For years, I preserved the two composition books from that debate. However, they were destroyed in a fire which occurred in my apartment a little over eleven years ago. Otherwise I would still have these books and could have quoted them here. This was the only time on the land, on the sea or in the air that any mortal ever could have stated that Buck Herzog was a better second baseman than Edward Trowbridge Collins, and that a team with the players Mann, Paskert, Flack, Deal, Herzog and Merkle was preferable to the 1919 White Sox. Of course this all occurred before the news of the scandal and 1919 World Series fix broke.

I Remember the Black Sox

Here is how I remember the fixed 1919 World
Series and the subsequent scandal which grew out
of it. At the time, I was a boy of fifteen and a
passionate White Sox enthusiast. The 1919 White
Sox were, unquestionably, one of baseball's greatest teams. In 1921, when seven of the blacklisted
players were being tried on criminal charges, Kid
Gleason, their old manager, was reported in the
press to have said:

"I think the White Sox at that time were the
best ball club in the world."

The 1919 White Sox were, perhaps, the strang-
est of great teams. They constitute one of the most
dramatic chapters in baseball history, and have
become the dark legend of baseball lore and
memory.

To this day, this story is clouded and part of it
is locked away in files, in fading and mellowing
memories and in the grave. Not only did the
blacklisted men suffer: so did innocent players.
The psychic scars of that scandal remain, even to

this day. Eventually, the story will become clari-
fied and the facts more harmoniously fitted to-
gether. But all of this is different from what I have
attempted here.

This, then, is how I remember it from my teen-
age days when the White Sox meant so much
to me.

NINETEEN-NINETEEN was the big year for the White Sox.
The team was so good that its power and effectiveness
could almost deceive a fan. They were strong in every department. Besides their outstanding stars like Joe Jackson,
Eddie Collins and Ray Schalk, they had sound, reliable players. There was Chick Gandil on first base and two highly useful infielders, Swede Risberg and Fred McMullin. Risberg
was tall, rangy and lantern-jawed. He had one of the most
powerful arms in baseball and could play shortstop more
deeply than any other shortstop of his time. McMullin was
a steady player, and whether the White Sox played him at
third base and Weaver at short, or Weaver at third and Risberg at short, they were strong on the left side of the diamond.

The champion White Sox were one of the most interesting
teams that I have ever seen play. They were a colorful team,
but their color was not due to eccentricity. Buck Weaver's
soiled uniform was, perhaps, their only noticeable eccentricity. They ran on and off the field like champions. They
went through infield practice with expertness. They were
colorful because they were so good. As a teen-age fan who
watched them intently and read from one to five sports pages
a day, I never knew or imagined that there was dissension
among them. When the White Sox were on the field, the unexpected could always happen. Every one of the regulars was
dangerous with men on base. The outfielders were accurate
throwers. Joe Jackson had one of the strongest throwing arms

of any outfielder of the period. In 1919, Happy Felsch made thirty-two assists and Nemo Liebold in right field was credited with twenty-six.

Now, in memory, scenes re-occur in my mind. Joe Jackson streaking back and spearing a ball over his head. Felsch going to his right or left and pulling in long flies. Eddie Collins making gloved-hand stops and fast throws. Ray Schalk tearing after a foul ball. Buck Weaver going into the dirt for a hot grounder. Risberg snaring a grounder deep over second base and getting the ball to Gandil or Shano Collins at first in time as though the ball were a bullet. Cicotte taking short steps off the pitching mound, dropping his glove by the base line, walking on into the dugout as though it were a matter of course that he should blank an opposing team and have its batters eat out of his hand.

And late-inning rallies. The stands cheering, pleading, hoping or encouraging. Joe Jackson, whose walk was tread-like, emerging from the dugout carrying three bats. One of them was black and the fans would call out:

"Come on, Joe, give her Black Betsy!"

The attendance at games was good. The fans were enthusiastic. The players were popular. After every game, fifty, one hundred or more fans would stand near the clubhouse to watch the players leave in their civilian clothes. Someone would call out praise and encouragement to the players. Buck Weaver was always greeted especially. He was, perhaps, the most popular on the team.

And the White Sox seemed like an unbeatable team when they went into the 1919 World Series with the Cincinnati Reds. In the American League, a team like Cincinnati would have done well to finish fourth. It was a patched together team with cast-offs like Maurice Rath, a predecessor of Eddie Collins as White Sox second baseman. If ever a World Series seemed in the bag, it was the 1919 Series. And it was in the bag, but that was the bag of the gamblers.

The story of how the 1919 Series was thrown has often been told. In the first game, Cincinnati knocked Cicotte out of the box and won, 9 to 1. I remember walking away from the Fifty-eighth Street elevated station and disappointedly reading the play-by-play account of this game. Rarely was Eddie Cicotte in such poor form. In 1919, he had been as consistent as any American League pitcher, with the possible exception of Walter Johnson. And the next day, the Reds took Lefty Williams, 4 to 2. The White Sox seemed unbelievably off form. And they were a team which played best when victories were needed. But I was far away from the hotel lobbies where players, sports writers and gamblers congregated. The thought that the games were being thrown never entered my head.

The third game of the 1919 World Series has become one of the most famous games in the history of baseball. I saw it. Dick Kerr, a small and frail-looking southpaw who had been a busher in April, shut out Cincinnati, 3 to 0, and the White Sox were back in the running. I saw this game from the left-field bleachers of Comiskey Park. No fan around me gave voice to the suspicion that the two previous games had been thrown. As is now believed, some of Kerr's teammates were trying to lose the game for him and they failed. Inning after inning, Kerr reduced Cincinnati. I tensely watched the last innings, hungry for the Sox to win but I did not have the same confidence in Kerr as I did in Cicotte and Williams. I went home pleased about the Sox victory. They were in form. They would now win the Series. Cicotte could not be off form two games in a row. The fact that the Reds were one up on the White Sox meant nothing.

I saw the fourth game, also. Cicotte was himself. He was opposed by Jimmy Ring of Cincinnati. From the beginning, the game was a pitchers' duel.

Cincinnati scored in the fourth inning. Cicotte, one of the finest fielding pitchers in the game, made a wild throw on an easy play. A Red reached second base. Larry Kopf, the Cincinnati shortstop, hit to left. I remember this play vividly even now. There was Joe Jackson. He fielded the ball on one bounce and got off a quick, accurate throw. As the ball sailed in, I knew that the Cincinnati runner would be out if he tried to score. He didn't. He merely made a stab at going on. And far away from me in the bleachers, there was the figure of Cicotte near third. He tried to stop Jackson's throw. The runner scored and Kopf reached second.

I wondered why Cicotte had done this. The play didn't seem right, especially for a player as smart as Cicotte. I spoke to Earl about this play. We both agreed that it was a boner. But I never imagined that this play was deliberate. When Cicotte confessed to having helped throw the Series, he spoke of this play. Rumors did circulate through the bleachers during the game, which Cincinnati took, 2 to 0. However, these had nothing to do with gambling or crookedness. Word passed from lip to lip that there was bad blood between the Reds and the White Sox. It was said that the Sox were after Greasy Neale, the Cincinnati right fielder. One story was that he and Happy Felsch had had a fist fight under the stands. Some said Neale had won; others said it had been Felsch.

After the game I was dispirited. It looked bad for the White Sox. But Earl and I walked around to Thirty-fifth and Shields, went under the stands and watched the players leave the clubhouse. Swede Risberg and Chick Gandil were supposed to be the two toughest players on the White Sox, and we were hoping to see a fight, with either Risberg or Gandil cleaning up on Greasy Neale. We saw no fist fight with a White Sox player soothing my sense of loss by pasting a Cincinnati Red.

Cincinnati won the fifth game. The White Sox took the sixth and seventh, and the teams returned to Chicago with Cincinnati leading 4 to 3.

My uncle wrote a note to one of the priests at my high school asking that I be excused from classes to see the eighth

game of the Series. I recall that in this note my uncle remarked that a boy doesn't always get a chance to see a World
Series ball game that he will remember all his life. I was excused. I sat alone in the bleachers. It was a sunny day. There
were many empty seats in the big stands and bleachers. I
watched the teams go through fielding practice, impatient
and hopeful. And then the game began. And in the first inning, Lefty Williams was knocked out of the box and Cincinnati led, 4 to 0. Jackson failed with men on base in the first
inning, but he slammed a home run into the right-field
bleachers later in the game. Each time the Sox came to bat,
there was hope. But the Reds won, 10 to 5, and the unexpected had happened. The White Sox lost the World Series
to a team which seemed to be so inferior to them.

Nineteen-twenty was another year. The White Sox were
battling all season for the pennant. I was still as ardent a fan
as ever. During the summer, I worked as a clerk in an express office. I read the baseball news and box scores every
morning on the elevated as I went to work. Often on my
lunch hour, I read more about baseball from an early edition
of an afternoon newspaper. I carried the batting averages of
every White Sox player in my head. I knew the total number
of home runs the team had hit. I bought box seats for Sunday
games when they were home and sat very close to the diamond, watching the practice and then the games. I never
heard a fan voice any suspicion about the 1919 Series, and
I never imagined that it might have been fixed.

Early in September, 1920, a Chicago newspaper printed a
story about an alleged attempt to fix a game between the
Chicago Cubs and the Philadelphia Phillies. This led to
charges, accusations, denials, and finally a big baseball scandal blew up. Baseball's dirty linen was washed in public. A
grand jury began an investigation of the allegation concerning the Cub-Philly game, and this snowballed fast. Charges
appeared in the newspapers that White Sox players had de-

liberately thrown games. I recall not wanting to believe this. Also, I anxiously wondered who the accused players might be. Five to seven and then eight players were supposed to have been involved in this plot with gamblers. And while these stories were printed, the White Sox went on battling for the pennant. They had a chance to win and I kept hoping that they would.

And then as the last week of September began, the fact of crookedness was clear. On September 23, the *Chicago Daily Tribune* carried this headline: BARE FIXED WORLD SERIES

Assistant State's Attorney Replogle, who was conducting the grand jury investigation of the baseball scandal, flatly declared that the 1919 World Series had not been on the square. It was quite clear that there was plenty of hot fire behind the smoke, and I didn't want to believe it. I hoped against hope. The guilty players were named in the papers. They were: Joe Jackson, Happy Felsch, Buck Weaver, Swede Risberg, Chick Gandil, Fred McMullin, Eddie Cicotte, and Claude Williams.

I had a box seat ticket for the game of Sunday, September 27. It was a muggy, sunless day. I went to the park early and watched the players take their hitting and fielding practice. It looked the same as always. They took their turns at the plate. They had their turns on the field. They seemed calm, no different, no different than they had been on other days before the scandal had broken. The crowd was friendly to them and some cheered. But a subtle gloom hung over the fans. The atmosphere of the park was like the muggy weather. The game began. Cicotte pitched. The suspected players got a hand when they came to bat. The White Sox won easily. Cicotte was master of the Detroit Tigers that day. One could only wish that he had pitched as well in the 1919 Series.

After the game, I went under the stands and stood near the steps leading down from the White Sox clubhouse. A small crowd always collected there to watch the players leave. But on this particular Sunday, there were about 200 to 250 boys waiting. Some of the players left. Lefty Williams, wearing a blue suit and a gray cap, was one, and some of the fans called to him. A few others came down the steps. And then Joe Jackson and Happy Felsch appeared. They were both big men. Jackson was the taller of the two and Felsch the broader. They were sportively dressed in gray silk shirts, white duck trousers and white shoes. They came down the clubhouse steps slowly, their faces masked by impassivity.

A few fans called to them, but they gave no acknowledgment to these greetings. They turned and started to walk away. Spontaneously, the crowd followed in a slow, disorderly manner. I went with the crowd and trailed about five feet behind Jackson and Felsch. They walked somewhat slowly. A fan called out:

"It ain't true, Joe."

The two suspected players did not turn back. They walked on, slowly. The crowd took up this cry and more than once, men and boys called out and repeated:

"It ain't true, Joe."

This call followed Jackson and Felsch as they walked all the way under the stands to the Thirty-fifth Street side of the ball park. They left the park and went for their parked cars in a soccer field behind the right field bleachers. I waited by the exit of the soccer field. Many others also waited. Soon Felsch and Jackson drove out in their sportive roadsters, through a double file of silent fans.

I went back to the clubhouse. But most of the players had gone. It was getting dark. A ball park seems very lonely after the crowd has cleared away. Never was a ball park lonelier or more deserted for me than on that September Sunday afternoon. It was almost dark. I went home. I sensed it was true. But I hoped that the players would get out of this and be allowed to go on playing.

Two days later, Cicotte and Jackson confessed to the grand jury. Felsch and Williams followed with confessions. Charles A. Comiskey, owner of the White Sox, suspended seven players. Chick Gandil, the eighth of these players, had quit baseball at the end of the 1919 season.

Cicotte admitted to having been paid $10,000 as his share in the conspiracy. Jackson got $5,000 according to his confession. The players were supposed to have received $100,000 in all. It seems, however, that they were doublecrossed by the gamblers with whom they conspired and they did not get their full share. The details of the pay-off have never been made completely clear. Among those mentioned as involved in this deal was Bill Burns, a one-time major league pitcher of mediocre ability; Abe Attell, a former featherweight champion, and Arnold Rothstein, the New York gambler.

The eight players were indicted and subsequently tried on a conspiracy charge, but they were acquitted of criminal charges. Judge Kenesaw Mountain Landis, the first Commissioner of Baseball, outlawed the eight for life.

In 1922, several of the players, including Jackson, Risberg and Williams, attempted a barnstorming tour. The coach of my high school team, St. Cyril, knew the players and signed up to play on their barnstorming team. One afternoon, he brought Lefty Williams out to our practice session in Jackson Park. Williams, wearing a White Sox uniform, pitched to us in batting practice. He threw us all straight balls and let us hit. He did not talk to us. Swede Risberg stood watching. He didn't talk to us, either.

The "Black Sox," as they were called, opened their barnstorming tour in Chicago. They played at a small park in Grand Crossing, at Seventy-fifth Street and the Illinois Central tracks. The park has since been torn down. A crowd of about 2,000 saw this game. Joe Jackson hit one ball over the railroad tracks.

The barnstorming trip was a failure.

My interest in baseball changed after this. For years I had no favorite team. I was growing up, and this marked the end of my days of hero-worshiping baseball players. Many fans felt betrayed. I didn't. I felt sorry. I wished it weren't true. I wished the players would have been given another chance.

All of the eight blacklisted players except Joe Jackson, Buck Weaver and McMullin are still living. Jackson has become one of the legends of baseball. He is reported to have been illiterate, and stories are told of how he was without shoes when he broke into the minor leagues. The "Say it ain't so, Joe" story has become a legend; some sports writers have denied that it ever occurred. The story is told of a crowd waiting outside the courthouse in Chicago while Jackson confessed to the grand jury. When he came out, boys are supposed to have called to him:

"Say it ain't so, Joe."

But this kind of an incident *did* happen at Comiskey Park as I have described it here. Had I not been shy, I would have called out, as did many men and boys.

I can recall Jackson vividly. He was tall and lean and stood pigeon-toed at home plate. He bent his knees and waved his bat and stepped into a pitch with one of the most graceful and powerful swings in baseball. Babe Ruth learned from his batting stance. Ty Cobb called him the greatest of all natural hitters. In 1911, his first full year as a big-league regular, Joe batted .408. He was a subject of particular pride to White Sox fans. In him, they had on their team one of the greatest of all baseball players. The defection of Joe Jackson hurt Chicago fans more than did that of any of the others.

The Perfect Catcher

Ray Schalk seems to have changed from a scrappy ball player to a mellowed old-timer. If the newspaper accounts of Ray in 1919 are true, he took what happened very hard. The years have softened that hurt and the anger he felt. Of all the White Sox regulars in the 1919 Series, Ray fought the hardest and played up to his top potential.

I met Ray when I was working on the Buck Weaver interview, which is included in this volume. The present piece is a consequence of that meeting. The dream and hope of every old ball player of the first rank is election to the Hall of Fame. But some only receive this recognition when they are gone. Ray did not have to wait until it was too late. And anyone who saw him catch knows that Ray only received his due.

BEFORE a recent Sunday afternoon game between the Dodgers and the Braves in Milwaukee, I was on the field. The Dodgers were taking their practice and the Braves were in the clubhouse. A short, plump man with glasses, gray hair and clad in a gray suit called to me from the side of the Braves' dugout.

"Tell him who I am Jim, so that I can go down in the dugout and say hello to Charley Grimm."

I was embarrassed at having to identify the man for an usher so that he would be permitted onto the ball field. He was Ray Schalk, the old-time White Sox catcher, and a member of the Baseball Hall of Fame.

In 1946, Babe Ruth picked his own all-star team for the *Saturday Evening Post*. Said Ruth: "For catcher my man is Ray Schalk, durable little iron man who caught for the White Sox for many seasons . . . to me he was the perfect catcher." And once, years ago in a letter to a sports editor, Ty Cobb wrote:

"I consider Ray the all-time catcher on any team . . . he is my idea of the perfect catcher." And when Eddie Collins selected his own all-time American League team, consisting of players he had seen and played with or against, he declared that the choice of his catcher was easy: It was Ray Schalk.

Today, in his sixties, Schalk is hale, healthy and prosperous. For many years, he was the proprietor of a big bowling alley on the southwest side of Chicago, and only this year, he sold out his interest. When the news of his retirement from the bowling alley was printed in the newspapers, I telephoned his home. Ray was at Purdue University, where he helps out with the coaching every year. Mrs. Schalk answered the telephone, and, speaking of Schalk's retirement, she said:

"You know Daddy. He'll have to do something else."

He does not easily take to the idea of sitting at home and doing nothing. His work at Purdue is very important to him and gives him a continuing contact with baseball. He puts on a uniform and works out with the students. He goes to all of the Old Timers dinners in Chicago, likes to take in the races, and sees a ball game now and then. The years have been good to him. He is prosperous and without financial worry. His physique and voice are robust. He speaks with the same confidence that he possessed years ago when he was so widely regarded as the kingpin of backstops. Every Monday night, he bowls in a league. The teams are given the names of big league clubs. Ray, who spent so many years with the White Sox, is on the team named after the Pirates. But he was one bowling alley proprietor who admits that he isn't a good bowler. He averages around 154 and jokes about his bowling as he does about his hitting when he was a big-leaguer. One night, he started off good, with three strikes. But then he blew up.

"You can't call strikes here the way you used to at Comiskey Park, Ray," a spectator called to him.

Ray shook his head and agreed.

He told a story he likes to repeat to every new person he meets. One day he was speaking to a colored employee at his bowling alley, talking of the bases he stole in the American League.

"Mister Schalk, you ain't stole no bases. You never got on base to steal any bases."

"I was a base on balls hitter," he said.

But one year, Schalk did hit .282.

Ray, like almost all old-time ball players, likes to talk about baseball and to reminisce about his past. At the time of the big world series scandal, the newspapers printed stories about a division between the eight "Black Sox" and the remainder of the team. Ray admits that in 1920 the guilty players all stuck together, but he denies that he bore them any animosity. Usually he will not talk much of the series. It hurt him deeply.

"Those men suffered the tortures of Hell. They suffered enough," he repeats wherever the subject is brought up.

Other th'an Buck Weaver, he had not seen or heard from the other players in years. However, a couple of years ago, he told me:

"I hear Lefty Williams is around here working somewhere. But I don't know where. I can't locate him."

He likes to talk warmly, of Kid Gleason, his old manager.

"He was for the ball player," Ray repeats.

One winter afternoon I went with him to the offices of the White Sox at Comiskey Park. He recalled the past and talked baseball with young Chuck Comiskey, (a man who seems much more serious and pleasant than many of his early press notices might suggest), Johnny Rigney and Johnny Mostil. Rigney, a Chicago boy who went to St. Mel's, a Christian Brothers high school on the West Side of Chicago, was one of the Sox's most promising pitchers in the 1930's. He was about on a par with Monty Stratton whose career was so unfortunately cut short when he accidentally shot himself while hunting. Rigney married the Comiskey daughter, retired from active play and now directs the White Sox farm system. Mostil, his assistant, succeeded Happy Felsch as the regular center fielder in 1921. During the twenties, he was one of the best center fielders in the American League, a steady hitter, a fast base runner and a good lead-off man. His lifetime average was .301.

"No, I don't think baseball players should take their wives with them on spring training," Mostil said.

"Johnny here is a bachelor," Ray laughed.

Rigney joined in to kid Mostil.

"Those days," Schalk said, rocking back on his chair and with a new note coming into his voice, "seem like only yesterday."

"Yes, I remember the day I broke in," Johnny Mostil said.

He was playing second base; Eddie Collins had gone off to war and Mostil was in his place.

"Ty Cobb was on first base. He called to me, 'I'm coming

down, busher.' I was thrilled just to be playing in a game with Cobb. Buck Weaver was at short. He called over to me that I shouldn't take this. He would. Buck took the throw."

"Cobb used to say, Johnny," Ray recalled, "that you played center field between two traffic cops. With Falk in left and Bill Barrett in right, they'd wave to you and yell, 'Come on, Johnny, get it, get it. Come on, Johnny.'"

They laughed.

"Yes, it seems like yesterday," Schalk said.

He turned to Mostil:

"Remember those heavy blue uniforms, Johnny?"

"Yes, I played one game in one in the heat in Moline."

They spoke about the old uniforms. Then Schalk said:

"We had a good team. They behaved themselves pretty well. We'd play a little cards and go to shows. There was not much cutting up or problems of discipline."

"I thought that was the team that was crooked," Chuck Comiskey said.

"I wasn't talking of that. But it was a good team," Ray said.

On another occasion, he said:

"I lived and slept and played with those fellows."

By this, he seemed to me to be conveying a feeling of pity and regret as well as nostalgia. His baseball life was a good one, but yet it would have been much better except for that fixed world series.

Schalk is concerned about old-time ball players and has done things to help them quietly and unobtrusively. He was one of the founders of a small and little publicized organization called Baseball Anonymous. There are a few hundred members. They have a yearly dinner at which an old-timer is the guest of honor. Red Faber and Joe Benz were guests of honor at such dinners. Also, awards are given to promising high school players. One recipient was Fred Lindstrom's son.

Baseball Anonymous was founded as a result of the deaths

of Bill Cissell, American League infielder in the 1920's, and
Red Ormsby. Cissell was broke, had hit the bottle heavily
and died a sick pauper. Red Ormsby was found broke and
dead in a cheap hotel. Schalk visited Cissell in the hospital
just before he died, then he saw Tony Piet, a former big-
league infielder who was also hospitalized. This led to the
founding of Baseball Anonymous. Today, there is a pension
plan for players and many of them can look forward to a
cushion of security in their old age. Also, baseball owners
contend, and I have no reason to refute them, that various
old ball players have been quietly helpful. But there are other
meanings to Baseball Anonymous.

Security in old age is not a mere question of dollars and
cents, a roof over your head, an escape from the degradation
of poverty. Old age presents us with one of the greatest
psychological tests we face in life. Old-time ball players can
feel useless, discarded, wasted, done for. There are hun-
dreds who will never make the Hall of Fame. The idea of
Baseball Anonymous is valuable in this sense. For a few of
them it gives them a feeling of belonging. In addition, Baseball Anonymous has found jobs for a couple of retired
veterans, permitting them to feel an added sense of dignity
in their final years. They are not mere pensioners; they are
working at jobs, supporting or helping to support themselves
and their families. Today, Bobby Feller is heading up a per-
manent organization of ball players. This, plus the pension
plan, will be meaningful for retired ball players in the future.
However Baseball Anonymous, on a small scale, met this
need for a few old-timers in Chicago.

In 1955, I took a road trip with the Dodgers. In Chicago,
Bill Roeder of the *New York World Telegram and Sun* and
I had a small dinner for Ray and invited a few sports writers.
The purpose of this was to have Ray and Roy Campanella
meet; they did not then know one another. Campanella
couldn't join us for dinner but did afterwards. No notes were

taken and we were not trying to get the two of them together in order to cook up a story where every word they said would be written down and decorated. It was to be a natural meeting of a great catcher of the past and one of today. However, Bill Roeder and Mike Gaven of the *New York Journal American* did write good off-day stories of the meeting.

Schalk and Campanella were pleased to meet one another and they had good baseball talk. They talked of catching and Ray, while actually believing that it was harder in his day and that the players were better, was too polite to say so. In reference to records, he whispered to me a remark which I have quoted elsewhere.

"I don't want to hurt his [Campanella's] feelings, but the trouble with him is that he never played against Ty Cobb."

"We had a great infielder on our team, Eddie Collins," Ray said at one point in the conversation.

"We have Pee Wee Reese," Campy said.

Also Ray remarked:

"I caught spitters. I was always catching spitters."

Campy said that he had caught spitters in the Negro League and added:

"In my league, I hit more spitters than I catch."

They talked technically about catching. Ray told Campanella that he admired his catching, a genuine statement. He named a few catchers in the National League whom he had seen on television and whom he considered to be bad receivers. Campanella agreed. One of these catchers is now back in the minor leagues. Ray talked about how this young catcher did not handle his glove right or know how to block bad low throws. Schalk, I might add, used a smaller glove than most catchers of his time, and handled it as though it were a fielder's mitt. Campanella remarked that sometimes on a difficult bad pitch:

"I'll just hold my glove out and push the ball on the ground."

And on foul balls, Campanella said that he takes one look at the stands, in order that he can protect himself at the last minute, when he is chasing a foul fly.

"How do you give signals. Do you give outside signals?"

Ray meant signals flashed on the outside of his knee. Campanella doesn't give outside signals.

"I used to," Ray said.

He got up, bent forward and put his right hand on the outside of his knee to demonstrate how he gave such signals. Few catchers do that, but Schalk was allowed to by his managers. He laughed and said:

"When you bend down and can't get up, then you know you're through."

They laughed.

Pee Wee Reese, who was eating in the dining room came over and met Schalk. Ray managed in Indianapolis after he ended up in the big leagues, coaching one year for the Chicago Cubs when Rogers Hornsby was manager. Ray told Pee Wee that he had recommended him to Clarence Rowland and Reese had almost been bought by the Cubs. Reese appears satisfied to have gone to Brooklyn instead.

Ray and Campy proudly showed one another their gnarled hands and Schalk asked the Brooklyn catcher about the operation on his hands. They talked about pitchers, and other details of catching. We invited Rube Walker and Dixie Howell to the table and they sat listening very attentively. Bill Roeder, Mike Gaven, John Drebinger and I were on the sidelines, saying little. Campy told Ray about some of the Dodger pitchers, among them Newcombe who was then hot. Ray had caught some pitchers whom he wanted to talk about, also, among them Ed Walsh, Lefty Williams, Cicotte.

"I caught four no-hit games," Ray said, quite proud.

These games were pitched by Death Valley Jim Scott, Joe Benz, Charlie Robertson and Ted Lyons; as is known, Robertson pitched a perfect game.

Schalk also told how he discovered Lyons. One year when he was on a spring training trip in Texas, he was asked to look at a young college pitcher. Ray caught warm-up pitches from the kid without taking his coat off. He immediately sent a telegram to the late Charles A. Comiskey Sr., then owner of the Sox. Lyons was signed up.

"I paid for the wire myself and never got my money back," Ray laughed.

In all, Ray and Campanella talked for an hour and a half to two hours. The next morning, Ray telephoned to tell me how much he had enjoyed the evening and how he liked Campanella. To him, Campy is a real catcher.

Of course, fans and players who saw Schalk catch have said as much for Schalk. No catcher could receive higher praise than Ray did from Ty Cobb, Eddie Collins and Babe Ruth. He is usually credited with having revolutionized the art of catching. When he broke in with the White Sox in 1912, he weighed 140 pounds; during the best of his years behind the bat, his weight was 155. Most catchers in those days were big and slow. Fast and agile, Schalk was all over the field. He followed the batter down to first base and backed up the first sacker; sometimes he blocked a wild throw at first and checked the runner from gaining an extra base. Today, this is standard practice, but in 1912 it wasn't. When ground singles were smashed by the first baseman, he would trail the runner and back up the base. If the runner overran first base, or made a start for second base, the right fielder would throw past the first baseman to Schalk; the runner who had made a start towards second, would find himself trapped off the base and a hit would be turned into an easy out.

Baseball writers and players repeatedly attested to Schalk's ability to handle pitchers. When he was a rookie, he caught Big Ed Walsh with ease. He is reported to have done this without having given Walsh one signal. I might add that he lists as the best pitchers he ever caught, Ed Walsh, Doc White, Reb Russell, Red Faber, Lefty Williams, Eddie Cicotte and Ted Lyons. Once when advising young catchers, he told them to take the pitcher into their confidence. That was his style. He never had a powerful arm, but he made up for this by accuracy in throwing and speed in getting the ball away.

"Ray threw a very soft ball back to the pitcher," Red Faber says.

He holds the record for the most assists made by a catcher in one league, 1810. And when he was playing, he had to contend with some of the best, the fastest and the cleverest base stealers in all baseball history, among them Ty Cobb, Eddie Collins, George Sisler, Clyde Milan, the old Washington outfielder, and Fritz Maisel, third baseman for New York when the team was called the Highlanders.

Schalk was lively and peppery. He kept a team on its toes. He knew the game thoroughly and did well and expertly everything that a catcher needed to do. With the possible exception of Bill Dickey, no catcher seems ever to have been his equal on foul flies. And he was faster than Dickey. Once he caught with ease a ball thrown from the top of the Tribune Tower in Chicago.

"I caught hell from the Old Roman, Mr. Comiskey, for that," he remarks, chuckling.

Schalk was born in Harvey, Illinois, on August 12, 1892. There were six kids in the family. Thirty-five dollars a month was a good take for his father when Ray was a kid. The Schalks moved to Litchfield, Illinois, when Ray was six. As a boy, he worked at many odd jobs, delivering papers, lugging coal, collecting dandelions and at anything else which would make him a few pennies. Sometimes he earned a dollar a week. He loved to play ball and always wanted to catch. He and other Litchfield kids cut the grass for their own diamond, and often had only one bat, a Hillerich model with a picture of a bulldog on it. Teams were organized by wards and the rivalry between them was dangerous. But Ray was a catcher, something exceptional among the young ball players of Litchfield. He could cross the tracks unmolested because catchers were badly needed. He caught his first semipro game at the age of sixteen and after this, he used to earn a dollar of a week end catching for one of the teams around Litchfield. In 1911, before he had attained his nineteenth birthday, he was signed up for $65 a month to catch for Taylorville in the Class D Illinois-Missouri League. He didn't last out the season because Milwaukee, of the American Association, bought him for $750. With Milwaukee, he got about $125 a month.

In 1912, Kid Gleason, White Sox coach, scouted him and Ray was bought by the Chicago White Sox for $10,000, a big sum in those days. Also included in the deal were two players, Block, a catcher, and Lena Blackburne, the infielder who had come up to the White Sox heralded as "the $11,000 beauty." Years later in 1928, when Schalk was relieved as manager of the White Sox, Blackburne succeeded him.

When Ray reported to the White Sox on August 11, 1912, he looked as much like a mascot as he did like the new catcher. He reached the ball park at about eleven-thirty in the morning; Shano Collins and Rollie Zeider, the infielder, put him at his ease. Once on the field, Doc White, the veteran pitcher and a one-time nemesis of Ty Cobb, told Ray that he was catching. Thus he was behind the plate in the first game of a double-header, and also caught the first big-league game he ever saw. He got one hit. Ira Thomas, a slow-footed catcher, stole a base on him, but he nailed the fleeter Stuffy McInnis.

Bill Veeck, Sr., who used to write sports under the name of Bill Bailey, covered Ray's first game for a Chicago newspaper. In his story the next morning, he stated that Schalk should be watched further: on the basis of this game, Veeck could not decide if Schalk was or was not worth the money paid for his services. Schalk appeared in twenty-five games in 1912, and fans at Comiskey Park were beginning to notice him before the season ended. In 1913, he figured in 128 as a first-string backstop and it was clear that he was a star and not just another catcher. Catching has never been quite the same since then.

As he looks back on his career, Ray says that the man who probably helped him more than anyone else was Kid Gleason. He also said that Hal Chase helped him and that after Eddie Collins came to the White Sox in 1915, he became a better catcher. "Collins always caught the signal for a steal and gave me the sign. All I had to do was throw the ball to second base." He thinks that Collins was the most intelligent ball player he ever encountered. He also says that no pitchers were too fast or tricky for him.

There is a much publicized story about Schalk which I'll risk repeating here. One morning in 1916, Ray was excused from morning practice by his manager, Clarence Rowland. In those days, morning practice was regular. He sat in a shady spot in the stands at Comiskey Park watching his teammates go through their paces. A number of teen-age kids had sneaked into the park and they were spread around, also watching. A cop told the kids to beat it. They vanished. Ray continued to watch the practice. The policeman told him that he should beat it, too. No one was allowed in to watch the practice. Ray identified himself. However, seeing this, the players on the field egged the cop on, said that it was a secret work-out and told the cop that the intruder was not Ray Schalk. The cop took a good look at Ray and decided that this young boy couldn't be a ball player, let alone Ray Schalk. Schalk was kicked out of the ball park as a juvenile. That afternoon when the policeman discovered his mistake, he was profuse with apologies.

Schalk talks also with an affectionate memory of Charles

A. Comiskey, Sr., and likes to call him the Old Roman. His years in baseball were among the golden days of ball playing as far as the art and science of baseball are concerned. A majority of the stars elected to the Hall of Fame were his contemporaries—Cobb, Speaker, Collins, Wagner, Lajoie, Home Run Baker, Ed Walsh, Johnson, Evers, Heilmann, Maranville, Alexander, Eddie Plank, Hornsby, Babe Ruth. He belongs with them in Cooperstown. Not only was he a great player, he was an interesting one, and on a club of interesting and great players.

Baseball Players Called Her Ma

The days of Babe Ruth and all the others of his era are gone but Mrs. McCuddy's Tavern is still in the same place, across from Comiskey Park. A wonderful woman, Mrs. McCuddy, who has been mother and hostess to two baseball generations.

ONE day in 1912, the late Charles A. Comiskey, then owner of the Chicago White Sox, took a boy in his late teens across the street from Comiskey Park to a frame house next door to a saloon on West Thirty-fifth Street. He spoke to a Chicago-born woman of Italian descent, more or less as follows:

"Ma, this is Ray Schalk, and I want you to feed him and take care of him."

At the time, Schalk was a country boy in the big city, and looked so juvenile that he could have been more easily taken for a bat boy rather than the great catcher he was quickly to become. When the White Sox were playing at home, Schalk would report to this woman for lunch every day before he went across the street to put on his uniform for the

123

game. He would sit out in her garden eating big plates of food, and finding a substitute sense of home in the glow of her warmth and hospitality. They became lifelong friends.

The woman is Mrs. Elizabeth McCuddy, and she still lives in the same frame house. The neighborhood has changed but she has not moved. It is home to her. About two years or so ago, the house was almost destroyed by fire. She had it repaired and was happy to return to it as quickly as she could. She lives there with her son, her daughter and two dogs. She has many memories. For years, she has seen the crowds flow by to go to the White Sox ball games, and sometimes the roar of the crowds can be heard in her home. In other days, there were the crowds, and the roar. Then, the cheers would be for Babe Ruth, Ty Cobb, Joe Jackson, Buck Weaver, Harry Heilmann. She was their friend, she saw them often and most of the ball players called her "Ma."

"Mother," Babe Ruth often used to say to her, "you're the best woman in the world."

Two years ago, Ray Schalk took me to meet Ma McCuddy. When we entered, she had a mild and affectionate reprimand for him, he had not phoned her of late. He apologized and said that he would phone her more often. We sat down to talk. The home was warm, cozy and its atmosphere seemed especially hospitable with a blizzard raging outside. There was the Christmas tree, a dog by a stove, a puppy penned up in the kitchen and full of life, two daughters talking and buzzing about to get us things, and Mrs. McCuddy sitting and rocking, talking with Schalk about the old days when he was young and acknowledged as the greatest catcher in baseball.

Mrs. McCuddy is now gray, slender and medium sized, but she still looks youthful for her age. She has a clear skin, soft hazel eyes, and enjoys good health.

Her husband owned a saloon next door to the family home on Thirty-fifth Street, but he died over thirty years ago. She raised and supported a family of three girls and a boy, washed towels for the White Sox ball club, held open house for baseball players, fed them, washed for them, boarded their sons, loaned them money, listened to them when they needed a friendly ear, and sat there amidst them when they would let off steam in boyish release. They knocked at her door day and night but it was always open. Today the tavern which her husband once owned is back in the family, it is clean and well kept and her son and her two daughters run it. On summer days and nights when the crowds pour by for the ball game, many fans stop in for a glass of beer and for McCuddy hot dogs. Some fans will not buy hot dogs at the ball park, preferring the ones that Ma and her daughters make.

"Two seasons ago," one of her daughters said, "a man with his hair getting gray stopped at the bar with a boy and told me that when he was a boy, his father stopped in with him for a glass of beer and bought him a root-beer. He wanted to do this now with his own son."

"Yes, but it's a new crowd now," Mrs. McCuddy said. "We had good times. And Ray, I remember you when Mr. Comiskey brought you to me. You were just a skinny kid."

"I can remember it as if it were yesterday," Schalk said. "Those were good meals, I used to sit out in your garden and eat and I never ate better meals, Ma."

"We gave you what we had. The players always took pot luck and sat down to the table with us, and ate what we ate. Ray, I got a Christmas card from Nick Altrock."

Ray Schalk asked of Altrock's health. They had both heard that he had been ill.

"He said that he was well," Mrs. McCuddy said. There was a sense of pleasure and affection in her voice.

She likes to hear from the old-time ball players and is gratified when they remember her.

"I washed Nick's shirt." A daughter told the story. During the last War, Altrock was in Chicago with a group of old-timers for a War Bond Rally. The Washington Nationals were playing the White Sox and a coach was dropped. Altrock was ordered to stay with the team until there was a replacement of another coach, and he had only one nylon shirt with him.

"Every day at four o'clock he sent that shirt over to me to be washed."

In the kitchen spaghetti was on the stove. Charles A. Comiskey II, grandson of the Old Roman, and others in the White Sox office had phoned over to the McCuddys for spaghetti for lunch. Now and then, Mrs. McCuddy reminded her daughters to watch the stove, or would look to me and say:

"Give the man something!"

We talked more of Altrock.

"He came to see me often. He used to be Santa Claus for my children. He would dress up for it and he looked the part. But he fell on my Johnny's train one Christmas. We were giving Johnny a train that year and when Nick came dressed up he sat right down on it. But we were able to get the train fixed."

Later I saw Nick Altrock in Florida. He was reminiscing about his early days in baseball. I mentioned Mrs. McCuddy and his eyes filled with a warm glow of memory, and his smile, so familiar to baseball fans, grew charming.

"Did she ever tell you that I was Santa Claus for her children?" he asked.

And he wanted to know how she was and also wanted her to know that he was well.

"We used to have fun and good times at her place," he said.

"Yes, Nick Altrock came here," Mrs. McCuddy told me. "They all did. They were good men. They were all good men. And you couldn't find anyone who looked more like Santa

Claus than Nick. Did I tell you, Ray, that he sent me a Christmas card?"

The previous summer, Ed Walsh had been in Chicago for an old-timer's game. He had been one of her favorites.

"He looks young. He hasn't a gray hair on his head. I don't know why he doesn't come back here and live. I told him he ought to.

"There used to be good times here," she continued. "But sometimes, they used to play ball and golf in my house. I came home one day and the rug was pulled back. The furniture was pushed into corners and they were playing a ball game here. They broke some of my furniture."

That was a day in the 1920's. When the White Sox were rained out and several of the young ball players wanted to play, they brought a bat and indoor ball over to the McCuddy's and went to it in the living room. The house was really wrecked.

"And golf—they played golf in here. I had a special putter they used. Babe Ruth used to come over here and use it. He and the others ruined one of my rugs and I had to buy a new one. He was a big, fine man. I liked Babe Ruth. He could eat. He ate here with us."

Sometimes when Babe Ruth was playing in Chicago, he would send a message across the street.

"Tell Ma to put six bottles of beer on ice—it's two out in the ninth."

"We had good times when he was here. There was fun. There was a poor little boy. Nobody knew his name. They called him Teddy Bear. I can still see Teddy Bear. He didn't know who Babe Ruth was and you know how the kids were with him. Babe Ruth was good to them. He gave Teddy Bear one of his gloves. And poor little Teddy Bear didn't know what it was worth. A man wanted to give him a dollar for it. I said 'No.' I told Teddy Bear to get five dollars for it. He might as well have gotten something. He was such a poor little kid. I don't know what happened to Teddy Bear. Babe Ruth liked him and was good to little Teddy Bear."

Another time, Babe came with his first wife after a game. He left her outside on the sidewalk talking with a fellow in white pants. Babe socialized, talked with Ma, drank some beer, and every once in a while looked out. His wife was still there.

"She likes White Pants," Babe said.

Then he left.

Johnny Mostil, one-time fleet-footed White Sox center fielder, knocked at the door. He had come for the spaghetti dinner being cooked for the staff at the White Sox offices. He was invited to sit down and have a bite to eat. He was in a hurry but did have a cup of coffee.

"How is Chuckie?" he was asked.

"Chuckie" is Charles Comiskey II, the present vice-president of the White Sox.

"We had him when he was a baby. We took him out every Sunday," Ma said.

"You never come and see me, any more," Ma told Mostil.

He apologized and said that he would drop by very soon.

"But that's all right. I see you waving to me when you go by on Thirty-fifth Street."

Mostil left with the spaghetti and Ray Schalk spoke of Kid Gleason.

"He was good to us ball players."

"He used to come over here, too. He was a fine man, one of the finest men. He came over here one day to me and told me one of my daughters was misbehaving. She was sitting near the White Sox bench and causing trouble. 'I'll soon put a stop to that,' I told him. But next day, Kid Gleason was back here. He asked me why I had let my daughter go back to the ball game. She had misbehaved even more. It wasn't my daughter at all but one of the girls in the neighborhood.

We had given this girl some dresses and Kid Gleason had recognized the dresses. But what I liked about him is that he came to me."

The name of George Uhle, the one-time Cleveland pitching star, was mentioned.

"Remember Uhle and the pig, Mother?" one of the daughters asked.

"I do," she said. "Uhle was a good man, too."

Uhle was once pitching in an exhibition game at Comiskey Park. Harry Heilmann and other stars were also playing.

"And they bought a big pig for me to cook for them after the game. I put it on the fire and went to see the ball game myself. In the second inning, Uhle said he was sick. He said he had stomach trouble. Oh, he looked sick, and he had to leave the game. He came over here to lay down. When we got here after the game, there he was at the table, eating pig and he wasn't sick at all. He seemed like he was figuring to eat the whole pig himself. He had grease on his hands and face, and looked up at me and asked me, 'Ma, do I look like a pig?' "

Fans may remember Art Shires, who came up with the White Sox and who was much in the newspapers for a brief spell. He styled himself "The Great Guy" and he was constantly getting into trouble and scrapes.

"He wasn't bad. He was just wild," Ma remarked. "I remember him the first day he came. He knocked here at my door, and looked like a country boy. I asked him what he was looking for and he said he was looking for Comiskey Park."

"Why boy," I told him, "it's right in front of you."

"Old Mr. Comiskey liked Shires. Shires took my daughters downtown that very day. He needed luggage. He didn't ask about prices and picked out fancy valises. He bought hats and bags to match for my daughters. When he was asked for the money, he said he was a ball player and to send the bill to Mr. Comiskey. There was a lot of worry, but Mr. Comiskey, he liked Shires and the bill was paid.

"Some of them used to come to me and tell me that Art Shires was a bad one and advised me not to loan him money. But I did. When he needed money he came to me. Once he wired me from some place in Pennsylvania for two hundred dollars, and I sent it. But he always paid me back."

On a subsequent visit which I paid to her, she talked more of old ball players.

"There was that Italian from San Francisco, what was his name? A quiet man, he's dead now? Tony Lazzeri. He was a quiet one. He wrote me once from California, to buy him an electric toaster he wanted to give as a wedding present to someone. I wondered why he wanted an electric toaster shipped all the way to California when he could buy one there. But then, I remembered he always had thrifty habits and I used to get gifts for the boys wholesale.

"They all came here. They'd leave a five or a twenty-dollar bill on the table and eat as much as they wanted and talk. We'd have friends, and politicians and business men coming and I treated them all the same. One night, Nick Altrock was here and he talked to a Monsignor. Well, you know Nick and the way he talks. But the Monsignor liked him and they went on talking. He didn't mind the way Nick did a little cursing. And Joe Jackson was a good man. He was simple. He didn't talk much. He used to come here sometimes and he'd sit here and take his shoes off."

She was a good friend of the late Harry Grabiner, one-time Secretary of the Chicago White Sox.

"After my husband died, I had to support my children. I washed towels for the White Sox for twenty years. I was ready to quit, but Harry Grabiner said to me, 'Ma, you've done this for twenty years, you might as well do it for twenty-five years.' So I did it for five more years before I stopped.

"And they all came here. They had fun. We had good times. Ty Cobb, I knew him. He came here. They were all good men, fine men."

She mentioned an old-time star.

"His son was a bad one, though. He was wild. I boarded him." She shook her head from side to side. "He used to tear the house up. He destroyed things. I was glad when he left. One day, one of my daughters wanted to take a bath. And so did he. He was big, so he picked her up and dumped her in a bathtub full of water and said, 'There, you had your bath.' He locked her out of the bathroom. He was a wild one, always destroying furniture, but I boarded him. He went to college. He wasn't a ball player.

"And the young Comiskey. Did I tell you, we had him every Sunday? My daughters wheeled him in his baby buggy. The other day after we had a snow storm, I was outside seeing about my sidewalk, and he was across the street in front of the ball park, doing the same thing. He was getting together a ground crew to shovel off the sidewalk. It was only nine o'clock in the morning. He tends to his business. He saw me and waved and called over to me.

" 'Ma, don't forget that you saw your grandson out at work early this morning.'

"I like that about him. He tends to business."

Mrs. McCuddy is a woman of warmth, character and courage. At almost any gathering of old ball players, one can find among them, a player who fondly remembers her home, her hospitality and good times he had at her place. And stories are sometimes told of her. A few years ago, after the tavern was closed, a drunk rang her bell. Baseball players used to do this at all hours. But this was a stranger. She told him that the tavern was closed. He put one foot in her door and insisted that he be admitted and given a drink. She grabbed two revolvers and chased him along Thirty-fifth Street. He was last seen fleeing across Thirty-fifth Street and Wentworth Avenue as fast as his legs would carry him.

Not many of the modern players seem to know Mrs. Mc-Cuddy. It is the old-timers she knew, and it is they whom she remembers with a kind of maternal warmth. It was they whom she fed, and for whom she held open house. Now they are like ghosts of the past. Across the street the new crowds roar for Minnie Minoso, Nellie Fox, Mickey Mantle and the other players of the moment. Many of the old-timers are dead. But they are alive in Mrs. McCuddy's memory and in her feelings for the past when taking some care of them was part of her business. Still young in heart and enjoying good health, she rocks in her chair and remembers them. To her, they were good men who sometimes had to be fed, and taken care of, and given a passing or wayside home to come to, to sit in and talk and play and be themselves. The social history of baseball cannot be told or written without mention of Ma McCuddy and her family. Baseball players called her "Ma" with real affection because she was for several decades, a mother to many of them. She created a little way station where there was love, kindness, good cheer, fun and understanding. She has meant much to some of these players, and hence to the game itself. It is no exaggeration to characterize her as one of the living legends of baseball.

On Baseball Scouts

*The importance of the good scout to a major
league organization cannot be overestimated.
The scout holds much of the future of a club in
his hands. With this in mind, I interviewed and
spoke to some scouts, desiring to learn what they
look for in a prospect and to present this in their
own language.*

MUCH has been written about scouts, the system of baseball scouting, and the dramatic discoveries of stars
by scouts. Here I do not intend to repeat and to rehash what
is already known. Rather, I wish, merely, to give the reader
some idea of what scouts look for and what they see, mostly
in their own words. The scout, as Fresco Thompson, Dodger
vice-president, remarked to me in a discussion of scouting,
must see more than the fan does. He should be competent
to grasp many details instantaneously and be able to see
more than one play or movement on the same play. He should
see a ball game, or even a practice session as though he were
possessed of four or six eyes. If good, he requires the capacity

to see promise and potential capabilities or defects and weakness in many kinds of detail. A trained baseball man, a good scout watches a ball game like a connoisseur and a true expert. Speaking of this aspect of baseball, Andy High, one of the chief scouts for the Brooklyn Dodgers, told me that he likes to watch a ball game alone so that there is no one to distract him from concentrating on the details of play by talking and discussing the game.

In 1956, Zinn Beck, former National League infielder and now a scout for the Washington Nationals, said:

"I always look in their eyes. Real good eyes have a bit of sparkle. Hornsby had the best eyes I've seen. Hornsby and Mr. [Clark] Griffith. There is a lot of glitter in his eyes."

This is a significant detail. Once a major-league scout signed a player who had two fingers missing on his glove hand. And another scout jokingly declared:

"I once signed a blind man." Then he told the story of this episode.

He saw a young player hit seven home runs in ten days, and it seemed as though he had come upon a real good prospect. He signed up the boy and hastened on to another town, searching for more ivory. Suddenly, this player went into a terrific slump. He went to his manager and said that he couldn't see the ball. His home runs had been hit in daylight. Under the lights, he couldn't hit. Examined by a competent occulist, it turned out that he was night blind. He was fitted to thick-lensed glasses but these were of no help. After playing along with "the blind slugger" for a year, and having him undergo further examinations, the scout had to give up on his prospect.

One scout also said that he tries to get into the dressing room or clubhouse when he is watching a player.

"I like to see them under the showers. They might have a physical blemish that you can't see when they're in uniform."

He pretends to be talking to the boy's manager or coach,

but all of the while, his eyes are roving over the boy's body. Of course one of the obvious physical limitations of a prospect would be whether or not he is muscle bound. The first serious defect Paul Krichell mentioned to me was this one— muscle bound.

"There's a lot more to scouting than I had realized," Zack Taylor, the old catcher, said just after he had taken a scouting job with the Chicago White Sox. Taylor spent thirty-seven years in uniform as catcher, coach and manager. Ray Schalk watched Taylor on the bench and remarked:

"Zack, you're a student of baseball."

Scouting gave Taylor new insights into the game to which he has devoted his life. He also stated that he does not look for sensational performance and spectacular plays. It is even possible that he or another scout might overlook or pass up a boy who goes five for five in a game and turn in a more favorable report on a player in the same game who had gone hitless.

"It means more to a baseball scout," Taylor emphasized, "to look at the actions and intelligence and baseball instincts of a player. This is especially the case if you are watching a young boy. In Double A or Triple A and big league ball, the results mean more. But in scouting young fellows, we go by their actions, instincts, baseball intelligence, smartness more than by the results."

And Zinn Beck said:

"With an outfielder, we want to know if he can run and throw. If he can and if he can hit, we know that we've got a good prospect. An infielder, of course, has got to be able to run and throw, but he can get by with less hitting than an outfielder. But if he has power, so much the better. You also look at the faults and if they have a major fault or a minor fault. Slowness of foot or a bad arm would be a major fault in an outfielder. A bad stance can be a minor fault. Any hitter with good eyes should learn to hit!"

On the question of hitting, Paul Krichell spoke of inability to hit a ball across the letters as a major fault.

And:

"In a young pitcher," said Zack Taylor, "we look for a boy who can throw the ball hard. Every pitcher who throws the ball hard doesn't have a good fast ball. The ball must 'move,' and you must stand behind the pitcher to see it."

Other scouts make the same point. Sometimes instead of using the verb "move," they say that the ball must be "alive"; it must have a hop to it.

"We look for this," Taylor continued, "in a young pitcher because when young pitchers start out in baseball they all make mistakes. And a good fast ball can't be hit consistently. As a pitcher gains in knowledge of how to pitch then he really becomes a pitcher. He has his weapons, knowledge and a fast ball. You can teach a pitcher how to throw a curve, but he has to be gifted by God with that fast ball. A proof of what I say is Feller." (He was talking while Feller was still an active player.) "He's still a great pitcher. He went through the game with that fast ball, but he accumulated knowledge. He was what we call a 'thrower,' but now, he learned to pitch in spots and he developed a great curve ball, one of the best curve balls I ever saw."

Taylor also mentioned hungry ball players—players wanting to play above all else.

And Paul Krichell summed up what he looks for succinctly and cryptically. While similar to what I have quoted above, his views are nevertheless worth presenting. For as is known, Krichell was one of the greatest of all scouts. For an outfielder —good arm, takes good cut at the ball, has power, can run, has speed. Infielder—a good arm, speed, a good pair of hands. How does an infielder throw? Does he peg "straight as a string" or is there a hop in his ball? And what does he do when a batted ball takes a bad hop? Catcher—good hands, good arm, fair hitter. Pitcher—a fast ball.

Speaking of serious weaknesses, Paul Krichell said that the most serious of all is "no guts." This is most fatal, and he spoke of one big fellow who was courageous otherwise but who shook like a leaf on the ball diamond. He and practically all scouts emphasize mental attitude—whether it is good or bad. And in Krichell's book, a most important virtue was the desire to make good and to overcome faults. If a hitter can't hit a curve ball, he regarded this as a serious defect. And Fresco Thompson remarked that running is the most important thing in a well-rounded ball player.

Essentially, the scouts all seek the same qualities. But what makes a good scout? Jack Schwarz of the New York Giants organization said that a good scout also must have "good sense, the judgment to know a major-league ball player when he sees one. He must have confidence, be able to get along with the family of a promising player and be able to sell the merits of his own organization. He should be a self starter and, above all, show common sense."

"Sometimes," said Zinn Beck, "we're more valuable when we reject players. We save the club money."

And Paul Florence, a scout for the Cincinnati Reds, added on this that there is even a danger of a scout becoming negative-minded and seeing only faults.

Some years ago in an interview with J. Taylor Spink, Paul Krichell spoke of what the good scout should be. Besides the qualities already indicated, which Krichell mentioned, he said that a good scout should be a man who has played big-league ball and knows from experience what is involved in big-league ball. He stressed the difference between knowing a ball player in the making, sensing development and recognizing ability in the finished product or the developed ball player. Further he should have "Judgment . . . in business, in relations with young men and with older ones, too. He must have tact. Yes, you might say a little cunning, too. Often

you have to act fast and outwit other scouts . . . He has to
become accustomed to quick jumps, discomfort, bad food,
bad trains, terrible hotels, getting up at five in the morning . . . And your good scout must be a 100 per cent organization man . . ."

This is important because the basic change in the profession of scouting today as against the past is that the scout
now works for a big organization, and scouting has become
a highly systematized enterprise.

The Brooklyn Dodger organization gives each scout a
thick handbook which has been prepared by Fresco Thompson. This contains not only information about scouting, but
also, instruction on a system of grading and classifying players with a code system and instructions that will be helpful
and useful to the scout in selling the merits of the Dodger
organization as against those of other big league clubs. For
almost every good prospect who is a free agent today has a
choice of more than one organization with which he may
sign. In many instances, the cash offers or bonus will be the
same or roughly so. In some cases, also, the prospect will
be a college man with training and other abilities so that he
can think confidently of a successful life outside of baseball.
He, and often his parents, must be convinced, sometimes of
the very merits of a baseball career, and more frequently, of
those of a particular organization, the Dodgers, the Yankees,
the Baltimore Orioles, the Chicago Cubs. And each organization has and must have selling points on its own merits as
against those of a rival. For example, the Yankees can point
out the possibilities of a young player getting extra world
series money. But to the contrary, the Baltimore Orioles can
tell a prospect that his chances of reaching the big leagues
and playing regularly are better with their organization,
which needs talent, than it is with the Yankees who are
glutted with it. The Dodger scouts can argue that besides

their first division standings and pennants won in recent years, they own or have working agreements with two clubs in each minor league category. Thus, there is more room for advancement in the Dodger organization. The Chicago Cubs can argue that they play no night ball at home and night ball is one of the beefs of many ball players. Each club has its sales arguments, and the scout must know how to present these in the best possible light to a young prospect and his family.

And today, there is an increasing burden of clerical work imposed on the scout. Usually, they must submit many reports, and some scouts send in reports on every player they see. Big league clubs keep a file card system on players. Thus in the Dodger files, a player is marked Average, or Average Plus. He might be marked Plus as a runner or because of some other especial capacity. Along with this, there are specific comments. For instance, on a pitcher, it might be noted: "fast ball, alive from belt up."

In the cards used by some scouts for the evaluation of a prospect, there are the following headings—Team, Arm, Power. Best Assets. Hustle. Change (of pace or change up in regard to a pitcher). League. Speed, Hitting, Disposition, Aggressiveness, Curve, Control. Also, the type of ball played and the military status of the boy is to be reported on. And there is space also for additional comment. Each young ball player of promise in America has now become the subjects of many cards filed in many big-league front offices.

The scouts also follow the players signed by rival organizations and cards are kept. Thus in one major-league club file there was a thick record of cards on Herb Score while he was a minor leaguer and the property of the Cleveland Indians. This provides information which can be useful when the rookie comes up to the big leagues, and it also furnishes data which are important for trades. Whenever unknown minor leaguers are involved in trades, these players almost invariably have been thoroughly scouted and there are many reports on them in the files. Two or more reports a year are filed on promising prospects, and often more than one scout for an organization will see these players. In passing, one of the most interesting aspects of these files is that of noting the different impressions and judgments of the same player as he is reported on by different scouts.

Scouts usually work at least five or six months a year, hitting the road. They cover wide areas, usually by car, and they see high school, college, American Legion, semipro and minor league baseball. As a matter of fact, an enterprising scout will never pass up a baseball game, and often they will see two or more games in one day. Zinn Beck tells how once he was driving through Barneside, Georgia, en route to see a ball game in another town. He saw a sign "Ball Game To Day." Having the time, he stopped to watch the game, and picked up an outfielder named Johnny Marion, brother of Marty Marion. Johnny Marion never made the big leagues, but he became a minor-league player and manager. This is typical of a baseball scout. They go over back roads, to villages, hamlets, anywhere that they might see a ball game and find a promising ball player.

The scouts cultivate friends in their territory, are to be seen at the local Elks Clubs, speak at Rotarian luncheons and elsewhere. They never know from where they might get a tip. Often they use part of their expense accounts in giving presents to friends who have tipped them off. And as is obvious and well known, the competition among them is keen. I went to my hotel in a Florida city accompanied by a scout with whom I was going to have dinner. Then he planned to hit the road to go to North Carolina where he was scheduled to make a speech. We stopped by the hotel desk and the girl behind it mentioned the name of a man who was coming to that hotel. The scout immediately changed his plans, and took a room for the night at the hotel.

"A Yankee scout is coming to town," he told me. "That means there's a ball player in this vicinity. I've got to see my friends and find out who he is. I know that girl. She tipped me off. I'll have to buy her a box of candy."

And one winter in Florida, an ex-major leaguer and an instructor at the school said to me passingly:

"I see them everywhere—Yankee scouts. The scout and the bird dog—you see the two of them everywhere."

A story, illustrative of competitiveness among scouts, is told about Leon Hamilton. At one time, he worked for the New York Yankees; now, he is a Brooklyn Dodger scout. He and four or five other big league scouts were all trying to sign up a farm boy who was under age: his contract had to be approved and signed by the boy's father, an old farmer. In their bidding for the boy, the scouts were all restricted by baseball regulations and they could only go up to six thousand dollars in their offer. The rival scouts had seen the old farmer ahead of Hamilton. They had made their offer and presented their arguments. Hamilton then saw the father, and noted one thing said. The old farmer remarked that while the other scouts had offered money, they had not shown him any cash. This gave Hamilton an idea. He phoned his home office for an O.K. Then, he went to a bank and got thirty-eight-hundred old one-dollar bills. The reason he wanted old rather than new bills is that they would take up more space. The day of the decision came. All of the scouts had made appointments to see the old farmer and get their answer. Hamilton, knowing that farmers arise early, appeared at the farm at about 6:30 A.M. He was carrying his dollar bills in a sack. Reminding the farmer of the latter's remark about showing cash, he dumped the thirty-eight-hundred old dollar bills on the kitchen table.

"The money is yours if your boy signs with me," he said.

He got the boy. However, while he was talking, a young brother of the boy grabbed two fistfulls of dollar bills and held them over a hot stove. Hamilton sweated nervously. If the child dropped the money into the hot stove, he would have been the loser and would have to make up for the burned money. Fortunately, this did not happen. But then Hamilton faced a second problem. The old farmer signed the contract and took the money. But Hamilton needed a second signature acknowledging receipt of this money. The farmer balked at this. He didn't mind signing once, but he did not want to sign twice. Hamilton had to do some persuading before he got the signed receipt, and since he had used his own money, he needed this second signature in order to be recompensed for what he had laid out.

There are endless stories and anecdotes about scouts, the competition, and the way in which the stars were discovered. In an issue of *This Week*, the writer, Harold Parrott, told an interesting one about the Yankee scout, "Vinegar Bill" Essick, the Yankee scout who signed Joe Gordon. He was trying to sign a young prospect named Johnny Lindell. The night he called on Lindell's parents, Essick played a few selections from Brahms. And the parents hearing the scout at the piano, decided that after all, baseball couldn't be so rowdy. Johnny Lindell was signed, and his batting helped the New York Yankees to win a world series.

Most scouts are old-time ball players, and some have been great stars. Thus, George Sisler was a scout for years. Old ball players become scouts generally because they want to stay in the game, and they need jobs after their retirement. Often, scouting is the road to a new career in the game, a job as manager or coach or a front office job. When Fresco Thompson was through as a player, he had a chance to become a scout, and today he is chief trouble shooter and a Vice President of the Brooklyn Dodger organization. In scouting, there is a continuing drama. The discovery of a prospect is only the beginning. Then follows the career of the prospect, and the scout is judged by results. Generally speaking, they are being increasingly curtailed in the power to offer money to prospects; the front office usually steps in at that point. But the money spent on talent depends on their judgment and their own jobs depend on their discoveries. If they make many costly mistakes, they can go packing for a new job. They do and must watch the career of their boys, and often this is not solely because of material and economic reasons. They gain prestige because of their discoveries. And they like many of their prospects. Talking to them, you find them possessed of a homely wisdom; they are almost like common man philosophers. And their satisfaction is perhaps akin to that of a teacher, who sees students of his, discoveries of his, go out into the world and make their mark. The drama of the scout's life thus extends forward, and the full meaning of a seemingly routine day's work becomes a story of intense interest years later; it becomes part of the history and tradition of baseball, the game which most scouts love. The scout sits in a stand on a sunscorched diamond located in a Georgia hamlet. He sees a strapping young fellow who catches his eye because of grace, hustle, a throw, a slide, a pitch, a cut taken at the ball, a home run hit. Or he sits in a stand watching college kids. He has seen, perhaps, thousands of games. But he watches. A big kid takes a toe-hold at the plate and swings. The ball sails out of sight. Such power. Maybe he has found a ball player. His name might be Lou Gehrig. It might be another name.

In Paul Krichell's office at the Yankee Stadium, there were a number of pictures of ball players. There are players he discovered. I list some of the names. Lou Gehrig, Whitey Ford, Leo Durocher, Phil Rizzuto, Charlie Keller, Mark Koenig, Tony Lazzeri, Tommy Byrne, Billy Johnson, Red Rolfe, Hank Borowy, Billy Werber, Johnny Murphy. The list is longer. But when Paul Krichell pointed to those pictures, he revealed a modest but justified pride. The discoveries of the good scout become an inseparable part of the history of the game.

And years after he has first seen the boy he discovers, that meeting, that ball game becomes like the first act of a story or drama. This, I should guess, is the major satisfaction a scout finds in his work, and this is what he beats the bushes to attain.

Miscellany

Lowdermilk . . . Alexander . . . Gehrig, et. al. There are so many more who could have been a part of this catch-as-catch-can thesis, but when I started, I thought most of a pitcher who couldn't get the ball over the plate, a pitcher who did nothing else but get the ball over the plate, and a sturdy block of cement at first plate that crumbled and withered as if by some mysterious alchemy.

SOME book written about baseball should contain some reference to a one-time pitcher named Grover Cleveland Lowdermilk. He was nine years in the big leagues and played with the St. Louis Cardinals, the Chicago Cubs, the St. Louis Browns twice, the Cleveland Indians, the Detroit Tigers and ended up with the White Sox in 1919 and 1920. All told, he appeared in 121 games, winning 21 and losing 39. But Lowdermilk is more remembered than many a pitcher with a much better record. Probably, he is mentioned more frequently than Bill Doak, Al Mamaux, Joe Benz, Bob Fromme, Jimmy Lavender or Claude Hendrix although they all won

more games—and were better pitchers—than Lowdermilk.
You will find modern ball players using his name, and not
in vain, and any time you mention it, there is almost instant
recognition.

Lowdermilk was a big fellow, born in Sandborn, Indiana,
and who knows—he might have been a great pitcher. But
this is an "if." When Lowdermilk went in to pitch, perhaps
anything could happen, but one thing usually did occur.
Batters walked to first base, and he was quite capable of
burning the ball past the batter and out of reach of his
catcher. My memory of him is vague but what I can recall
is the sound of the ball cracking into the boards below the
screen in back of the home plate. He threw the ball at those
boards as if he might be flinging hand gernades at the Huns.
Quite obviously he threw strikes, but I can't remember them.
I can recall bases on balls and wild pitches and the ball
smashing into the backstop. And therein resides the fame of
Grover Cleveland Lowdermilk. Even today, a wild pitcher is
referred to as a "Lowdermilk." He enriched the language of
baseball with his name. Fame is that capricious.

And if there ever was a wilder pitcher than Lowdermilk,
I won't believe it. Lowdermilk seemed so wild to me that he
was almost like a nightmare.

Today, however, with the platoon system, he might be
a useful man on a ball club. He could be used as a dead
certainty whenever a manager's intellect decided that a
batter should be purposefully passed.

✳   ✳   ✳

One of my grammar school classmates, a boy named Dick
Buckley, gave a Saint Patrick's Day party in 1917. His aunt
was at the party with her fiancé, a big, young and quiet man
named Sullivan. He did not talk much but when I asked him
a few questions, he told me that he was a Three Eye League

pitcher. He went up in my estimation immediately. I said I hoped that he would make the big leagues, preferably, of course, with the White Sox. And he did, in 1919.

He was a southpaw with good stuff. Lefty Sullivan started one game, against Walter Johnson. But Walter Johnson did not beat him and put him out of the American League. Lefty was bunted out. Somehow or other, he could not field a bunt and throw the ball to the first baseman. He would fling it away, possibly to right field. He just could not snare a bunt, probably because first base was too close.

For years he was one of the best semipro pitchers in Chicago, and in those days there were good semipro teams in and around Chicago, just as there were in New York and elsewhere. Sometimes one failing is enough to keep a promising player out of the big leagues.

* * *

On a chilly Sunday early in the 1939 season I went to Yankee Stadium to see my first game of the year. The sports pages had been full of stories about Lou Gehrig. He was not himself. Something was wrong. He looked as though he were through. But you did not quite believe it. You did not want to believe it. Merely watching Gehrig play, as I often had, you could sense something of the man's earnestness. He seemed to be such a decent and likeable man. And he was continuing to make such a phenomenal record of playing in consecutive games. Reading the stories about him during the spring training period of 1939, I sometimes thought that the reporters must have been short of copy. When the season started, Gehrig would hit his stride. He was so strong and healthy. He overpowered the ball, but he had, in addition, made a pretty good first baseman out of himself. His effort and seeming sincerity could only win admiration from one who merely went to ball games and watched as I did, not caring if the Yankees won or lost. Let me add that I almost never seem to see them lose and it sometimes becomes almost monotonous.

It was a dull day. There was no sun. The Yankees won with ease. But Gehrig was sluggish. He swung without power. By accident he made a hit. The ball, by a fluke, popped out safe towards left. He couldn't run; he dragged to first base. In the field, a ball went by him because he could not bend and stop it. Here was no veteran slowing up. His reflexes were so far off that you could not but observe the fact.

I didn't know that was to be one of Gehrig's last games.

The season continued. The Yankees were off to another pennant. I went to a mid-summer game, with two doctors, one of them my younger brother. Outside the ball park, I had bought a newspaper. Sitting in the stands while the Yankees took their batting practice, I looked at the newspaper. The report on the examination of Lou Gehrig at the Mayo Clinic, had been released and served as the basis of a front-page story.

"Lou Gehrig has infantile paralysis," I said.

"What?"

Reading on, I remarked:

"The medical report gives the diagnosis—amyotropic lateral sclerosis—not polio."

The two doctors exploded.

"That shouldn't be published."

"Why?"

They explained to me that this was a rare form of paralysis which, so far as was medically known, was incurable.

"He probably won't live two years."

The typical course of this disease was described to me by the doctors.

I watched the ball game feeling both shock and awe. At the time I was reading about neurology and questioning my brother and other doctors about paralysis because I was

working on a novel in which one of the characters was to
suffer a stroke. This all only deepened my feelings of sadness.
I felt more than sympathy for Lou Gehrig, whom I did not
know. In him I saw the biological tragedy of man, striking
one who was strong, healthy, and, judging from all I had
read and sensed he was just completely decent. A year before
I had seen him on that same ball field, swinging, and he had
looked as healthy as ever, even though his average had slid
down to .295. It had seemed like an off year for him.

With this news of his disease, I thought that not only was
he condemned to death but he must know it. At a ball game,
you do not think of your problems, let alone death.

But already, and even though Gehrig was not with the
team, you sensed him there as an unseen presence.

Gehrig returned to the Yankees. Before each game, he
came out of the dugout, walked to the plate carrying the
card with the batting order. Already you could see the hitch
in his gait.

On July 4th, there was a Lou Gehrig day. Babe Ruth and
other old teammates came to honor Gehrig. Ruth put his
arm around Gehrig's shoulder. Gehrig spoke through the
microphone, and at one point, his voice almost cracked. He
mentioned the things he could be thankful for and said that
he was the luckiest man in the world. His words were simple.
The talk was, apparently, unprepared. But nothing like this,
as meaningful and spoken with such moral bravery, was
ever uttered through a microphone from the home base area
of a big-league ball park. Courageously, and when he should
have had only a short time to live, he said his uncomplaining
farewell not solely to his baseball career, but to life itself.

The ceremonies over, he walked back to the Yankee bench
with that hitch in his gait. And to sit in the stands, watching,
listening, knowing that the sentence of doom was upon him
took your thoughts into deeper channels than those of baseball.

Soon the game started. Di Maggio, Dickey, Rolfe, Crosetti, Joe Gordon, Keller were on the field, playing as though they might be forever young.

Stricken by something beyond the control or power of man, Lou Gehrig gave an example of fine manly courage and moral bravery. He should be remembered for this even more than for his hitting and for the record he established.

*　　*　　*

Before the 1915 season was half over, many fans knew that the Boston Red Sox had a young southpaw pitcher who could go with the best of them, and who was just about as good as Dutch Leonard, one of the Red Sox's aces. His name was Babe Ruth. I was aware of him and knew that he was an exceptional hitter for a pitcher. By 1916, it was unmistakable! Babe Ruth was one of the best southpaws in the business. And one day in 1917, when the White Sox were battling the Red Sox for the pennant, they filled the bases. Ruth came in to relieve Dutch Leonard. He struck out Joe Jackson and Happy Felsch and saved the game.

In 1919, I saw him hit a ball over the right-field bleachers in Comiskey Park. The next year, he was with the New York Yankees and he was revolutionizing baseball with his home-run hitting. There was a three-way pennant race between Cleveland, the White Sox and the Yankees. With Ruth in the outfield, the Yankees were to become contenders from one season to the next. Miller Higgins had in his line-up the first Yankee Murderer's Row—Babe Ruth, Meusel, Pipp and Home Run Baker.

On the last Yankee Western trip and before the World Series scandal broke as it soon would, the contending Yankees and White Sox played a Saturday game before an overflow crowd. Fans were let out on the outfield and roped off from the playing space of the outfield. Ruth as much or more than the pennant fight had pulled out this crowd. Also, he was to face Eddie Cicotte and sports writers had pointed out that Babe Ruth had never hit a home run off the White Sox shine-ball ace. In my personal experiences as a fan, this was the specific game which set the change in baseball marking off the Babe Ruth era from that of Ty Cobb. Ruth had already become the Babe Ruth who is now a legend, and he was hitting home runs in an unprecedented manner. That season, he smashed out fifty-four. He had already been nicknamed the Bambino, and the overflow crowd was mainly due to his drawing power.

The White Sox won that game easily. Bob Shawkey, a southpaw, started for the Yankees. The Sox began pasting the ball in the first inning. They went ahead and never were caught. They peppered two-base-hits into the crowd. Ruth hit no home runs and Cicotte's record against the great slugger was preserved.

After the game, I watched the players come out of the clubhouse as I usually did. As I was, myself, leaving the ball park, I saw Ruth. A crowd of over a hundred kids had him not only surrounded but almost mobbed. They pushed, shoved, scrambled and yelled so that Ruth could scarcely move. Wearing a blue suit, and a gray cap, there was an expression of bewilderment on his moon face. He said nothing, rolled with the kids and the strange, hysterical and noisy little mob slowly moved on to the exit gate with Ruth in the center of it. More kids rushed to the edge of the crowd and they, also, pushed and shoved. Ruth swayed from side to side, his shoulders bending one way, and then the other. As they all swirled to the gate, Ruth narrowly escaped being shoved into mustard which had been spilled from an overturned barrel. Ruth and the kids left the park, with the big fellow still in the center of the crowd of kids.

Probably, he left them to go to Mrs. McCuddy's across the street from Comiskey Park.

✳   ✳   ✳

I can understand a regular baseball writer, who covers the Dodgers year after year, either liking Don Newcombe and being for him, or disliking the big pitcher and roasting him. But it would be pointless and in bad taste for me to take sides in the case of Newcombe versus sports writers, or possibly the world. I made one trip with the Dodgers, have spoken a few words to him, and have seen him in hotels, clubhouses, trains, and on the field before games as well as when he is on the mound. I enjoy seeing him pitch and believe that he has the capacity to be a great pitcher and to last a long time. How he pitches is more interesting than the way in which he reacts under the pressures of newspaper stories when he loses, especially if he loses or is knocked out of the box in a big game. No pitcher is a Superman, and they all lose, are taken out of the box or are shelled into the showers; all, or nearly all, have lost big games. Jack Coombs and Lefty Gomez never lost world series games, but that is exceptional for any pitcher who appears in four, five or more world series games. Coombs, in passing, was the first Dodger ever to win a world series game, which he achieved against the Boston Red Sox back in the 1916 World Series.

Newcombe is the kind of pitcher who overpowers the batter. He has speed and control, and when he is right he keeps throwing many strikes and keeps ahead of the batter. His difficulties are probably not all psychological. He was very fast in the final game of the 1956 World Series, or at least he looked fast to me from my seat in the press box. Tommy Holmes, veteran sports writer, remarked of Newcombe after that game that he is one of those fast-ball pitchers who sometimes seem to have too much speed. And on such days, the ball comes in straight. It comes with so much speed that it does not move or hop. Such pitching is tailor-made for the Yankees, especially Yogi Berra. This is probably one of Newcombe's troubles, and certainly it is not worth all of the ballooning it receives in the sports pages, let alone the man-handling of a service station attendant.

It has often been written that Newcombe is just about the hardest working pitcher on the Dodger team. And it is true. He is not lazy; he only looks lazy. He works like hell running, and keeping himself in shape. But he is a big and somewhat awkward man, and big fellows are touchy, as small men often are. Just as he looks lazy, so does he seem insensitive, but he isn't. He is overly-sensitive and takes remarks and criticism too hard. So he is good copy for circulation and bad copy for himself and his popularity. He seems to fight himself, and this is just about one of the worst things you can do, not only in baseball but in life in general. But the war of Newk against Newcombe suggests to me a paraphrasing of the philosopher Hobbes who wrote of the war of all against all; Newcombe seems psychologically engaged in warfare against himself and against all. The pity of this is that he should easily go on pitching winning ball, perhaps for as long as ten more years. He can pile up one of the best records of any pitcher of his time. But while he throws a fast ball, he hurls a very slow phrase. When he is right and in the box, he has stuff on the ball, plenty of it; when he has lost a big one, as they all do, he doesn't even seem to have a roundhouse outcurve. And certainly he cannot then throw verbal curves.

During the practice session at Yankee Stadium before the third game of the 1956 World Series, Newcombe was brooding, semi-communicative and in a withdrawn sulk; the day before, he had been taken out of the box. The papers were on his neck and stories about "choking up" had been printed. Hurt sullenness was on the big pitcher's face. Instead of having almost lost a ball game, you might have imagined that he had lost the final struggle of life. But more than choking up, I would guess that he is shy and lacking in the kind of self-assurance which a man can only give himself. This is not so exceptional or unusual, especially in a pitcher. Baseball pitchers are a temperamental confraternity of specialists. Many of them have excesses of temperament. One of the nicest guys I have met in baseball is Russ Meyer, and on the occasions I have seen him he has been both pleasant and intelligent. But from what I am told as well as what I read, he can play Halloween with a clubhouse just about as efficiently as any pitcher in the business. Before a game at St. Louis in 1955, Russ was sitting alone in the Dodger dugout. He picked up an old baseball, looked at it carefully, and said, speaking to himself and to no one:

"Just think of it. This little ball causes all of the trouble."

To a pitcher, especially, that little ball causes all of the trouble. It gives him sore arms, and on days it seems to be capable of more eccentricities and tantrums, as it were, than the most temperamental of pitchers. It won't hop; it won't curve; it won't slide; it won't shoot down; it won't get over that plate, or else it will collide with a bat and ergo—the pitcher is taking his shower or drinking a bottle of coke or a can of beer in the clubhouse. Pitching is harder today than in the past. Some of them, such as Newcombe, or Roberts or Pierce are as good as many of the pitchers of the past. It is perhaps easier for a pitcher to go off the handle now because hurling is rough going. Any .220 hitter, let alone Yogi Berra, can wreck a well-pitched game. In 1917, a 4-0 lead was a big margin; today, with a 4-0 lead, Newcombe, Sal Maglie, Robin Roberts, none of them are safe and able to coast. And the terrible injury to Herb Score of the Cleveland Indians only dramatizes the physical danger which pitchers face.

We don't know so much about what we really mean if we say a pitcher chokes up. At least, I don't. But we possibly have a clearer idea in our minds if we use words like "fighting yourself" and "over-anxious." And we know what we mean when we say that a player can bring the wrong part of his nature onto the ball field. It's a platitude to say that you can only win today's ball game, not yesterday's. You can state this differently by observing that you have got yourself licked if you allow the past to control the future. But the past of a few lost ball games can play hell with a pitcher like New-combe. If he learns this in the sense of assimilating it in his own thoughts, he is going to go down as one whale of a pitcher; if he does not, his fast ball and the games he won will be forgotten and he will be remembered for his rhubarbs. But he is not only an outstanding pitcher; he is an interesting pitcher to watch. He pitches a damned good ball game.

*　*　*

There are games you have seen, or plays, or innings or players which remain fixed in memory. They might remain in memory in a partly disassociated or fragmentary way. Sitting in a ball park years later, various of these memories will drift back to you. I jot some of these down at random. For this kind of remembering is one of the pleasures of baseball.

I think of Nap Lajoie at the end of his career when he was with the Philadelphia Athletics. No team today could have done a better job finishing last than did the 1916 Athletics. That was their style, their *metier*. I recall a Sunday double-header which they played against the White Sox. As usual, the Athletics dropped the first game to the White Sox and they had done a real good job to lose the second. Late in the game, in the eighth inning, Lajoie stood at bat and deliberately banged foul balls. Each time he hit one, he laughed. But as a ball player, he was everything they say of him, at least in my unprofessional opinion.

In 1920 on Labor Day, I happened to sit in the box seat next to the Tiger dugout. The White Sox put in a tall, gookish-

looking rookie pitcher named Shovel Hodge. Inning after
inning went by. I could hear the Tigers on their bench beefing
about Hughie Jennings and repeating:

"He's got nothing."

But it looked as though the rookie had a no-hitter. Late in
the game, the no-hitter was spoiled, but Hodge won. It
seemed as if the White Sox had a new pitcher who was going
places. But I don't think Hodge ever again pitched as good
a game in the majors. He was going places—back to the
minors.

And watching Alexander pitch. He had an easy motion,
and scarcely a windup. And he let the ball go sidearm. He
usually seemed to have control of the game and could win it
as easily as a hungry ball player can put away a steak.

And George Sisler. He was a clean cut and trim looking ball
player, one of the most graceful ever to play. But it was sad
to watch him when he was finishing up with the Braves, so
slowed up that he might have had lumber in his thighs.

Sitting in the stands, watching practice and then the game,
memories of this character come and go irregularly and by
a process of association. But memories can play tricks on you.
Thus, I have for almost two years been convinced that I saw
Rube Walker, Dodger catcher steal a base at Wrigley Field.
He didn't but I consistently believed that he did until I
checked the fact in a record book. And then there was Babe
Herman playing a night game in Hollywood back in 1941.
He was lucky the park was small. He did not run. He got to
first base by sheer will power.

And watching Sam Crawford, who is now in the Hall of
Fame, with his easy swing, propelling the ball on a line, sometimes for extra bases. Crawford was a star and an interesting
hitter to watch.

And there are so many more scenes and players. Bob Feller
firing the ball past the Yankee hitters. Walter Johnson, Eddie
Plank, Dizzy Dean. The Yankees winning ball games year

after year. Bill Dickey once hit a home run with the bases full
in the ninth inning, to crush the White Sox. When you think
of baseball, scenes, plays, names, games crowd into your
memory. But no matter how many games you have watched,
you want to go back. You might see a play you've never wit-
nessed before. But the hope of the unusual is but one of the
reasons why you want to see more games. Merely to see a
good game, that is enough in itself. Because you like baseball.
You've liked it for years. And you'll probably like it all of
your life.

School Days—Diamond-Type

I was curious to know what baseball schools were like. Through the kindness of Dick Johnston, Assistant Editor of SPORTS ILLUSTRATED, *I was able to get an assignment to go to Florida and investigate the schools. I found much pathos, many boys hungry to achieve what is beyond their capacity —success in the big leagues. The human features of the baseball school interested me, perhaps more than the instruction. At all events, I present what I saw and heard and what I think of the schools.*

"I'VE seen kids like that before," Virgil Trucks remarked. "You couldn't keep him in school."

Trucks was speaking of a sixteen-year-old kid from Buffalo named Benedict Trawinski. Trawinski was crazy for baseball. That's all he wanted to do, play ball. Along with a brother, he was on teams around Buffalo, but he was impatient and wanted to get on, to be seen by scouts, to learn more about the game, and to play in Florida when there still is snow on the diamonds in Buffalo. He went to a baseball school. That was how Virgil Trucks happened to be speaking of him, for that year Virgil was the head of the school and it bore his name.

Trawinski was well built for his age and looked like a ball player and a possible prospect. He practiced at shortstop as though he might have been in a world series, and talked it up, chattering ceaselessly. He was an inarticulate kid, and could talk of little else but baseball. He gave the impression of wanting, and wanting like all hell to make it.

The first game which the kids and young men of the Trucks School played that year was with a team from Lakeland, Florida. It was a raw cold night and you shivered, watching and hanging around the local field in Auburndale, where the game was being played. Trawinski started at shortstop for the Trucks school. In the first inning, he walked and got to second on a wild pitch. When another ball was thrown past the catcher, he went around third and tore for home. But he began to slide too soon. He momentarily checked himself —always a bad thing when sliding—and then abruptly he was writhing on the ground.

The previous spring, Bobby Thomson had broken an ankle on a similar slide, and had sat out most of the regular season while a Milwaukee Brave. Trawinski was more fortunate. He got off with a sprain which was not too bad. He was able to play before his course in the school was up. But he learned something by his mishap. Inexperienced, he might never make it, but he most likely will never again hesitate during a slide. This was finding out the hard way.

Trawinski was one of several hundred aspiring ball players scattered about Florida at winter baseball schools. They were, or mostly pretended to be convinced, that in baseball they would find their chance to gain fame and fortune. They paid their money for the privilege or opportunity of working out and playing before the critical eyes of big-leaguers or veteran ball players who were the instructors or directors at these private schools. Most of them played and practiced hard, watched, listened closely to whatever instruction they received, and the hope of making the majors was in their minds. I doubt that many of them from the schools in that year or any other year will make it, but this was their dream and their ambition.

I was going about the schools on an assignment but I had picked it myself and was curious as to what the schools were like. I went to one of them unintroduced, and one of the aspiring players immediately asked me if I were a scout. And others at the schools asked if I knew when any scouts were coming. Some of them lived from day to day, hoping a scout would show up, see them and sign them to a contract. Then they would not have had to go home, back to a job. They would have been on their way. In Kissimmee, Florida, I asked one of the young player-students what he thought of the school.

"What do I think of it? It's our future."

At a meal in Kissimmee, one of the boys at Sid Hudson's school said:

"Big leaguers think in five thousands the way we think of five dollars."

The baseball school is a relatively new institution. The record isn't clear as to its origins but apparently Ray Doan, promoter of the House of David teams, started the first one in Arkansas in the 1930's. Rogers Hornsby was early associated with him. And in 1939, when Doan moved from Hot Springs, Arkansas, to Jackson, Mississippi, he advertised Babe Ruth as a member of his faculty.

Jersey Joe Stripp seems to have operated the first baseball school in Florida, and most of these institutions have since located in that state. However, more schools are springing up elsewhere, and while January is the big month, schools are operated at other times, including spring and summer. In

1937, the majors got interested when Joe Engel, president of the Chattanooga Lookouts, established the Washington Nationals Baseball School at Winter Garden. In 1955, Jack Rossiter, a Washington scout, ran a school in Cocoa; Ed Lopat had one in St. Augustine. There was also a school run by Eddie Miller. These schools, excepting that of the Washington ball club, were privately run for profit. Almost anyone who paid could attend. There was no way of screening the aspiring players in advance. They came from all over America and even Canada, and the large majority of them really had no chance of success in baseball. As is known many of the major-league clubs had their own schools. But the Yankees, or the Dodgers at Vero Beach, give instruction to players signed up to play in the farm systems. The Washington school is a means of finding prospects to be signed.

The baseball schools, despite the dislike and even opposition of baseball men, appear to be firmly established; they are here to stay. They may even gain somewhat in importance, and become one source of prospects. Definitely, they do provide at least a few prospects for minor and independent leagues. Scattered among them any year are young players who have already had some minor-league experience, usually Class D. Because of injuries or for other reasons, they go to a school hoping that through it, they will get a new chance.

It is to the interest of the private schools to find prospects. This not only enhances their prestige, but some of them, at least, charge a commission or fee from any team signing one of their boys. There is one instance of extreme school advertising in which quite patently extravagant claims are made by a school director. The advertisements of this particular school claim a high percentage of contracts for its students or attendants; this attracts many to the school. But the advertisements of other schools have been more modest, promising instruction by big-leaguers but not holding out big promises of contracts. Some scouts either will not go to the schools or else they do so with a jaundiced eye and a disinclination to find any prospects at the schools. Others visit the schools and look as they will elsewhere and anywhere. At Sid Hudson's School in Cocoa, for instance, I met Paul Florence and two scouts. In a game at Orlando played between a team of the Washington Nationals and the Rossiter School, I met or saw other scouts, including one from the St. Louis Cardinals. All scouts will visit the Washington school. The Nationals sign up any prospects at their school but scouts can get an early line on these boys.

I will deal more with the general character of the schools below, but before I do, I think it well to give some sense of the boys and young men who go to the schools. As I have indicated, they come from all over the nation and even outside of it and they pay their expense of travel and fees or tuition. The Washington Nationals charge no tuition and provide meals, but the hopefuls they accept pay their own travel expenses. Those who are signed up are refunded their costs of transportation. These hopefuls travel to the school by bus, private auto, train or plane, and most of them are full of determination and dreams. Some of them are mixed up, and now and then, you can see one who would benefit more from a psychiatrist than a retired big-leaguer. But mostly they are average boys and young men, young ball players from local and sandlot teams. Among them there is as much variety in character and background as you will find on a ball club, especially, perhaps, during spring training. They are like young ball players, except that many are not good enough to achieve this status.

A chap named Harry Bode who attended the Washington Nationals school at Winter Garden, was a checker from Anchorage, Alaska, and he went to Florida by airplane. Another young Canadian traveled seven days and nights by bus to reach one of the schools. There was Jim Costellas, seventeen, who came to America from Athens, Greece, at the age of fifteen. He went to night school while he worked and he earned the money to attend a baseball school by working in a doughnut establishment. He was hoping to be signed by a scout, and he was as good as most of the American-born boys even though he had been playing ball only two years. A young southpaw from the state of Washington had worked in an aircraft plant and had had a bad year at home, pitching. He went to one of the schools wanting once and for all to know if he had the stuff to make a big-league pitcher. His self-doubts had put him in bad shape.

"Well, he had better know that he hasn't got the stuff," a big-league pitcher said to me after I had spoken of the boy.

The entire staff of the Washington school believed that they had found a good prospect in a nineteen-year-old lefty first baseman named Tony Gatch. He was a chemical worker in Chicago and his father was opposed to his becoming a ball player; the elder Gatch was a steelworker. Gatch's mother told him to "buckle down to it." He was signed to a contract and ticketed for Class AA baseball with the Chattanooga Lookouts. However, he was released during the season of 1956, after having been optioned to Orlando.

A young Southerner named Daniels was recommended by Ty Cobb, and impressed Joe Engel and Zinn Beck. While they did not want to sign him, they tried to place him in a minor league club outside the Washington Club, but they failed.

There also was a catcher, Gerald Weber, who was signed and then released by Orlando, and was re-signed by Gainesville, Florida, in the Florida State League.

Then there was a twenty-eight-year-old tool and die maker who gave up his job in a Midwest plant that paid $2.82 an hour, hoping that he might be signed to a contract in Class D ball at a salary of perhaps $125 per month. He was a first baseman.

"He ought to go home," said a major-leaguer teaching at a school.

And there was a carpenter from Dayton, Ohio, named Fuzzy Fosnaugh. At Winter Garden, he was the life of the camp. Everyone liked him and got a laugh out of his antics. Fuzzy went home without a contract. A third baseman who belonged to the Yankees' Binghamton Club went to Ed Lopat's school in St. Augustine. He attended the school in order to get into condition and to improve in his fielding and throwing. He played with Binghamton but has not as yet come up to worry Andy Carey or any other Yankee third baseman.

A cable operator named Bernard Henry Marchena in Curaçao, Dutch West Indies, wanted to be a ball player but knew that he had only an outside chance. He played outfield in an amateur school at home. The crowd of aspirants at Lopat's school all called him Chico. In baseball, it appears that many players from the Caribbean area are, and with a lack of imagination and originality, all called "Chico." This Chico could not hit well, but he improved. He writes me to this day, and informs me that his hitting has improved. Some months ago, a letter from Chico brought the news that he had hit .770. Chico also said that even though he would not get a contract, he would learn and be able to teach players in his own league. He is more than satisfied that his attendance at the school in St. Augustine was worth the time.

From farms, small towns, big cities they came. They still do. They are all chasing the rainbow that Ty Cobb, Tris Speaker, Lefty Grove, Bob Feller, Fred Lindstrom, Ray Schalk found. They want to become big-leaguers. And if they fail, they will at least act and play-act as though they were on their way to finding that rainbow. For while many come and go, they can act like ball players at a school. With their dreams and hopes, and with all they have read of baseball, ball players and spring training, they do get to Florida and even to the very places, or places near to where the big teams play. They condition themselves like real ball players. They talk about their arms, their throwing, their stance, their aches and bumps. They go through each and every motion. Living together in barracks, they could be as the rookies who go to Vero Beach, including those who will one day be up there in the big show. In other words, they go through a course in conditioning, practicing and playing similar to that of the professionals during spring training. The instruction they get deals with the fundamentals of the game and is mostly good. But since they pay (except at Winter Garden), all must be treated equally and given the same amount of time as well as opportunity to play in ball games. A plate-shy screwball who even had difficulty in getting his bat off the shoulder was equal to a promising boy who might have been a prospect. A business man over thirty, with the paunch beginning to show also was equal. You pay your money and you play your three or five innings.

Among those instructing at the schools when I visited them were Virgil Trucks, Zack Taylor, former catcher, Chuck Stobbs of Washington, "Boom Boom" Beck and Pete Appleton, ex-pitchers, Ellis Clary, Joe Fitzgerald and Joe Haynes of the Washington coaching staff, Cal Ermer, the Chattanooga manager, Hudson and Ted Lepcio of the Red Sox, Ed Lopat, Enos Slaughter and Gus Niarhos.

The boys were taken seriously, and efforts were made to correct faults. However, now and then, you will find an instructor who finds the golf links more appealing of an afternoon than a crew of kids and young men yearning to be a Yankee with some of them even desperate to attain this status. Interest varied from instructor to instructor. Virgil Trucks would watch the boys more than he seemed to and, especially with the pitchers, he was able to tell them much, more than they could profit by. He did not have much by way of pitchers to work with. Chuck Stobbs came to his school, helped out and stayed with the boys in the camp where they lived. He looked as young as some of them and out of a uniform he could have been taken for one of the student players. But Stobbs' staying in the camp was an especial treat. Old Zack Taylor was earnest, sincere and watchful, constantly explaining, even to the point of telling the boys how to walk with a spring in their gait. Enos Slaughter would play a pepper game with the boys as though he were in the outfield in Yankee Stadium, outyelling them and also snapping them into greater enthusiasm. Ted Lepcio, whom on sight I mistook for one of the aspiring pay-to-learn players, looked as young as they, and I began asking him questions about himself, his background and the reasons why he had come to the school. He laughed at my mistake.

Zack Taylor spent a great deal of time teaching catchers how to move out from behind the batter to take a pitch-out. This is not as easy as it looks when you see Yogi Berra or Roy Campanella doing it; at least, it wasn't for some of these boys. Another difficulty which young catchers have is covering the plate. Zack also told the boys how he had once been talking in Florida with Jimmy Archer, old-time Club catcher who was famous for his squat throw. Archer had said that in order to perfect himself in catching foul balls, he used to throw oranges into the air and catch them. Zach had done this and advised the boys to do likewise. At another school, Gus Niarhos spoke of covering the plate, explaining how the catcher should place himself and tag a runner coming home to score. The boys did not learn this too easily. Many young catchers move up from the plate and find themselves trapped into making a desperate lunge to tag the runner out. Even under instructions, young catchers persist in such faults.

Besides instruction, the schools offer young players an opportunity to practice and to play daily. This was most welcomed by those who came from large cities where they were lucky to play two days running. A big-league ball player has spent thousands of hours throwing and catching and hitting a ball. For every time he has swung at a pitch in a game, he has taken at least several cuts in practice. It is this great difference between someone who merely plays ball and a big-leaguer who plays all the time that the young players are trying to bridge.

At least two of the schools have acquired umpiring and trainer adjuncts. Art Passarella, who was associated with Lopat, annually takes a small group of student umpires. He trains them and if they show promise, he tries to get them jobs umpiring in Class D leagues. In 1955 he took only four young umpires, all of whom admitted that they had once dreamed of becoming ball players before they realized they would never succeed. They took up umpiring to stay in baseball.

Gus Mauch, the Yankee trainer, was teaching student trainers at the Sid Hudson School. He had eleven under his wing in 1955, one a chiropractor who traveled about 150 miles a day by auto to the school. A second was a doctor who wanted to work with athletes and another a Turkish bath masseur who wanted to better his position economically.

Clearly there is in the schools something of the pathos of ambition. Of 125 boys who attended the Washington camp, six were signed up. It was likely that eight more would be placed with minor league teams. One hundred and eleven went home without contracts. The vast majority who go to the private schools and pay tuition do not get contracts and go on to make the grade. But even so, the boys like it. They have their dream of training and acting like the big-leaguers, and this, at least, some of them want.

Opinions about the relative worth of the schools differ among the scouts. But as I have mentioned, most baseball men do not like or favor the schools. Some prefer clinics, which are also growing in popularity. The clinics are usually run on weekends under the sponsorship of newspapers, and they admit boys from 8 to 10 to 18. At such a clinic in Brooklyn, Lopat was picked out from among 1,000 boys, signed up and thus began his baseball career.

In 1955 the *Sarasota Herald-Tribune* conducted a series of four weekend clinics which were highly successful. Nineteen present-day and former ball players assisted in this work. From 200 to 400 boys were on hand, and they were coached and given tips on fundamentals of the game.

Colored boys were not excluded and, for the first time, boys of both races played together in a ball game at Payne Park in Sarasota. Four former big-league batting champions —Eddie Roush, Paul Waner, Heinie Manush and Billy Goodman—were among the instructors along with Nick Altrock, Heinie Groh, Early Wynn, Wes Ferrell and Hoot Evers. Both the boys and the players loved it and the event attained much local prominence.

The clinics are undoubtedly cheaper to run than the schools —the *Sarasota Herald's* cost about $500 in all—and they give the scouts a quick and easy look at a mob of rookies. Washington's school-operating expenses amounted to $15,000 a year, money well spent if only a few stars are found. Wynn and Hudson, in fact, did get their start there.

One of the criticisms directed against the schools (as opposed to the clinics) is that most of them are privately operated, and for profit. Actually, the profits are not large. For Hudson it was like taking a baseball refresher course every year, and Lopat has enjoyed himself immensely. At the schools some of the big-leaguers seemed to be generally sympathetic to the hopes and problems of the students.

The last weekend at the Washington camp, there was an atmosphere of dispiritedness. A dark-haired boy sat on a bench in the locker room. Others were dressing. An attendant collected Chattanooga Lookout uniforms which had been used in some of the games. These borrowed baseball suits were being returned for those to whom they would belong —players with contracts.

"Ma, I'm coming home—unsigned," a dark-haired boy said aloud and in a tone of half irony.

And in the early afternoon, a player stood all alone at home plate with bat in hand, swinging again and again at an imaginary ball. He had not given up. He was practicing his swing for the future.

He, too, like most of those who went to baseball school that year, went home unsigned.

Watching a young pitcher in the box at Auburndale, Trucks said:

"I was like that when I broke in. You couldn't stop me. I could have thrown the ball through a brick wall. But I was wild as a March hare."

From the boys of eight and nine on, the clinics and the schools give a picture of baseball, its hopes, its spirit, its joys, its suffering and dreams. The colored boy pitching in Payne Park, the high-school kid eager to break in, the minor-leaguer, Virgil Trucks, Ed Lopat, Paul Waner who is honored in the Hall of Fame, and old Nick Altrock—a span of generations. You see those who want to do it, those who are doing it now, and those who have done it and who remember backwards to the days when they went through the process step by step that these new generations now seek to repeat.

But two incidents tell me much about the baseball schools. In Auburndale, Florida, Dick Wakefield came out to watch the boys and he gave them odd bits of advice on hitting. He was already out of baseball, and casting about for something to do. He is an intelligent fellow interested in economics. But there he was, still young enough to play, and he had thrown away the chance to go on doing what these kids would have broken an arm and a leg to achieve. A big bonus baby, he had not had the baseball ambition to pursue a career. Wakefield had never had to pay as these boys were in order to play and hope that a scout would start them off in Class D. The pathos I mentioned above was marked, merely if you saw Dick Wakefield in shorts, standing by the batter's box, watching the kids who were trying so hard to impress him. Now and then, he commented or illustrated a point by demonstrating with a bat.

The second episode concerns Ed Lopat, a very nice and modest guy. Ed was picked up as a first baseman in a newspaper clinic held in Brooklyn. Running the school, he would come on the ball field in his gray Yankee uniform. Ed had made it. He was hoping with confidence to go on with the world champion Yankees and to win 200 ball games before closing out the books.

The kids in the schools wanted what the boys who played with Fred Lindstrom wanted. In those earlier years, of course, baseball schools were unthought of. The schools are but one of the changes in the baseball world. As to the opinions about them, and the disapproval of front office men and many others in baseball, it is unnecessary for me to judge. I found them humanly interesting. In some ways, I could compare them to actors' schools and writers' conferences where many go hoping to become stars or writers. There is a parallel pathos of ambition and mediocrity or less. In the case of actors' schools, however, much can be taught. Little can be taught in writing, or at least that is my opinion. How much baseball can be taught? This is a question which will produce a great variety of answers from baseball men.

But concerning schools and ambition for fame, it is not generally realized but there are more persons in these United States who want to be writers than there are who want to play baseball. About five or six years ago, one estimate was that there are 8,500,000 aspiring writers in the nation. In the meantime, the population of the nation has been increasing.

Buck Weaver's Last Interview

Recently I was speaking with a baseball man who knew Buck Weaver. He shook his head with regret and remarked that he wished Weaver had been reinstated. He is convinced that Weaver played his best in the 1919 World Series and that Buck was caught in a net of circumstances. Whatever the true story is, Weaver paid a lifelong penalty and was disbarred from doing the one thing he could do well. Now he is no more. But baseball fans remember him and still regret that his was such a painful destiny. I have tried to tell something of his story as I have been able to piece it together.

SHORTLY after noon on a day in January, 1956, a slender man of sixty-four years of age was walking along West Seventy-first Street on the South Side of Chicago, on his way to see an income tax consultant. He began to fall to the ground and clutched a picket fence. A passing motorist saw the stricken man, stopped his automobile and rushed to give what aid he could. But before he could be reached, the old man dropped to the sidewalk. A small crowd collected. The police were called. The body was taken to a hospital and there it was said that the man had died of natural causes.

The next day, the obituary page of the *New York Times* carried over a seven-paragraph story, the following head:

"BUCK WEAVER OF 1919 'BLACK SOX' IS DEAD: 3RD BASEMAN ONE OF 8 BARRED FROM GAME."

For years, Buck Weaver had been a baseball legend. Now and then, I would ask a baseball fan:

"Do you remember Buck Weaver?"

Generally, I would be answered:

"Do I remember Buck Weaver? He was one of the greatest third basemen who ever lived. He got a raw deal."

Fans in American League towns, and especially in Chicago where he played with the White Sox from 1912 to 1920, thought of him with sympathy and affection. As is well known, Weaver was one of the eight White Sox players suspended by the late Charles A. Comiskey, White Sox owner, late in the 1920 season on the grounds that they had allegedly thrown the 1919 World Series to the Cincinnati Reds. The evidence against Weaver has always been vague and unclear. It was charged that he had been approached by Eddie Cicotte, pitcher, and one of the eight "Black Sox" and asked to participate in the series fix. Also, it was alleged that he had been present when the conspiracy was discussed by the involved players, and, hence, he knew of the plot but did not talk. Since Weaver's death, Chick Gandil, White Sox first baseman in the 1919 Series, granted an interview to a writer from *Sports Illustrated* and he declared that Weaver attended a meeting of the guilty players. Gandil further asserted that Weaver wanted to collect the money from the gamblers immediately. But George Davis Weaver is dead now and cannot speak any more. When news of the scandal broke in the press in September, 1920, it was asserted that Fred McMullin, substitute infielder, left a package of money at Weaver's home. This was never proven. Most baseball men with whom I've talked believe that Buck was a victim.

There were also other rumors and stories. One is that Buck refused to take a lie detector test. According to a second story, Weaver, after the 1919 series, is supposed to have gone hunting with a teammate of previous years. Buck seemed troubled and not at all himself. Finally, he is supposed to have broken down and told the story of the "fix" but, also, to have insisted that he had done nothing himself to throw the games.

It does seem certain that Buck had what is termed "guilty knowledge." But his distress while hunting is easily understandable. His knowledge, then, could only have left him in a moral quandary, faced with the risk of being considered a squealer and, possibly, a goat. For had he told on his teammates, he could not have been certain that he would have been believed. During Buck's playing days, it seems that there was considerable talk of thrown games among players and in baseball circles. In *McGraw of The Giants,* Frank Graham writes that Hal Chase's manager in Cincinnati, Christy Mathewson, charged Chase with not having given his best efforts to the club in 1918. Graham declares that Mathewson meant throwing games. Matty also suspended Chase for indifferent playing. Chase was tried, but Mathewson was in France, and ignored cables requesting a deposition. The testimony of other players was inconclusive, and Chase was exonerated. But there are other stories about the Mathewson-Chase incident which, to my mind, have not been printed. Mathewson is reported to have been advised by a baseball writer that if charges of crookedness were made against Chase and not proven, Chase could have sued and collected heavy damages. For this reason, it is believed that Chase was exonerated. In 1919, Chase was first baseman for John McGraw's New York Giants, and Mathewson, returned from France, signed up as coach. Frank Graham comments on this strange coincidence: "Chase grinned inscrutably when he heard" that Mathewson was to be coach. Towards the end of the 1919 season, Chase dropped away from the Giants. So did Heinie Zimmerman, the third baseman. When the Black Sox scandal broke, Chase never denied allegations of crookedness made against him, but Heinie Zimmerman did. At all events, both players were let out of baseball in such a manner that they could not sue. And Mathewson did not press the charges against Hal Chase to the point where he was out on a limb.

Buck Weaver knew only baseball. The code by which he grew up cast scorn and opprobium on a squealer. He must have heard tales and rumors of other thrown games prior to 1919. These, if there were such—as seems to have been the case—were not reported. What should a player like Weaver have done? And had he told of the "fix," could he have felt safe in his own career? There could have been the word of seven against one. With Buck dead after having suffered for years because of his suspension from organized baseball, I most certainly do not want to accuse him. But there was a cloud over him. Withal, his failure to report this "guilty knowledge" is more than understandable. And he well could not have known what to do.

Up to his death, Weaver consistently maintained his innocence. He and the other players were indicted by a Cook County Grand Jury in the early twenties. The evidence against Buck was so insubstantial legally that the presiding judge, Judge Hugo Friend, wanted to dismiss the indictment against him. Likewise Judge Friend found the evidence against Happy Felsch too insubstantial for conviction. Lawyers for the other indicted players feared that if this were done, the defense of their clients would be damaged. Weaver agreed, therefore, to stand trial. Judge Friend consented to this, but also declared that, were Weaver to be found guilty by the jury, he would overrule the verdict. All of the defendants were acquitted. Weaver periodically applied for reinstatement in organized baseball, but his efforts were in vain. Two Baseball Commissioners, the late Judge Kenesaw Landis and Governor Happy Chandler, rejected his appeals for the clearing of his name and his reinstatement in organized baseball. He had wanted to do this before he died. Many fans supported him in his effort.

In the fall of 1954, I went to Chicago to interview Buck Weaver and to get him to tell his story in his own words. After some difficulty, I located him through his old and loyal friend, Marty Bleeker, a tavern keeper on the South Side of Chicago who is a familiar and popular figure among Chicago's baseball old-timers. Buck came to see me in my room at the Morrison Hotel.

He was a thin, pale, gray man in his sixties. He dressed on the sporty side, and there were small red blotches on his face. He smiled easily and readily. During his playing days, he was always smiling and kidding on the field. Buck's smile as well as his great playing ability made him one of the most popular White Sox players of his time at Comiskey Park.

In answer to the contention that he should have talked about the alleged conspiracy, he told me:

"Landis wanted me to tell him something that I didn't know. I can't accuse you and it comes back on you and I am . . . a goof. That makes sense to me. I didn't have any evidence."

He went on to say:

"All I did in that series was field 1.000 and I hit something like .336. I'd have hit .600 if I had any luck. There wasn't a game that they didn't spear one or two line drives. But that's the breaks. In the court session, it lasted a month . . . all I can say is the only thing we got left in the world is our judges and our jurors. I was acquitted in court. The judge even wanted to throw my case out of court—the other attorneys feared it would hurt their case. The judge said: 'I'll let Weaver go into court, but if his case is convicted, I'll throw his case out of court.' "

He spoke of his visits to the office of the late Judge Landis, the Commissioner of Baseball.

"He was a funny man. I'd come in. He'd say, 'Sit down, sit down!' He had that big box on his desk full of tobacco. He knew I chewed tobacco, too. He'd give me a chew of tobacco. I appealed I don't know how many times, maybe a half a dozen times. But he didn't have the guts to tell me to my face. He said he'd send me a letter. He didn't have the guts to tell me to my face."

According to the *Chicago Daily Tribune,* Landis, in his decision rejecting Weaver's appeal, wrote in part:

"I regret that it was not possible for me to arrive at any other conclusion than that set forth in the previous decision that your own admissions and actions in the circumstances forbid your reinstatement.

"You testify that preceding the world series, Cicotte, your team's leading pitcher that season, asked you if you wanted 'to get in on something—fix the world series,' and you replied: 'You are crazy; that can't be done.' "

When Weaver was suspended, he had one more year to play on a three-year contract. He filed suit for breach of contract. The case was finally settled out of court. Joe Jackson also filed suit. The jury decided in his favor, but the judge overruled the decision.

"I sent a letter to the Commissioner. I says Mr. Comiskey settled for my 1921 contract. But that shows that they're wrong and I'm right. But still they paid it and I can't do nothin' about it."

He was disappointed that he received no answer from the Commissioner.

"I never threw a ball game in my life," he said with passion

and a ring of sincerity. "All I knew was win. That's all I know."
And several times, he repeated:
"I can't do nothin' about it."
Weaver believed that if he were to have had his name
cleared, he might have become a scout, or else helped kids to
learn the game. He prided himself on having discovered Nick
Etten who played on one Yankee World's Championship
team. Following his disbarment, he played semipro ball with
the Duffy Floals in Chicago and was rarely seen at social
events where sports people gather. Almost every day, during
the off-racing season, he went to a saloon near Sixty-third
Street and Cottage Grove Avenue and in the back room, he
played pinochle with some cronies. He did not drink. He had
no children of his own, but raised two children of relatives.
In recent years, his wife was ailing and he took care of her
and was usually home with her almost every evening. All he
wanted from life was to support and care for Mrs. Weaver,
see his cronies and clear his name. About the latter, he was
pessimistic and at times, when he talked to me, bitterness
came into his voice.

But about the game of baseball itself, he felt love, not bitterness. He talked of baseball enthusiastically and with a
sharp and clear baseball intelligence. Baseball was a way of
life to him as well as a profession. He lived the game and
thought of it on and off the field. And because of his feeling
for the game, the mark against him hurt.

"A murderer," he said, "even serves his sentence and is let
out. I got life."

Speaking of the game, he said:

"What are the qualifications you have got to have to be a
ball player? You got to run. You got to throw. You got to hit.
You got to field. You got to think. If you can't meet all of
these qualifications you ain't a hundred per cent ball player."

He was not only a fans' player but he was also something of
a ball player's player. And many who saw Weaver play be-

tween 1912 and 1920 would readily agree that he met all of these qualifications. In his last few years especially, he had developed into a highly polished big-leaguer. Lean and of medium height, he almost invariably had the dirtiest uniform of any player on the team. When he broke in with the White Sox in 1912, he was an erratic shortstop. He would throw many balls away. Fans even spoke of his daily error and for a while, some of them nicknamed him "Error-a-Day Weaver." Buck said that he couldn't explain why this was so. Once he was shifted to third he rarely made a wild throw. When he broke into the American League, he was a weak hitter. In his first year, he batted .224 in 147 games. But when he became a switch hitter, his average picked up and in his last season, 1920, he hit .333 in 151 games.

"I couldn't hit 'em high. I couldn't hit 'em low. I couldn't hit," he said, speaking of his early years in the American League.

During one off-season he was visiting Oscar Vitt, the Detroit Tiger third baseman, at the latter's cabin in California. Buck was chopping wood. He noticed that when he chopped left-handed, he always hit the groove in the wood; when he swung the axe right-handed, he missed the groove. This led to his decision to bat left-handed.

"But I didn't start swinging right away," Buck explained. "First I just stood up at the plate like this." He illustrated his stance with his feet close together. "I let them pitch to me. Then, I practiced taking one step forward like this. Then I practiced my swing like this. I didn't try to hit the ball. I just wanted to get my swing and my confidence. Then, I practiced getting away, runnin'. I got my confidence that way. And then I knew I could hit anything. I'd have the ball always comin' in to me. If a left-hander was pitching, I'd bat right-handed where my power was. The ball would still be comin' in to me. All of them pitches would be comin' in."

Fans may still remember how Buck often played a shorter third base than most of his contemporaries.

"I didn't know nothin' about the National League. I didn't play in it. But I knew the American League. You take this situation. There's a man on first. There's a man on second. There's a man on third. I'm playing third, right on the line with the base. I know the speed of each of them runners. I know how fast the batter can run. I know the speed of the ball. So I get the ball. I know what to do just like that. If I played back a few feet, I'd be licked on a dragged bunt. And I could get the hard ones, too, where I played."

Buck stood up and showed me how he could pick up a bunt with both hands and without bending his knees.

Following his death, the Associated Press reported comments of Ty Cobb on Weaver as a third baseman. Calling him "the greatest third baseman I ever saw," Cobb also remarked:

"Weaver was one third baseman I didn't try to bunt against. I was supposed to be a fast man getting to first base but I knew better than to lay one down in Weaver's direction. There was no chance of beating out a bunt to him. He'd throw you out every time." Weaver was supposed to have a standing bet with Ty Cobb that any time Ty bunted towards third base, he could throw him out.

"Buck just wasn't the type to be in a crooked deal like that and certainly there wasn't anything wrong with the way he played in the 1919 series."

"One year," Buck also said in our interview, "a baseball writer asked me why I played shortstop in fifteen feet closer than he thought I ought to. I explained it to him this way. 'I'll play where I stand. You play fifteen feet behind me. I won't make more than one or two errors than you make. And I'll have a chance to get runners out. You see it in the assists.' "

Speaking of players of the past and the present, he asked:
"Who's a shortstop today?"

"Rizzuto was."

"I'll give you that. But in our day, who was the shortstop
for the Red Sox? Scott. And who did the Yankees have?
Peckinpaugh. And the Tigers had Bush. Who did Cleveland
have? Chapman. Who did the Athletics have? Barry. Do you
have shortstops like that now?"

He spoke of the salaries today as compared with salaries in
his day. Perhaps there was a touch of bitterness here. He began with the White Sox for $1,800, and in 1920 his salary was
supposed to have been $7,500. He said that he would be
ashamed to tell me what some of the White Sox players
earned, especially the ones who, along with Weaver, were
barred late in 1920 because of the thrown World Series of
1919. Ditch diggers, he said, today make more than some of
these players did. The game is played differently now. Today
it seems to him to be all a matter of money.

"I was playing in a game in St. Louis in 1917. Sisler hit one
along the ground. I run in and scoop it up. But I don't throw
this ball. I hold it. There were ten perforations in it, one, two,
three, four, ten perforations. I ran to the umpire and said he
had better look at Sisler's bat. He had driven nails in it and
filed them down."

And Ty Cobb.

"That was a fellow, that Cobb. And they say he was a dirty
player. That base line belongs to the runner. Take Baker. He
was a little bit slow. A man is coming in. He jumps high for
the ball and comes down on that line and it belongs to the
runner. So what happens? He gets spiked. When I went up
for one and came down, I spread my legs and I didn't get
spiked. To me Ty Cobb was not dirty.

"And I used to hit the ball with nothin' and two on me.
Some batters need three strikes to hit. I could hit with one.
Here's why I do it. When the pitcher has nothin' and two on

you, you know he's going to waste one. The infielders know
it. So what do they do? They relax. So I have nothin' and two
on me and the infielders are relaxed. They throw it outside
or inside, but what difference does it make? I'd hit it and be
off and the infielders were relaxed. They'd ask me how come
I done a thing like that. I'd say, 'I don't know why I done it.
I must have been a goof.' "

Weaver was born in Pennsylvania in 1890. His father was
a laborer in the iron works. Back in 1910, he was playing
semipro ball. A team of barnstorming major-leaguers, managed by Charley Dooin, then manager of the Philadelphia
Phillies, played against Buck's team. And a scout named Kennedy came to watch the games.

"I didn't know nothin' from nothin'. Kennedy, the scout
from Philadelphia saw me and he asked me to sign a contract
for $125 a month. *One-hundred-twenty-five a month!* Why
I never seen that much money."

During the winter, Kennedy shifted from Philadelphia to
Cleveland and hence, Weaver signed a Cleveland contract.
But he heard nothing about his contract, and the 1911 season
opened. Two or three weeks went by and he had not received
word. He wrote a letter to the National Commission and was
mailed a check for $62.50.

"Boy was that money!"

He was sent to play at Northampton, Massachusetts. Suddenly he discovered that when a batted ball was two feet
away from him, he would lose sight of it. He told his manager about this, and he was never able to understand how
this happened to him. His manager told him he was through.
He thought that he was through. He was released and went
to Philadelphia to see Dooin. He saw a game on a Saturday
afternoon, the first big league game he ever saw.

"When I seen them fellows hit and run, I said, 'Hell, I can
play.' "

He spoke with Dooin and then was offered a contract to

play with York, Pennsylvania, for $175 a month. He played in the outfield and ran in on line drives. The fans hollered for him to be put in the infield. Dooin had the choice of taking Weaver or a pitcher and he passed up Buck. But Ted Sullivan, White Sox scout, bought Weaver for $750. In 1911, he was sent to play with San Francisco in the Pacific Coast League.

"I didn't get nowhere in spring practice. They had Oscar Vitt playing third base. I'm a goof. I didn't know nothin' from nothin'. Oscar was sick. He would field a few balls and call it a day. So I practiced. I didn't know they considered Vitt the best third baseman in the league. I said to myself, 'Brother, I can take your job.'

"I sat on the bench for about three weeks. One day the center fielder got hurt. The manager says to me, 'Georgie, can you play the outfield?' I told him, 'I can play any place.'

"A ball was hit just over the infield. I run. I keep running and make the catch right here off the ground." Buck stood up and illustrated. "And then I come to bat and swing. The ball sails and hits the fence. I make a two-base hit. The next time I bat, I hit the fence again. See, I got the breaks. But after that, I told myself, 'Georgie, my boy, now you're in.' "

He reported to the White Sox at Waco in the spring of the next year.

"When I joined the Sox, I didn't know Kid Gleason from the man in the moon. That's how green I was."

Gleason hit grounders to him. He missed one and chased it and called to Gleason to hit them harder. Gleason slammed the ball at him and every time he missed, he called for Gleason to hit the grounders still harder. In later years, he and Gleason laughed over this incident.

He spoke warmly and admiringly of Gleason as a man who was for the ball players. He remembered other players of his day with affection and friendliness.

"We had a kid on our team," he also said, "a third baseman

named McMullin. He comes to me one day and says to me,
'Buck, can't you get sick for a couple of days?' He was dying
to get into a ball game. So I made myself indisposed for a
couple of days to let him play. Then I went back in there
myself."

At the end of a long interview, he flashed at me his own
winning smile. But there was something wounded and sad in
Buck's smile. Buck wanted his reinstatement but felt that
nothing could be done about it.

When we rode down in the hotel elevator, I suggested
seeing him again for dinner, but he refused, saying that he
always spent the evening with his wife.

"You know," he added, "she was a good hair pin."

Ironically, there was an Old Timers dinner held in Chicago
on the evening of that same day when Weaver died in the
street.

Two of his old White Sox teammates, Red Faber and Ray
Schalk, were present. According to Dave Condon, Chicago
sports writer, both were visibly shaken. Faber said:

"I played baseball with Weaver, and I played cards with
him, and I found him as honest as could be. No one can ever
be certain about 1919, I guess. Weaver was a wonderful
competitor, a fellow who played baseball because he loved it.
Buck Weaver and Lena Blackburne were two I knew who
never wanted to leave the field not even in practice. I guess
the last time I saw Buck was about a year ago, out at
Schalk's."

And Ray Schalk, who generally refuses to talk about the
thrown world series, remarked, as he often has done on other
occasions:

"That incident caused Weaver the tortures of Hell."

And an old-time baseball fan, who, like myself, used to see
Buck play when we were boys, wrote me:

"Last Thursday evening on my way home from work I
stopped at Seventy-ninth Street and Emerald Avenue at the

Undertakers Chapel where Buck Weaver was laid out. It was about 6:00 P.M. No one was there at the time except the Undertaker's assistant. Inasmuch as Buck was not a Catholic and the Chapel is used mostly by non-Catholics, nevertheless they had kneelers by the coffin. I knelt down and said a few prayers for him. Contrary to some places it did not seem *cold* to me. He looked, outside of thinning gray hair and that is all, that he could get right up and don a uniform and play third base for the Sox again. I don't think he was more than five pounds heavier than when he was playing ball. It sure was a shame to see him go from this world without getting his name cleared."

Many baseball fans had similar feelings when he passed away.

Like many others who saw him spear hot ones at third with graceful ease, who cheered and watched him, I also considered myself as one of those who was in Buck Weaver's corner. And now, on reflection, I have a hunch that when Buck said to me, "Landis wanted me to tell him something that I didn't know. I can't accuse you and it comes back on you and I am . . . a goof. That makes sense to me. I didn't have any evidence," he was telling his real story. I suspect that he did not know what to do. And because of a moral dilemma he suffered a lifelong torment. Could he have accused? And had he, would he have been a "goof?"

Now, it is all over and long ago. But Buck Weaver was a great ball player and very likeable. He was caught in a net of circumstances as are many characters in tragic novels. For to him, baseball was a way of life, and his barring was a supreme defeat.

"Those fellows suffered Hell," Ray Schalk often says. Buck did.

Death of an Idol

Baseball men still speak of Eddie Collins with much respect.

"He was a great ball player. He was first class and a gentleman," Clarence Rowland recently remarked to me.

ONE morning several years ago, I read in my morning newspaper that Eddie Collins had died. Even though I never knew him personally, I felt as though a friend were dead. Boyhood memories crowded upon me.

We American men are a nation of frustrated baseball players and the literature of our childhood was of play-by-play, morning-after stories and box scores. These box scores, in the days of our boyhood, read like documents of history. When Eddie Collins stole six bases in one game in 1912, he had achieved a kind of immortality for some of us boys. The feats of Ty Cobb, Walter Johnson, Tris Speaker and other stars of those days were tickets to immortality. And many of us boys hungered to do what they had done, and even to surpass them. But there is more than the lost desire for glory in boy-

187

hood memories of baseball. There is the remembrance of fun, of physical release, of days spent playing in the sun when nothing else but a base hit, a run scored, a fly ball caught mattered. And there is the memory of long afternoons spent in the bleachers or grand stand, watching batting and fielding practice, waiting for the game to begin, and then living out the drama of the game, inning by inning, play by play. Hope or frustration hung on a decision of the umpire, a ball or a strike. One had root-beer, pop corn, peanuts and hot dogs. One watched with a full concentration of emotion. The gestures, movements and mannerisms of the players down on the field were significant. The green field spread out and the teams moved on and off. There was the crack of the bat. The cheers, shouts, booes. There were the sudden moments of excitement with rallies, surprises, unexpected turns in the course of the game. And one or more of the players was one's favorite, one's hero. One of mine was Eddie Collins.

Sitting in my hotel room and reading of his death was like bidding farewell to the dead dreams of my boyhood.

Eddie Collins was purchased by the White Sox ball club for $50,000 after the end of the 1914 season. In 1914, after he had batted .344, he was given the Chalmers Award as the most valuable player in the American League. When I saw his picture in the morning newspaper, and read that he had been sold to my team, he instantly became another of my baseball heroes. With Collins in the lineup I was now sure, one day, to see the White Sox play in a World Series and become world's champions. I looked at his picture over the obituary notice and remembered this. I recalled how my uncle used to take me to games at Comiskey Park in Chicago and I would feel sorry for him. I would gaze about at other men in the stands, and pity them. They could only come and watch ball games. They couldn't be big-league ball players. They couldn't be like Eddie Collins. I imagined that they must be unhappy. And then, my own hopes would take on wings. When I grew up, I would be out there on the field. I dreamed of becoming another Eddie Collins and of succeeding him as second baseman on the Chicago White Sox. Since he batted left-handed, I even tried to switch, and I adopted his stance at the plate. Whenever I could, I played second base. I even imitated his walk, and would stride along Fifty-eighth Street swinging my arms as he did when he walked.

From 1915 on, when I looked at the White Sox box score, my first concern was to find out what Eddie Collins had done, how many hits he had made, how many assists and put-outs. This habit persisted until he retired from active play in 1931. It was as though he played ball for me. In my imagination, I lived in his career. He became my model. He was an alert, smart and clean baseball player. I tried to play the same way as he did. And in 1920, when the "Black Sox" scandal was exposed, I was proud that he was not one of the eight White Sox players accused of having thrown the 1919 World Series to the Cincinnati Reds. When I read in the newspaper that one of the accused players had said that he had not even approached Collins with the proposition to throw games, I became very proud. Not only was he a great player: he was incorruptible.

All this came back to mind after I read of his death. The irrevocableness of his going saddened me. Many former friends of mine are no more. But the death of some of my friends did not bring me any deeper feeling of sadness than did the death of Eddie Collins. Let me repeat myself here: I felt as though a friend were gone. Once, he had been young, slim, strong and healthy. He had grown old and weak. Time had conquered him. Time had washed over all that I felt and dreamed about baseball. And bound up with all of those thoughts and feelings of my boyhood, there was the image

of Eddie Collins, trim in a White Sox uniform. Our boyhood
dreams die many times. Mine died once again that morning
in my hotel room.

I recalled Eddie Collins streaking down the base lines to
try and steal second. I would be on my feet. Others would
stand. There would be shouts and a sense of drama would
hold us fans. He would hit the dirt in a hook slide. Often, he
would make it. He was one of the fastest and smartest base
runners of his day. I remembered him trotting in from the
field at the end of an inning. Other recollections came to me.
I recall him more vividly than I do any other ball player
whom I saw in my boyhood.

Eddie Collins was slender, wiry, and he weighed about
155 pounds. His movements were quick, sometimes nervous.
Wearing his uniform neatly, he looked very trim on the field.
Often at the plate, he would touch some chewing gum stuck
on the peak of his cap. He stood at the plate with his left knee
bent inwards, swinging his bat slightly downward, and then
holding it on his shoulder to await the pitch. He had one of
the sharpest batting eyes in his days. It was very difficult for
a pitcher to strike him out, and he drew many bases on balls.
He could hit to any field. He often shot singles to left field,
drove out long ones to left center, dumped balls over the
shortstop's head, or dropped Texas Leaguers into dead
center field. At other times, he would pull solid hits into right
field. He was a good bunter and, in fact, he set a lifetime
record of sacrifice hits with 513. He beat out many infield
hits, especially slow rollers to the left side of the diamond.
During twenty-five years as an active player, his average
was .333.

He was also a fine fielder and frequently led the league in
fielding. He made many plays look easy, although he did not
possess that perfect gracefulness of Napoleon Lajoie (whom
I also saw play). Whenever Collins had time on a hard
grounder, he closed his legs to field it, or even bent down on

one knee. Whenever possible, he played a ball in the easiest manner possible. His style of play was both aggressive and methodical. He always seemed to be aware of the situation on the field and thought very quickly. It was always my impression that he was a team player. Only recently, Clarence Rowland, Sr., one of Collins' managers, confirmed this in conversation with me. As a captain, he was constantly rushing to the umpire to protest. He would gesticulate nervously before the men in blue. But in the many times I saw him play, I never once saw him put off the field. I liked the way he did things on the field. And I gloried in the fact that he was an unquestioned star, considered by many to have been the greatest of all second basemen. Rogers Hornsby named Collins as his all-time second baseman.

In 1925 and 1926, Collins managed the White Sox. By that time, my interest in baseball had waned considerably. I was working my way through college and was absorbed in my own intellectual development. I still read the box scores, but rarely went to see a game. My boyhood baseball ambitions had given way to other hopes. But one night, I went to the Trianon Dance Hall at Sixty-second Street and Cottage Grove Avenue. Collins, White Sox Manager, happened to be the special guest of honor. He appeared on the stage and handed out prizes to couples who had won dance contests. As I stood among the crowd and watched him, there was a catch in my throat. My youthful sophistication fled in a second. I was not then a reader of the *American Mercury:* I was a Chicago boy who loved baseball and thrilled at the sight of my favorite player in a blue business suit. Collins was very shy on the stage. He seemed out of place. Trying to speak, he was at a loss for words. At the end of the brief ceremony, he gave one of the prize winners an awkward, friendly pat on the shoulder. He disappeared from the stage the moment the ceremony ended. He had not known how to act. He belonged back on the ball field. But I was moved by his shyness, and,

I wanted to find him and talk to him. But I was too shy myself.

I last saw him play in 1925. He had slowed up considerably. A few years earlier, I had been concerned about his slowing up. Each year, I had hoped that he would have another good year and that the day of his fading would be postponed. He had been having a bad season back in 1918. Before he joined the armed services, he had been hitting only .275. I had then thought that he was past his prime. When he returned in 1919, I wondered if he would come back. I feared that he might not make it. But he hit .319 in 1919, and played a major part in a pennant winning team. After the final world series game, I watched the players leave the clubhouse under the stands at Comiskey Park. I was disappointed that the White Sox had lost. I saw Collins stride off in a baggy blue suit. I wondered was he now going to go down. Had he had his best years? This thought grew melancholy in my mind as I walked away from the stands in the fading autumn afternoon.

My account here should suggest what the drama of baseball meant to one American boy. And I suspect that I was not singular in the way in which I looked upon baseball and dreamed of it. It was no mere game. It was an extension of my inner feelings and hopes. My favorite players were like my ambassadors to the world. They were doing what I was too small to do. Collins was the one I was fixed upon, among my many favorites. He was the image of my boyhood dreams of grandeur and accomplishment. We never lose our boyhood. It hangs in our minds. The death of Eddie Collins brought this back to me with a certain keenness and clarity. And it also brought me another regret. I had always hoped that I might some day happen to meet him and tell him how much I admired him as a ball player and what his career meant to me.

There is not only fun and relaxation in baseball for a boy. There is also a poetry about the game. And the poetry of the game constitutes part of its appeal. It becomes a part of ourselves. The spectacle, the movements, the sounds, the crack of the bat, the swift changes from routine dullness to sudden and dramatic excitement, all of this is part of that appeal. But the drama of victory and defeat, the playing out of a boy's unformed sense of grandeur, of hope, is also bound up with this poetry of baseball.

Sitting here at a table, this comes back to me once more. With it, I revive my memories of Eddie Collins. I wish that he were alive and able to read this article recounting how one American boy felt about baseball and about him as a player.

And to say farewell to Eddie Collins, whom I never knew, is to bid one more farewell to many boyhood feelings, hopes, dreams, excitements. But there is no final farewell to our past. Eddie Collins as a player and a sportsman became my model. He helped to form me into what I am. He played an important role in my life. Thinking of this, I conclude by expressing the hope that his own life was good and happy.

Red Faber

Why Red Faber? All I know—and it says so in
the record books—is that he was a pitching pro-
totype of his generation, now forgotten, when
the spitball and the stolen base were as common
as today's home run and the franchise shift. Faber
was a major part of White Sox baseball—pre-
World War I and post-"Black Sox" era.

R ED Faber saw twenty years of service with the White Sox.
He appeared in 600 official games, pitched 4,176 innings, won 252 and lost 210 games. His lifetime earned run
average was 3.08, and his pitching percentage figures out at
.545. Also, he won three and lost one game in the 1917 World
Series when the White Sox dumped John McGraw's New
York Giants in a six-game World Series.

In one of the games of that Series, Faber happened to be
on second base with Buck Weaver on third. Red lit out and
stole third base but Weaver still occupied the bag.

"Where are you going?" Buck Weaver asked.

"Right out to pitch," Faber said, for his futile steal ended
the inning.

195

During his active career, Faber was a hard, mean, tough pitcher. What he always wanted to do was to go right out there to pitch and win. Ray Schalk caught many tough pitchers, but he says that Faber was probably the toughest pitcher he ever handled.

"He threw a heavy ball," Schalk remarks.

"Cracker (Schalk's nickname) says I forced him to put a sponge in his glove," Faber said when reminded of Schalk's remark.

"When you wanted a pitcher to go in there and win, Faber was the kind of a pitcher to send in," Schalk reminisces. "He was always a sixty to forty per cent bet to win your ball game."

Faber was born on September 6, 1888, in Cascade, Iowa. As a boy, he liked to play ball, and he got his start in baseball at St. Joseph's Prep School in Prairie Du Chien, Iowa.

"I was taking a bookkeeping course. I was told I could get a job at $40 a month," he said, speaking of his ambitions in those days.

In 1909, Faber began his professional career with Dubuque, Iowa, winning seven and losing six. His manager was an old-time White Sox infielder, Frank Isbell. Faber thinks that his first minor league salary was $100 a month.

He was bought by the Pittsburgh Pirates, then managed by the left-fielder, Fred Clarke, and owned by the late Barney Dreyfuss. Red went to spring training with the Pirates broke. Needing money for incidentals and tips, he got a five-dollar advance from Clarke. He nursed this money along as well as he could. Finally it was gone. When he went to Clarke again broke, Clarke told him:

"You must be gambling."

He did not get into any games with the Pirates, and was loaned back to Dubuque, of the Three Eye League. Pitching against Davenport, Red threw a perfect no-hit game, and in August, 1910, he was recalled by the Pirates. Again he was not used in games. He was already throwing a spit-ball but says:

"When I was with the Pirates, they wouldn't let me throw no spitters. I don't know why but they wouldn't let me do it."

In May, 1911, he was released by Pittsburgh to Minneapolis in the American Association and in turn shipped to Pueblo of the Western League. He spent 1912 and 1913 with Des Moines of the Western League and was then bought by the White Sox. He is not certain but thinks that his purchase price was $3,000. He recalls that his first White Sox salary, for the 1914 season was $1,200. That year he won eight and lost eight.

"Do you remember your first game with the Sox, Red?" I asked.

"Yes, it was again' Cleveland. I win it but was relieved."

At the end of the 1914 season the late Charles A. Comiskey, owner of the White Sox, and John McGraw arranged to take two ball teams around the world. Faber went with the Sox to the Pacific Coast. Then, at the last moment, it developed that Christy Mathewson could not embark with the Giants. Comiskey had enough pitchers, but McGraw, needing a replacement, invited Red to go with the Giants.

On the world tour, he won four and lost one against Comiskey's Sox. Recalling the trip which took them to the Orient and through Europe, he speaks most of Australia. When I happened to tell him that shortly I was to visit that country, he said:

"Say, you'll like it. That's a wonderful country. It's the most like us that I was in. That's a wonderful, free, democratic country."

Again in 1924, he went abroad on a tour, that time revisiting Western Europe. But he liked Europe better the first time, before World War I.

"Everything was better then."

"The batter I had the most trouble with was a .250 hitter,

Jack Barry. Everybody else could get that son of a gun out, but I couldn't. I don't know why. But the batter who was easiest for me was Duffy Lewis (of the Boston Red Sox). He was a good hitter, too. I think he did get one hit off me one time when he was backing away from a pitch." He laughed. "I could always get him out."

"Did you ever pitch much to Rogers Hornsby, Red?" I asked.

"I struck him out. It was at an old-timers game at Comiskey Park."

"Yes," Ray Schalk remarked, "and Lefty Gomez on the bench said, 'After twenty-five years we learned how to pitch to him.'"

At the time of this interview, I was with Ray, Red and Martin Bleeker, a tavern keeper from the South West side, and long-time baseball fan and friend of Schalk, Faber and Buck Weaver. It was shortly after Weaver had dropped dead of a heart attack on a street. Faber and Schalk had been pall-bearers for Buck, and Marty Bleeker also would have served as one had he not been ill at the time. They were all moved and spoke warmly of Buck.

"He loved to play ball," Red said. "He was always laughing. Remember, Ray, one day he threw the ball away. He comes into the bench and sits down beside Rowland and says, 'Teach—we used to call Rowland Teach—don't worry, don't worry, Teach, we'll win this one.' That was Buck."

Schalk spoke of how he had received a clipping from a newspaper which claimed that Weaver would not talk to Schalk or Eddie Collins. All three of Buck's old friends denied this. Schalk remarked on how he would always go to say hello to Buck at the race track where Weaver worked. Schalk, Faber and Joe Benz, another old White Sox pitcher, and teammate of Weaver's, all appeared at a night given for Weaver by Marty Bleeker at the latter's tavern. Bleeker had worked hard trying to help Buck clear his name. Faber and Schalk remembered Buck with warmth of feeling.

"Read what Ty Cobb said of Buck?" Marty Bleeker asked.

Ty Cobb had been quoted in press as having said that Weaver was the greatest of all third basemen.

I asked Faber how he had used to pitch to Cobb.

"I did pretty good again' him. One time I struck him out on a spitter that broke in. It hit him on the hip and broke his hip."

"No, Red didn't have much trouble with left-handed hitters," Schalk said.

"Remember that game in New York when Cocky (Eddie Collins) made me walk Ruth. I was mad. I didn't want to walk him. But Cocky said you better do it. So I walk Ruth and I struck out that first baseman they had before Gehrig —who was he?"

"Pipp."

"Yes, Pipp. He was a pretty fair hitter. I struck him out in three pitched balls. I win that game 1 to 0."

At one point in the evening, Schalk began comparing Faber's record with those of pitchers who have been elected to the Hall of Fame. Ray was checking off those who had won less games than Faber. Among them was Ed Walsh.

"Walsh was a good pitcher," Faber said. "And Cicotte was a hell of a good pitcher. He had a good fast ball too."

"Red had a knuckler but he wouldn't use it," Schalk said.

I asked Schalk if Faber was difficult to handle.

"Red had one signal for twenty years when he didn't want to throw what I called for.

"If Faber wiped his right hand across the left side of his breast it meant that that signal was good enough. If he didn't go through this motion, then he wanted me to call for another pitch." Schalk had only two signals he gave Red, one for a fast ball and one for a curve or spitter.

"We fought a lot," Faber said, referring to himself and Schalk. "But after the game we forgot it."

Faber, like Schalk, thinks that Eddie Collins was probably the smartest ball player they ever knew. Like most ball players who knew him, Faber speaks with most affectionate respect of his old manager, Kid Gleason.

"He was tough. But the ball players loved him."

Many other players were recalled.

"That Sam Rice was a hell of a hitter. He'd make two hundred hits almost every year."

"And he was fast," Schalk said. "He'd beat out hits in the infield."

"He was a good hitter. That Sam Rice belongs in the Hall of Fame," Faber said.

"And Stuffy McInnis of the old $100,000 infield of Connie Mack's Philadelphia Athletics?" I asked.

"I learned never to throw 'em high to him. One day, I threw him one up here above his head and he cracked it over the third baseman's head for two bases. I learned never to give him anything up high. He was a good ball player."

"Red was a low ball pitcher," Schalk said.

"The best center fielder was 'Spoke' (Tris Speaker). Felsch was good and Cobb was good, but as a center fielder I give it to Spoke. Mostil was good, too. But Spoke had it on them. And he had an arm."

"He'd never throw it at the plate," Schalk said. "It would curve in there though on the hop."

Joe Di Maggio? Faber wouldn't comment. He was living outside of Chicago during Joe Di Maggio's best years and hadn't seen enough of him in his prime to comment.

"But say," he said, "that Rizzuto is one hell of a shortstop— the greatest. In the world series, I see him on television getting balls in back of third and behind second. He's the greatest. That Peckinpaugh in our day was good, but I didn't see most of the shortstops in our league."

Faber liked to pitch against Walter Johnson because this was more of a challenge. He recalls how, because of an error, he lost a 1-0 game to Johnson but then got his revenge the next time they faced one another, winning by the same score.

He also remembers how he beat Herb Pennock 1 to 0 in New York. He always tried for a shutout no matter how many runs ahead the White Sox might be. He felt that if he pitched a shutout, then he knew that he had done a good job.

"Bush (Donnie Bush, who managed the White Sox) had me starting and finishing games. He put me in the bull pen and wouldn't start me. If he would have let me start I'd have won fifty more games."

Faber says that he would not get a sore arm. However, he went into the Navy in 1918, contracted influenza and during the 1919 season he was about thirty pounds under weight. That season, his record stood eleven won and nine lost.

"My arm was all right, but I could only go four innings."

Faber did not pitch in the 1919 World Series which was thrown to the Cincinnati Reds. The young pitcher, Dickie Kerr, has often been described as winning two games which some of his teammates were trying to lose. It is often said had Red Faber then been right, he might have repeated Kerr's performance and won the Series for the Sox.

For only a few years, did Faber have good teams behind him. He won the majority of his games for weak teams. In 1921 he took 25 games and in 1922, 21 with poor teams. His record would have probably been sensational had he been fortunate enough to have pitched all his years for a club like the New York Yankees.

Red's last game was a shutout to win the 1933 city series from the Cubs. He didn't want to quit then but was practically forced to. However, the next season the Cubs wanted him.

"I'd have gone with them if I could have helped them."

He worked out and pitched batting practice, but decided that he had had enough. He was approaching forty-six.

Since his retirement, Red Faber owned a tavern and bowling alley in Grayslake, Illinois; he sold real estate and automobiles for Tony Piet, the former American and National

League infielder who now owns an automobile agency. When Ted Lyons was manager of the Sox, he returned to his old team as coach. At present, he works for Cook County with a surveying crew. He likes the work because it is outside.

"I learn, too," he said.

Red is still hale and looks in fine shape. His first wife died after twenty-three years of marriage. He remarried and is the father of a seven-year-old boy, Urban Charles Faber, Jr. He carries a picture of his wife and son, and with the same air of modesty which characterizes his reminiscences of baseball, he will show you the photographs.

Faber was not spectacular, nor could he ever have been called a colorful ball player. But he went on year after year, one of the best in his league. Following the Black Sox scandal of 1920, he was lost on a poor ball club. But for that, he would probably be in the Hall of Fame today. For at the time of the scandal, he was coming into his best years as a pitcher.

Stuffy McInnis

In my boyhood, you felt three times as impor-
tant if you knew a ball player. I wrote this piece
as a belated expression of thanks to the small kind-
nesses which Stuffy showed me in my boyhood.

J OHN "Stuffy" McInnis was most kind to me in my boyhood.
Stuffy broke in with Connie Mack's Philadelphia Ath-
letics as a young shortstop, but in 1911 he supplanted Harry
Davis as first baseman, completing what became a famous
infield of its time, the $100,000 infield composed of "Home
Run" Frank Baker, Jack Barry, Eddie Collins and Stuffy.
Baker and Collins have already been elected to Baseball's
Hall of Fame, but just as Tinker, Evers and Chance of the old
Chicago Cubs were elected together, so ought Barry and
McInnis be, in order to accord final and full recognition to
Connie Mack's great and once highly publicized infield.
Shortstops did not come any too frequently in those days,
any more than now, and for several years Jack Barry was
an outstanding shortstop on four pennant winners and three
World's Champions. Stuffy probably was not a great player,

but for many years he was one of the outstanding first basemen in the game, and he attained this distinction even though
he was somewhat handicapped by size. He was a short,
stocky man. Stuffy was a remarkable fielding first baseman
and even though right-handed, he used to be able to make a
double play of first to second to first very neatly and with a
manner of expertness. He was, I think, quite generally regarded as a smart ball player. I, of course, thought him to be
such because I knew him slightly and he was kind to me.
He was a good hitter even though he had no power. His active career carried him through nineteen years in both major
leagues and he wound up with a lifetime batting average of
.308. In his last active year, he was another of the hapless
managers of the hapless Philadelphia Phillies and appeared
in only one game. At the plate, he choked up on his bat and
usually hit to left and center field. He had a knack of dump-
ing in safe Texas leaguers into center and left center and
often hit to straight left. He was also, as I recall, a good
bunter. Stuffy, along with Wallie Schang and Joe Bush, shares
the record of having played on three different clubs which
won the World Series. Stuffy's clubs were the Philadelphia
Athletics, the Boston Red Sox of 1918, and the Pittsburgh
Pirates. With the Pirates in 1925, he was a rapidly fading
veteran who alternated with George Grantham at first base.
But when Grantham was ragged in the series against the
Washington Senators, Stuffy was inserted into the lineup in
his place and accounts of the games suggested that he helped
pull the Pirate infield together.

Stuffy was usually dangerous in the pinches. The substitu-
tion of "clutch" for "the pinches" is of a relatively recent date.
With men on bases in a tight game, he could often dump one
of his Texas leaguers in front of the feet of the on-rushing
center fielder and those hits were sometimes as good as gold
or as a home run is in today's baseball. It was his hit which
helped give Babe Ruth a 1-0 victory over Hippo Jim Vaughan
in Comiskey Park in the first game of the 1918 World Series.

The Chicago games were played in Comiskey Park rather than at the Cubs North Side Park, in the vain hope that with the games played in a bigger ball park, there would be larger receipts. The share of the winning Boston Red Sox in 1918 was the lowest per player in modern World Series history: it totaled $1,102.51.

My Uncle Tom had met Stuffy on one of his trips to the East. On a summer Sunday in 1916, Uncle Tom unexpectedly told me that he would take me to the double-header between the White Sox and Athletics. The Sox were at last a ball club battling the Red Sox for the pennant and the Athletics were settling down to a long rest in the cellar. Watching the Sox take the double-header, I thought that perhaps I was seeing my first pennant-winning team.

Between games, we went down under the stands behind the visitor's dugout, and my uncle asked for Stuffy. He came out promptly, carrying a bat on which he leaned as he talked with us. He called me Jim. I was thrilled. McInnis said that he was having dinner that night with Eddie Collins and also expressed the wish that he would be traded to the White Sox. He said that he would like to play with the Chicago ball club. I wished the same thing. Chicago had not had a real good first baseman since Hal Chase had jumped to Buffalo of the Federal League in 1914. In 1916, they had tried out Jack Ness and had used Jacques Fournier. Neither had filled the spot too well. I began to hope that Charles A. Comiskey would trade for Stuffy or else buy him. After the meeting with Stuffy, in fact, I would walk around or sit in school imagining Stuffy McInnis playing first base with the White Sox in a world series. The late Charles A. Comiskey could never have known how he let down one of his young fans by not procuring Stuffy.

I listened, all ears, as Stuffy and my uncle talked casually. I was anxious, nervous. For I was supposed to get a ball. Where was it? But just before he shook hands with us again and agreed to have dinner with my Uncle Tom in the East, he fished out a new and still glossy official American League baseball and handed it to me. I was more excited and my pride vaulted.

That ball, like the others I received, was used in games which we boys played in Washington Park. I never thought to save it as a souvenir. Nor did I even think of asking for an autograph.

After my brief meeting with Stuffy, I spoke often of him and bragged to other kids that I knew him. I was quickly able to convince myself that he was the greatest first baseman in the big leagues. But when I told this to other kids, they did not care. They wouldn't give me an argument.

In 1918, Stuffy went from the Athletics to the Boston Red Sox. Sometimes when his club came to Chicago, I would telephone his hotel. This was almost an act of courage, since I was usually very shy. I had to drum up my courage to telephone Stuffy. But I would force myself into this act of boldness. I'd ask him to take me into the ball park, and he agreed. I'd be way ahead of time by the gate, fearful that I had missed him. Waiting, I would become almost panicky, believing that he had already gone in through the gate. And this loomed in my mind as though it were a catastrophe. I did not have the courage to ask the attendant at the gate if Stuffy McInnis had come as yet.

Other players came. Some I could recognize. Fearful minutes dragged by. But then Stuffy came along and gave me a pat on the shoulders and took me inside of the ball park. In my own mind, this gave me a special relationship to baseball. I felt superior to most other boys and even to men fans. I knew Stuffy McInnis. And when he took me in free to see a ball game, I would get a seat in the grandstand behind the visitors' dugout on the first-base side. A new period of nervous waiting began. Would Stuffy forget to get me a ball? After the Red Sox came out on the field for practice, I would sweat through my worries. How soon should I go down by the dugout, ask for him and then for a ball. This became such a problem that I could not relax and watch the practice. Three, four or five times, I would resolve to get up and walk down by that dugout. I would lose my nerve and decide to wait a few minutes longer. Finally, and like someone who is afraid to dive, I would make the jump. But I did it too soon. He had not as yet managed to get the ball for me. Quite obviously, he pinched the balls from the club. And in those days, baseball clubs were more parsimonious about balls than they are today.

Invariably I had rushed down for my baseball too soon, and Stuffy would tell me to come back a little later on. I did. But again too soon. Finally I would get my baseball and then I could relax and prepare to enjoy the ball game. I might add that one of the players on the Red Sox at that time was Babe Ruth. But I paid more attention to Stuffy McInnis down on the field than to Ruth.

I always remembered Stuffy with a warm feeling of gratitude. As long as he played, I used to look at the box scores to see if he had made any hits in the ball game of the previous day. Whenever he did, I was pleased.

Years later, I exchanged a few letters with him. Then I was visiting at Harvard University after lecturing in that area. He was at the time coach of the Harvard University ball team, a position from which he has since retired. On a chilly day in April when even the sun seemed cold, I trooped to the athletic field to see him: he was immediately recognizable. He had taken on a few pounds and was gray, but he looked hale and healthy. He remembered me and my Uncle Tom, and, in fact, he talked almost as though I might even have been an old teammate of his.

"Those were good days, Jim," he said nostalgically. "We'll never have days like them again. Now it's all different. It's all money now."

He spoke of old ball players, Babe Ruth, Ty Cobb and others.

"Eddie Collins is not well," he said, shaking his head.

Then, he pointed to the kids in uniform who were out trying to make the varsity nine.

"They're different," he said with a complaining shake of the head. "See that fellow pitching."

Stuffy pointed to a college boy who was on the mound pitching in batting practice.

"I tell him, but it does no good. He can't be told. These kids today, they won't learn. You can't tell 'em. You can't teach 'em. It's not the same as it used to be. Those were good days."

He would leave me, go out on the field and talk with one or another of the players. Then he would return to speak with me for another moment or two, again to remark that the students out for his team couldn't be taught much.

"They don't care," he said.

It seemed as though he meant much more, and that today you did not find students or young fellows caring about baseball as their predecessors had.

I remained for about an hour or so. Stuffy spoke softly and very patiently to his players. But he kept shaking his head and complaining about the unteachableness of his squad.

Just before I left, he again said:

"Those were good days, the best we ever had."

Stuffy's name now is rarely mentioned in the newspapers. He is one of the many good ball players of another day who is largely forgotten. Some day, it is likely that he and Jack Barry will get a plaque in Cooperstown as members of the great $100,000 infield.

Personally, when I think of Stuffy, it brings back some of my happiest boyhood baseball memories.

A Visit to Cooperstown

This article was written on assignment from
SPORTS ILLUSTRATED. *I was very curious to see the*
Baseball Museum and Hall of Fame.

I think, however, that the story about General
Abner Doubleday is saturated with myth. It will
not stand up under sound historical investigation.
Cooperstown is one of the legends of baseball
which has been made real and concrete. Withal,
it is interesting to visit, if you are a baseball fan.

LONG before the Baseball Hall of Fame and Museum was
established in Cooperstown, New York, there were many
symbolic or mythical baseball Halls of Fame. Every real
lover of baseball and every sports writer who likes the
game has carried his own Hall of Fame in his mind. I
thought of this fact when my fourteen-year-old son and I
visited the Cooperstown Museum. As we looked at the
plaques, the old gloves, balls, bats, pictures and other exhibits, my own baseball recollections came back to me in a
slow flood of memory. There are the names of those who

were before my time as a fan, Pop Anson, A. G. Spalding,
Wee Willie Keeler. When I was a boy, I would sit at the
family dinner table listening to my uncles talk baseball, and
I used to hear them respectfully mention these great players
who preceded Ty Cobb, Honus Wagner, Napoleon Lajoie
and the other outstanding stars of my boyhood. There is an
oral tradition of baseball, which is passed on from generation
to generation: it has, in itself, served as a kind of mythical
Hall of Fame. I have seen most of the players now in the
Cooperstown Hall of Fame, when they were in the big
leagues. I was told of the others by my elders. I, in turn,
have told my son of all these players. His first school composition was about King Kelly, who is also in the Hall of
Fame. My uncles told me stories of Slide Kelly Slide.

We stopped before the plaque of Ed Walsh, the old
spitball pitcher. In 1911 I was seven, and on a sultry sunless Sunday morning in August of that year, my older
brother was walking along Wentworth Avenue in Chicago.
From the sidewalk he picked up a white ticket which,
fortunately, was a box seat for that afternoon's baseball
game at Comiskey Park. Both of us were admitted on the
one ticket. Sitting in the grandstand, we watched Ed
Walsh pitch a winning no-hit game against the Boston Red
Sox. This was one of my first and also most exciting experiences in my long years as a baseball fan. I went home
spinning on air. And as I entered the front door, I was told
that while we had been at the ball game, a new baby sister
of mine had arrived. I replied spontaneously and somewhat
as follows:

"Good, she will always be remembered because she was
born on the day that Ed Walsh pitched a no-hit game."

That was more or less the beginning of my own private
Hall of Fame. As the years went on, as I saw, lived, talked
and read about baseball, many others joined Walsh in the
Farrell Hall of Fame. Most of those players are now com-

memorated at Cooperstown. And there is Rube Waddell. He was in the minors with Minneapolis when I became a conscious baseball lover. As I have told elsewhere in this book, Rube Waddell once gave me a baseball. I learned everything I could about Rube Waddell, talked about him, his exploits and records enthusiastically, and was almost ready to fight anyone who said that Waddell had not been a great pitcher.

I read on Rube Waddell's plaque that he had won more than two hundred games in major-league competition. But according to my own memories, Waddell had won only one hundred and ninety-three games. I spoke of this discrepancy with Sid C. Keener, old-time baseball reporter and present director of the museum. Keener got out all of the record books from the world's best baseball library, created by Ernest Lanigan, and sat at his desk in the Hall of Fame room, figuring and checking how many games Rube Waddell had really won. It is generally agreed that Waddell belongs with Mathewson, Grover Cleveland Alexander, Walter Johnson and Ed Walsh. But the record books do not agree as to the total number of his victories. Two of them credit him with two hundred and three major-league victories: two others give him a total of one hundred and ninety-three. There is an equal discrepancy concerning the games he lost, but these we will forget.

Details and memories of old games are important and even treasured only by the fan who loves the game: to anyone else, they are meaningless. But of such memories and recollections is baseball made. The Baseball Hall of Fame and Museum is interesting and fascinating because of these memories. A visit to it is a release to one's old baseball memories. Again and again, Sid Keener will overhear a visitor recalling a game, a play, a player. He and I sat and talked and we did what the visitors do: we talked and we recollected about baseball.

In addition to the plaques, there are a great variety of

exhibits to be seen and most visitors do not miss one of them. In a case there is the first contract of Eddie Collins, signed by him and Connie Mack when Collins was a student and a varsity backfield man at Columbia University. Collins signed his own name to the contract, but played his first big-league year under the name of Sullivan. Among the most interesting of the exhibits are the gloves. You see the skin tight gloves used in the early nineteenth-century days of baseball, and various gloves used by players down to the present. The glove worn by Neal Ball when he made his unassisted triple play is on exhibit. The gloves of today are much different and bigger than those used thirty and forty years ago. Looking at the different gloves, you even wondered how a present-day player could make an error. There is also a collection of catcher's masks which pinpoint the evolution of masks. And there are numerous baseballs, many hats, world series rings and trophies, and, even more interesting, many pictures and photographs.

When I was a boy, I used to stand out in front of a cigar store at Fifty-first Street and Prairie Avenue in Chicago. I would ask every man who came out of the store to give me the picture of the baseball player which came with packages of cigarettes. I remember begging for these pictures on the day that Woodrow Wilson was first elected President of the United States. For some reason or other I, then eight, wanted Wilson to win, but I wanted those baseball pictures more than I wanted Wilson in Washington. Many of the pictures I collected, looked at, thought about and treasured, hang on a wall in one of the rooms of the museum.

You cannot remain long in the Museum, looking about, watching the other visitors, overhearing chance comments and remarks without sensing that the atmosphere is one of sentiment, nostalgia and even sentimentality. Many gray-haired men come and drift about from case to case. As they stare, their faces soften up. The past comes back to them. Boyhood, and young manhood glow in their minds once again. Those baseballs in the cases are the balls that many of them never pitched, caught or hit on a big-league diamond. The uniforms are the baseball suits they never wore. The plaques speak of the records they never broke, the lives they never led, and the boyhood dreams they never fulfilled. These are some of the reasons why the Museum is very popular. It is open three hundred and sixty-two days of the year, and annually, the number of visitors increases. In 1947, there were 37,036 visitors. In 1952, the number was 114,713. The next year it rose to 132,175, and it continues to rise.

Ball players, when elected, are deeply moved and some of them are even overwhelmed. And amusing incidents occur. Once, in the Hall of Fame, the late Cy Young and Big Ed Walsh sat talking. Walsh reminded Young of a game they pitched against each other many years ago, and that he, Walsh, had won.

"You never beat me in that game," Young said.

They grew angry and argued.

"I beat you that game. You never beat me and you never could," Young said in even greater anger.

The two old ball players almost came to blows.

The fans have their comments to make, also. One fan came, went through the Museum and then heatedly proclaimed to the director:

"This place is a phoney."

He went on to explain that he came from Cleveland and Bob Feller is not to be found in the Hall of Fame. He was calmed down when he was told that after Feller retired from active play, he would probably be elected. The man decided that the Museum is not a phoney. He looked at more exhibits and left liking the institution very much.

On another day an elderly couple showed up. The wife

was not interested in baseball. Calling her dear, the gray-haired husband said that he would only be a few minutes. She sat on a chair, waiting impatiently.

The few minutes became a half hour. She grew more nervous, and began mumbling complaints about her husband. Then she loudly told herself that her husband was just ridiculous. And every so often, the husband would come back to tell the bored and restless wife that he would be finished very quickly. She would upbraid him. He would go back and look at more exhibits, fascinated.

"What could have happened to Henry?" she finally asked aloud.

She decided that his mind was affected.

He kept her sitting there most of the afternoon. When they finally left, she was quarreling with him, and she was also definitely convinced that her husband had lost his mind.

An atmosphere of sadness is also to be felt in the Museum. I recall visiting the ruins of Mount Olympia, the site of the original Olympic Games. The stadium was washed away in a flood centuries ago. The cement starting line for the racers remains, however. There are ruins of temples and buildings. Athletics was bound up with the religion of ancient Greece. In America, this is not the case. Baseball is part of our culture. It is loved. It is also a big business. And yet some of our great baseball players are thought of in terms similar to the way in which the athletes of ancient Greece were regarded. There is one story of an Olympic runner who was winning his race. Nearing the finish line, his pants began to fall down. He could either have paused, pulled up his pants and lost the race, or else let them fall off and go on to be the victor. He won the race running stark naked. Ty Cobb played ball the way that ancient Greek ran a race. In all societies sports have been part of the life and culture of the people. But truly great athletes are relatively rare. Cobb was one of those rare athletes who were truly great. The way he played baseball revealed that to him it must have been a way of life. Besides his plaque, there are many pictures of Cobb in the Museum. And you see these pictures and the pictures of other baseball players of the past when they were in their physical prime. Now many of them are old. A number are gone. A sense of this, a melancholy feeling about the biological changes and tragedy of man seems to creep into the minds of many of the visitors. Ruth, Gehrig, Alexander, Mathewson, Eddie Collins are gone. The visitors, seeing photos of them in their prime and then realizing how their strength was ravaged, sometimes grow melancholy. This is especially so in the case of Gehrig who showed such moral bravery when he knew that he was doomed with an incurable illness.

Baseball historians have challenged the claim that Cooperstown is the real home of baseball. A commission of baseball men, in 1907, announced that our national game had been invented by General Abner Doubleday in Cooperstown. However, this decision was not reached by scholars, or after the application of methods of scholarship to the solution of this question. Although there is no space here for a discussion of the question, I will say that the baseball historians have sound and substantial ground for their skepticism about Cooperstown as the original birthplace of baseball. But even if this be granted, there is a certain appropriateness in the Museum being located in Cooperstown. It is an old and attractive village on the shores of Lake Otsego. Although its Main Street is like many another Main Street, there are old houses and there is a charming old church built in 1805. In the graveyard by this church lie the remains of America's first important novelist, James Fenimore Cooper.

A sense of an earlier and different America pervades Cooperstown. To go there is like breathing a little of the air of that earlier America. An important campaign of the Revolu-

tionary War was carried out near the village. Two other museums are also housed in Cooperstown, the Farmer's Museum
and Fenimore House, an historical museum. The Farmer's
Museum recreates an America of the early nineteenth century. In Fenimore House are early American paintings, life
masks of Thomas Jefferson, John Adams, John Quincy Adams,
and Lafayette and other early personalities in American history. Also there is the correspondence between Alexander
Hamilton and Aaron Burr, leading to their duel and the
death of Hamilton, one of our first great statesmen. In the
Farmer's Museum, you can see an old one-room country
school with a stove in the center, blackboards with simple
spelling and arithmetic lessons chalked on them, slates on the
old wooden desks and a dunce's stool and dunce cap near
the teacher's desk. School rooms like this were the source of
education of many of our forebears who ploughed the land,
fought our wars, and contributed to the growth and building
of America. When I stood in the old school room, a farmer
of over seventy years stood beside me, and said:
"I first went to school in a place like this."
    The country store, the farm implements, household uten-
sils, toys, beds, clothes of another day are to be found in
these other Cooperstown museums. Seeing them, one gains
an added and more concrete idea of how America has
changed and how the American Way of Life is still one of
changing patterns. And in one Hall of Fame room, there is
on exhibit a famous homemade old ball with the stuffing
coming out of it. It is somewhat smaller than the modern
ball. It was found in an attic not far from Cooperstown and
well might have been used for games of Town Ball, One-A-
Cat, or baseball in Abner Doubleday's lifetime. Baseball was
probably played elsewhere in the 1830's or early 1840's. But
it was also played in Cooperstown. The Baseball Hall of
Fame and Museum, seen in connection with visits to the
other two Cooperstown museums, can make more vivid for

us a sense of where we came from and how our life and even our sports are part of the changing patterns of the still developing American Way of Life.

There is a standard joke about the father who buys a Lionel Train set for his son as a Christmas present. The toy is for the boy. But comes Christmas morning and there is the old man on the floor amidst the tracks, engine cars, signals, electric motor and other paraphernalia. It is a question as to whom the toy is for, the father or the son? The father is playing with the train set he never had as a boy. I felt somewhat like the father of this old saw when I went about the Baseball Hall of Fame and Museum with my own son. For whom was the visit? My son liked it. But it appeared that I liked it even more than he.

Ty Cobb

Some years ago, my friend and publisher, James Henle of Vanguard Press was speaking with a boy interested in baseball.

"He knew almost nothing about Ty Cobb."

The present generation of players, sports writers and fans never saw Cobb play. But here is what Ty Cobb, the player, was like as I remember him.

It is impossible to over-praise his ability on the ball field. What they say about Ty Cobb, his feats and records, is true. If there ever is another Ty Cobb in baseball, this will be a most extraordinary happening. Ball players like Cobb are singular, rare, even among those who are indisputably great. I am very glad that I saw him play frequently.

Two years ago, while making the jump from St. Louis to Chicago with the Brooklyn Dodgers, I was having a beer with Roy Campanella in the club car. Campy took a sip of his beer, and remarked with wonder and incomprehension that he could not understand how the old-time ball players had made their high batting averages and phenomenal records. He said that he constantly reads the record books, but he couldn't understand how Ty Cobb could have stolen ninety-six bases in one season let alone hit .420 in one season. Try his best, as he did, Campy said he couldn't get higher than .330.

"They can't be that much better than ball players today."

Ty Cobb is generally regarded as the greatest ball player who ever lived. That was how he was thought of at the height of his career. The Chicago White Sox used to line-up at the dugout when Cobb came onto the field and they would flatter him with friendliness.

"Hello Peach! How are you, Peach," they'd keep saying.

As Schalk put it:

"The one thing we didn't want to do was to get him mad."

Mad or not, Cobb could demoralize a team when he got on base which, as is well known, was all too much for the opposition. In twenty-four years as a player, he made 4191 hits, one of his many records. His lifetime batting average of .367 is a mark which is at least equally as phenomenal as Ruth's sixty home runs and all-time total homers. Another of his records is a lifetime total of 892 stolen bases. But these and other records of Ty Cobb's are widely known and they have been printed in many places. Many of them, unlike Ruth's sixty home runs in one season, can never be bettered even by a player who would be the equal of Ty Cobb in every respect. Modern baseball conditions exclude such records. This is practically an absolute certainty. The game is not quite the same as it was then because of the lively ball, and no manager of the present would allow a player to attempt to steal as many bases as did Cobb. The difference between Cobb and either Jackie Robinson or Willie Mays as base runners could not be so great that in three or four seasons Cobb could steal as many or more bases than they have been able to in their entire major league careers. Most certainly, the difference between Cobb and an entire club of twenty-five players is not so wide that in one season, he could steal more bases in a season than the whole ball club of the present. In the modern lively ball game, a player of Cobb's talents and temperament would not play the game quite as Cobb did. Jackie Robinson, with all of his great ability and spirit, was not a Ty Cobb. But more than any other player of recent years, he reminded you of Cobb when he would get on base. He was allowed, at least frequently, to steal without signals. But in some of his seasons, he would go down the base paths less than half as many times as Cobb.

The records of the Cobb era and of the present era are not truly comparable. If it were not for the fact that these baseball eras shade into each other, it would be just as well if the records were kept distinct. If the records of these two periods could be interpreted as being the same, and if we compared them as standards of judging the quality of play, a good case might be made out to substantiate or warrant the conclusion that there had been a quite drastic decline in ability and that the game was probably on the downgrade as far as the over-all calibre of ball players goes. This is most certainly so for hitting in all particulars except that of the number of home runs. Today, a team like the Yankees, the Dodgers, or even the New York Giants, hit more home runs in one season than Cobb did in twenty-four. Cobb's total was 116. Averages, as is well known, are now much lower and perhaps with rare exceptions, permanently so. When Ted Williams signed his 1957 contract with the Boston Red Sox, he expressed the hope that he would hit .330 or .340. Thirty years ago, a hitter like Williams would have hoped to hit .360 or .370. Between 1909 and 1919, inclusive, Ty Cobb's lowest average was .368. In 16 out of 24 years Cobb hit over .340, and in one other season, he touched that mark. Besides the fact that many players swing more often for home runs, there must be other factors in this difference in records. Today many players swing for the fence. Other differences probably are to be found in the preponderance of night games, more travel, and in the defensive equipment of today as against yesterday. Back around 1911 or 1912, a one-handed catch was much more sensational than it is today. With larger gloves and the webbing in them, fielding is easier. This is especially so for first basemen. In a game at Ebbets Field, a grounder was hit foul to first base. Gil Hodges casually swept it in with his mitt. No one, perhaps, except a few of the writers in the press box noticed this play on a dead ball. In the old days, with the gloves then used, such a play, if not sensational would have looked at least near-sensational.

Arguments and disputes about the old-timers and the modern player do not have much meaning. They furnish copy for sports writers and offer a subject of conversation for many others. Those of us who were young then and have retained our interest in baseball can convince ourselves that in the old days they were better, and that it will never be the same. But this reminds me of a joke told in circles far removed from baseball, at least theoretically—that is a psychiatric joke. An old attendant of a mental institution in Germany was looking at the inmates with contempt, in fact, with disgust. He shook his head, pointed to the shuffling unfortunates in his care, and said with increasing disdain:

"Look at them! Who wants to take care of them? Such people! They're not what they used to be. In the old days . . ." His eyes lit up, and his voice softened with nostalgia, "in the old days, we had Bismarcks, Napoleons—we had *schizophrenics* then."

But be this as it may, Ty Cobb remains as something phenomenal and utterly extraordinary in the history of baseball. He would have established many records whatever the kind of ball was in use in his day. He had the natural equipment, the instinct, or intuition, the head, the daring and the interest to be what he was—a ball player of untold greatness. By 1911 when I was first learning about baseball, Cobb was 24, going on 25. He had by then become not only a baseball legend: he was an American legend of his era. It was a time when there were many great and near great ball players, Honus Wagner, Napoleon Lajoie, Tris Speaker, Wahoo Sam Crawford, Eddie Collins. But fans saw Cobb as apart as later they were to see Babe Ruth. It seemed that he had always existed and always would. This is one of the features often to be noted in legends about a living man. It was not that he dominated the game as much as that he seemed to personify baseball as it was then played. He was a big drawing card, comparable in that time to Ruth a decade or a decade and a half later.

"I think I'll go out to the ball park and see what Ty will do."

This and similar remarks were common. In batting practice, to some extent in fielding practice, he was watched. When the game started, many of the fans were interested in him separately, in addition to the game. He was for thousands, and still remains, the most exciting ball player they have ever seen on a major-league ball field. He was as exciting to those who booed him as to those who cheered. Many who went to watch him play did so with the hope that he would be humiliated. He generated antagonism as well as admiration, antagonism in a sense and to a degree that other great players, including Rogers Hornsby did not, and that Babe Ruth most certainly never did. Cobb has often been accused of dirty play, and there are many stories about him, among them the tale that he would sit in the dugout sharpening his spikes in view of the opposing team. These stories could be true, or partly so. But, it was not merely because of any such alleged actions that he generated antagonism. He showed temper and temperament on the ball field. From the stands he often looked like a "sore head" and I have heard many fans chant these words at him in derision. But the antagonism against him was stimulated by his superiority, his ability, his kind of baseball brilliance.

There are great ball players who are mechanically perfect, who do everything well and show their unmistakable abilities. There are others like Cobb. Cobb played with his full potential and you always sensed that. He gave himself to the game, and with a baseball intelligence that matched his daring. He may or may not himself been inwardly tense when at bat or on the bases: he made the opposing team tense and he conveyed a sense of tension to the spectators. Once he came to bat or got on base, many of the fans would appear to feel that they could not relax or take their eyes off him. If they did they might miss something. And it is almost needless to add that a defensive team could not relax with Cobb at bat or on the bases. If he could inch himself off base a few extra inches or another foot, he would be on his way and hitting the dirt to safety with his famous hook slide. If a first baseman was slow or absent-minded about the ball on an infield out and Cobb were on first, he might take an extra base and go from first to third. I recall a game in 1917 when Cobb was on first base. A throw got by Chick Gandil and the ball rolled only to the edge of the diamond. Cobb scored. If a fielder were a few feet out of position, Cobb would hit the ball past him accordingly. If he caught a first baseman or third baseman coming in fast for an expected bunt, he would smash the ball past the fielder. Holding his hands apart at bat, bending his head forward, he stood there and hit the pitch according to circumstances, with a batting versatility probably unmatched in the whole history of baseball. A sports writer, I believe, gave to Wee Willie Keeler (who was before my time), the phrase, "I hit 'em where they ain't." Cobb could not only do that: he could get them to be where they ain't. In other words he could maneuver a fielder out of position.

Possibly, in fact undoubtedly, there were players in his time who could run faster than he in a straightaway race. But he had a knack of getting away, getting a jump. And this was one of the reasons why he was so exciting. There was the element of surprise in what he might do. Added to every other talent there was mind. He played with his mind, and this you felt as you watched him. We can say that there are many kinds of ball players, including great ones. But even among the great ball players, there is something partic- ular to say of Ty Cobb. He played with brilliance.

Everyone who saw him play often can remember some- thing spectacular, unusual, surprising which he did. I re- call a double-header in 1917. Five times he made base hits either on bunts or balls hit to the infielder. In the ninth in- ning of the second game, he came to bat and parked the ball in the right-field bleachers of Comiskey Park, tying the score. That I did not like. The White Sox were in a pennant fight. But in the last of the ninth, Joe Jackson put the game on ice by hitting a ball into the same bleachers. On July 31, 1910, I saw Ty Cobb pull one of his most remarkable feats but I did not know it. I read about it in the Congressional Library in Washington years later when I was doing some research in old copies of the *Chicago Daily Tribune* on a different matter. Going through the back issues I also looked at the sports section out of sheer force of habit. The accounts of forgotten ball games played by the White Sox and Chicago Cubs held me, not only because it brought back memories of Tinker, Evers, Chance, Fred Schulte, Ed Walsh and Doc White, but also because many of these reports were written by Ring Lardner. Some of his stories were among the best accounts of ball games which I ever read.

I remembered being taken to a game by my father, along with my older brother, Earl; I was then five, going on six.

But I knew nothing about baseball then. I was a year away from being a fanatic fan. We sat in fifty-cent pavilion seats.

The game that day, between the Detroit Tigers and the Chicago White Sox, was the inaugural one at Comiskey Park, the then new home of the White Sox. When the park was built, there was a space left between the pavilion seats, and a picket fence was built in front of this space. The pickets were, however, far enough apart to permit an official baseball to bounce through them. With the bases full, Lee Tannehill came up to bat and slammed the ball over the head of the Tiger left fielder. The ball hit the ground and bounced through the picket fence for a grand slam. At the end of the inning, Cobb, playing center field for Detroit, took one quick look at the picket fence. He came up to bat in the Tigers' half of the next inning, and placed one over the head of the White Sox left fielder, Pat Dougherty, Sox outfielder, vainly tried to prevent the ball from going through a space in the picket fence, as Tannehill's had done. The latter's hit had tied the score. Cobb's won the game. This is a forgotten fact, which matches that of Babe Ruth calling his shot in the 1932 World Series. But if there is any one feat which reveals Cobb, the ball player, it is this one. It should be known more widely as one of the amazing and legendary feats of baseball. That was Ty Cobb.

During that particular series in Chicago, Cobb's play was sensational, and, as Ring Lardner, then a journeyman baseball writer, summed up the series by writing that it all would have been different if Ty would have stayed in Georgia. Baseball as a whole would have been different if Ty had stayed in Georgia and studied law. Averages, better fielding equipment, night games, more road trips, the lively ball and the whole shebang notwithstanding, it is rare that you see athletes like Ty Cobb. As a ball player, he was what the French call *quelque chose,* and on the ball field he had *je ne sais quoi.* It means the same in English—"I do not know what."

The Fans' "Inalienable" Right

Today's player seems equipped for sound. He picks up every murmur and whisper from the fan, turns it into his own personal vandetta, sometimes takes an ill-advised newspaper or magazine blast at his verbal tormentors, and then may possibly ask the management to send him to quieter pastures. Times certainly have changed. Ask Pop, especially if he saw how McGraw or Frisch or Cobb reacted to vocal abuse that may have gone a trifle beyond "the fans' 'inalienable' right."

BACK in the 1955 season, Duke Snider, Dodger center fielder, blew his top and declared that the Brooklyn fans did not deserve a pennant. This was a brief sensation in the newspapers. Duke explained his hot-headed insult, and all was more or less forgiven. But Duke had a point. Whether or not the fans of Brooklyn or any other big-league town deserve a pennant, a few insults to the fans now and then will not hurt them, and possibly, it might not be bad for the gate. The fans are not the Deity, and they are often less than fair,

227

just, gentlemanly and chivalrous on all and every occasion. There are fans who go to ball games in order to hurl the most abusive insults at players. At times, fans will become like a mob and yell with the spirit of a mob. And do not forget that there have been occasions when players have been pelted and some could have been seriously injured and have had their careers ruined if they had been hit on the head by cans or other heavy objects thrown at them on the ball field. At times at least, bottles have not been sold in ball parks, for fear that some fans would hurl them at a visiting player and conk him.

Many fans are irrational in a ball park, and they will rumpus, sometimes even to the point of a near riot, over a decision which seems to have been justly and honestly called. But if a raw decision is called against the visiting team, they may even applaud it. There are fans who can even be seated behind a pillar but who will yell bloody murder and scream in what is usually called unprintable language in protest of a decision which they either did not see or saw badly and at too great a distance really to know what happened. During the 1934 World Series, the Detroit fans, in a whooping display of sportsmanship, littered the field and Ducky Medwick was removed from a ball game at the suggestion of Judge Landis for fear of injury to the Cardinal star or else of a riot. John McGraw was once reported to have been escorted by police from the ball park in Cincinnati lest he be mobbed. Everyone who has attended many ball games knows that the code of King Arthur's Court does not control the language, the manners and, occasionally, the conduct of every baseball fan of this nation.

Baseball is the national game. Sentimental togetherness can become a national hypocrisy. Because a man pays a few bucks to see a ball game, he does not become St. Francis of Assisi. Because he plunks his dough into the box office and

pushes through a turnstile, he does not become wise, toler-
ant, clear sighted and infallible. Even a box-seat ticket is not
a certificate that a man has been transformed into one of
those rare persons who are the pure of heart.

The Brooklyn fans have been celebrated in circulation
building news stories not only as baseball enthusiasts, but
as fanatics and the unfairness of some of them has been hailed
as one of the veritable virtues. In Milwaukee, the hottest
baseball town in America, you see many fans who will cheer
when a Brave hitter fouls off one, and will remain silent if
Duke Snider poles the ball out of the lot. Every baseball
crowd has its quota of rabid fans who are about as aware
of fair play as a beagle is of Einstein's special theory of rela-
tivity.

Many an aging player, yesterday's hero, has walked off a
ball field with stiff and weary legs or a tired, limp arm while
hearing boos and jeers. More than one star has been hooted
by a crowd and then only a year or two later to be traded to
the club favored by the hooters and then to become a hero.
Sal Maglie was not always the hero of Ebbets Field. And had
Jackie Robinson, while still good, been traded to Milwaukee
and had he helped spark them to a pennant, he would not
have been booed in the beer town as he so often was.

Of course, all this is not so important unless it is blown
up like a balloon to make headlines. Some ball games are
tense and exciting. Players and fans both become taut. The
nerves of both or either can snap. And for many fans, who
are otherwise estimable citizens, patriots, model and perhaps
even obedient husbands, the ball park is a place to let go.
There are fans who get a kick out of calling Ted Williams
a bum or who liked to call Ty Cobb what you and your
neighbor would not call your mother. And of course, the
umpire is fair game. If he weren't, then we could square the
circle. The freedom to bawl out the umpire is sometimes

described as one of our most vaunted freedoms. There are times when it almost seems as if the privilege of killing the umpire verbally is guaranteed in the Bill of Rights.

And the American baseball fan is not peculiar in these displays and outbursts of the higher gallantry. As a matter of fact, American baseball as well as other sporting crowds are close to the category of saints as compared with some sporting crowds abroad. If you are an Italian bicycle rider and you think you can win France's great bicycle race, the *Tour de France,* it will not do you any harm if, before the race, you take out accident insurance, and have your old mother light candles and say a novena for your safety. One year, an Italian racer was pelted with vegetables, but French sports writers pointed out that this wasn't so bad; only soft vegetables were thrown at him. National feelings can overcome sports audiences at international matches with the result that the *gendarmes* or the *flics* are urgently needed.

Baseball is always lauded because it is a competitive sport. It is high praise for a ball player to be described as "a great competitor." And it is accepted that anything a player can get away with is O.K. To throw spit balls is O.K. if you aren't caught. Fans often have the same attitude.

This is part of the spirit of the national game just as rigging votes and swiping ballot boxes was once almost standard political procedure. A long time ago before the spikes of Ty Cobb had flashed on any big-league diamond, the late William Randolph Hearst might have been elected mayor of New York if some of the votes cast for him would have been counted instead of fed to the fishes in the bay. But cheating in elections is different from throwing a spit ball or letting the umpire's mistakes go unmentioned, if it permits you to score the winning run. Actually, some of the unfairness of fans and even their abusiveness serves as a safety valve. It is undoubtedly true that more than one little missus escaped from having her teeth knocked out or her eyes punched black

and blue because her loving husband could go to a ball park
to insult Ty Cobb, or to describe the antecedents of some
other star or to render loud and negative judgments on the
morality of a pitcher who shut out the home team. Perhaps
many a clerk might have performed mayhem on his boss if
he hadn't been yelling this loyalty out of his system from
the bleachers.

Except for a student of the game, or a connoisseur of spec-
tacles, baseball is less fun unless the spectators take sides.
And how can they take sides and at the same time act like
nine justices of the Supreme Court in solemn session. It is all
part of the pattern, the tradition, the atmosphere, the spirit
of the game. It is reasonably controlled and policed. Many
fans are fickle. This is their right. But such a right is not
God-given. It does not carry with it the duty and obligation
that each and every player must at all times and under all
conditions, and regardless of provocation, act with the calm-
ness of a psychoanalyst who takes insults from a disturbed
patient on a couch at the rate of twenty to fifty smackers
per fifty-five minutes. After all, this is not precisely a situation where there is sauce for the goose and cyanide for the
gander. We sometimes go to prize fights to see a man
knocked cold. Spaniards go to bull fights to watch a bull get
tortured and stabbed into eternity or a roasting oven. The
Romans went to the Colosseum to watch a gladiator get
what the bull gets in Madrid. The fan sometimes goes to
the park not to be a gentleman but to be the exact opposite
of one. But the ball player signs a contract to play winning
ball if he can. There is not a reserve clause requiring him
to smile like a television M.C. or a vaudeville stooge every
time that every bleacherite screams untruths about his
mother's honor. In brief, he can be expected to kick back
now and again. A player is better off if he controls his disposition, but we would all be better off, at least by assumption,
if we were perfect.

So—it's all part of the game, the sport, the pastime, the business. But a baseball bat is not a harp. And Ted Williams may one day thrum a harp with Billy Sunday, but that is a future prospect. In the meantime, competition, excitement, the grand old sport is not a tranquilizer. It seems only proper if the fans can cuss out the players, now and then, it shouldn't hurt for a player to cuss back. However, the irate ball player who does becomes, for a day or so, something parallel to the fabled man who bites a dog.

And to conclude and repeat—this is all part of baseball; it is all part of sport and sporting crowds. It isn't likely to change. There are fans who go too far, and there are others who become over-excited. But the fans, *en masse,* all of them are not always right. Some fans like a ball player or the visiting Club the way some ball players like an umpire, and some of these ball players think of an umpire as some doctors do about undertakers. Ask your doctor what he thinks of morticians and you'll get clear on this whole situation. And perhaps eons hence there will be more love in the ball park than in some of the T.V. commercials and nevermore will the howling, hooting, jeering at the ball park be heard. The Bronx cheer will become the Bronx lullaby.

But until then the order of things in baseball will include the shrieking out of "You bum," the snarling demand to "Kill the umpire," as well as the unprintables.

Sic transit gloria.

It's Either Fun or Compulsion

Why do many of us love baseball? I have never been able to arrive at an answer to this question which is full and satisfying to myself. But in our liking for the game, there is both fun and compulsion.

SOME years ago, an intelligent and scientifically trained German Jewish boy wandered into Columbus Circle in New York City. He had but recently arrived in America from Hitler's Third Reich. There was a large crowd listening to an excited voice on the radio. He also saw policemen here and there. In the background, there were roars and cheers. The young fellow did not understand English very well. He did not know what was going on. But the people in Columbus Circle were also excited, and now and then they would burst into cheers. The young man was terrified.

His memories of Germany returned to him, painfully. There had been crowds and roaring cheers in Germany. The voice of the Fuehrer had come over the radio. He had heard the menacing and monotonous shouting of *"Sieg Heil!"* On

233

coming to America, he thought that he had escaped from this terror, because America is the land of the free. But now he wondered—was it the land of the free? How could it be free when a crowd like this gathered in a public square, and, while guarded by the police, listened to a speech by an American Fuehrer, perhaps from an open air stadium?

The young fellow became sick with despair. He felt trapped. There was no escape in this world. There was no hope. There was no haven of freedom. He wanted to run, but there was no place to run. If he should leave while the American Fuehrer was speaking, what would happen to him? The police might arrest him. He stood listening, petrified. But still, somehow this crowd did not seem to be either frightened or regimented. Men laughed, talked and even argued. What was all this? He kept wondering. He wanted to ask questions, but, held back by fear, his accent, his poor English, he hesitated for a long time. Finally, his curiosity overcame both his fear and his shyness. He asked what was going on.

"World Series."

What was World Series? For a moment, he was more confused than ever. But then, he began to get some inkling of what was happening. A sports match was being broadcast. Suddenly, he thrilled and experienced one of his first moments of great joy in the new land to which he had come as a refugee.

"Any country in which the people gather in crowds to hear the report of a baseball game instead of a speech by Hitler is a free country," he has since often said.

Then and there, he became a baseball fan, and today he is a New York Giants rooter. In fact, he claims absolutely to have in his possession the ball which Bobby Thomson hit for his famous home run in 1951.

This was how one young man became a fan. With most of us, it is obviously different. We grew up on baseball. In one of my novels, I have described America as a nation of frustrated baseball players. Baseball was a love and an enthusiasm of our boyhood, and in many instances, our continuing interest in and love of the game is a means of retaining something of our lost or departed boyhood. Without baseball, the world would be different for many of us. Our boyhood habit of turning first to the sports pages to read about baseball still persists. I realized this fact strongly when I was in Europe and Asia. Americans abroad often miss the opportunity of getting the baseball news. I recall how, in 1931, when I was living in Paris, I would go once a week, regularly, to the reading room of the *Chicago Daily Tribune*, near the opera on the Rue Scribe, to read all of the box scores. The Paris editions of the *New York Herald Tribune* and the *Chicago Daily Tribune* carried summaries of the baseball news, but this was not enough for me. I felt a need to follow the players more closely and to read the box scores.

While in Europe in 1938, I had a friend save all of the box scores for me, and on my return, read every one of them. Traveling through Italy by car, going to Istanbul, tramping the Negev in Israel, I would now and then wonder what was happening back home in the big leagues. In May, 1956, I was flying from Djakarta to Singapore. I had not seen an American newspaper in Australia and Indonesia for a couple of weeks. However, I was given one by the plane hostess. I immediately looked at the baseball news, and read a story that Carl Erskine had hurled a no-hit game.

In Cyprus, I sat at a hotel bar with Homer Bigart, of the *New York Times*, one of our very best foreign correspondents. At the bar there were Englishmen with guns in holsters strapped on. Soldiers patrolled the streets, walking along with rifles cocked. A barricade had been thrown up and in order to get through it, I had to walk along waving my American passport.

"You know," Homer said, as we sat down and before we

got to politics, "I come from Pittsburgh. I want to go home.
The Pirates are in first place and I want to see them play."

By the time he did get home, I might add, the Pirates
were back to normal, which means that they were far from
first place.

Baseball has become part of the accepted order of things
in America. If the game ever died out, there would be a
widespread feeling that a hole had been cut in the national
existence. And for a large majority of fans, of those who like
baseball, it is the game itself which counts. Other matters
are of secondary interest. The financial problems, the financial policies of ball clubs, the fact that it is a monopoly, cut
little ice with fans. For them, the game exists largely as a
thing in itself.

Likewise, much of the publicity now dished out about
baseball is taken less seriously than the publicity men of the
clubs appear to believe. I would venture that the vast majority of fans do not take too seriously the claims that baseball is an important means of solving the problems of juvenile
delinquency, or that baseball is one of the bulwarks of de-
mocracy. And I would further venture that fewer than is
imagined actually think of baseball players, and especially
stars, as great heroes in national life. To boys, this is frequently true. But to men, this notion of heroism is quite
often a more than dubious proposition. Fans enjoy watching
games, rooting, taking sides, shouting and releasing their
enthusiasms and aggressions. Also, they have the acquired
habits of interest. And since most of them had hoped in boyhood to become ball players themselves, they admire those
who have been able to do what they couldn't. They admire
the skill, ability and precision of players, talents which they
themselves lacked.

Baseball—and this also applies to other sports—is something which can be understood. The events of the political,
the economic, the social world are complicated, and often

full of dangerous or menacing import. These events cannot be easily understood without much reflection or study. The world is so complicated that one feels a strain in trying even to be moderately well-informed. And the effort to know about the real and threatening world of today produces anxiety and unsureness. The comprehensibility of baseball is in sharp contrast with so much of the incomprehensibility of the serious news of the day. This provides another motive for an interest in baseball. It is a distraction. It is a self-enclosed world of competition and action in which the emotions can have free play without the consequences being dangerous. The disappointment over the defeat of one's team is easier to take than most of life's disappointments, even in Brooklyn or Milwaukee. Even rabid fans manage to take defeat with relative ease, unless they lost money betting on the game. Baseball is, to use a phrase of William James, a means of having "a moral holiday." And we all need a "moral holiday." It need not be justified on any other grounds than the simple one that many of us like it. But curiously enough, William James failed to understand some of the psychological values of baseball. The late Dr. Morris R. Cohen, one of America's great philosophers and educators, and friend and student of William James, once wrote the following in an article titled "Baseball as a National Religion":

> "When my revered friend and teacher William James wrote an essay on 'A Moral Equivalent for War,' I suggested to him that baseball already embodied all the moral value of war, so far as war had any moral value. He listened sympathetically and was amused, but he did not take me seriously enough. All great men have their limitations, and William James's were due to the fact that he lived in Cambridge, a city which, in spite of the fact that it has a population of 100,000 souls (including the professors), is not represented in any baseball league that can be detected without a microscope."

Our liking of baseball is linked up with a past. As we sit in the stands, we think of other years, other games, other players. We feel a sense of continuity with that past. Baseball has become a history-minded game. Over the years, it has acquired much tradition. Intense or exciting games have passed over into the legendary side of baseball tradition. Babe Ruth's home run in the 1932 World Series, Grover Cleveland Alexander's famous strike-out of Tony Lazzeri, Tris Speaker going back for a fly ball, Merkle failing to touch second, Ty Cobb's feats, Honus Wagner, all this is now wrapped up both in baseball tradition and legend. And fans, every time they go to a ball game, hope that in some way, the game they are to see will be "a historic game," like Don Larsen's perfect no-hitter. Most of them grew up, as I did, hearing by word of mouth, the tales of historic games before their own time. They hope to acquire memories of "historic games" to match the ones they heard of but never saw.

This is all part of the attraction for and interest in the national sport.

Men have always been interested in sports. For boys and youths, sports constitute a challenge. The physical exhilaration, the sense of achievement in sports affords a sense of quite full satisfaction. The possession of skill or the chance to witness or watch others who possess that skill is a pleasure in itself. And baseball is a game in which many skills are called into play. Grace, speed, power, timing, judgment are all necessary. There are many examples of this even in a dull or lop-sided ball game. It was always pleasing, for instance, to watch Joe Di Maggio gather in a fly ball, no matter how close or how one-sided the game might have been. I could cite endless other examples, as could other sportswriters.

But we can boil all of this down to a simple sentence—we like baseball. We like the atmosphere of a ball park, the practice sessions, the warming up of the pitchers, the moment when the home team runs out onto the field for the first inning, the sound of the crack of the bat, the alternating moments of rest and action, the ball arching out to a fielder, or else lifting, rising and disappearing from sight as it goes out of the park, the thrill when a catcher receives a fast ball—briefly, we like baseball. And without rationalizing or devising arguments, we think that perhaps our national life might have been the poorer without it. No other sport is quite the same to many of us. Baseball is a lot of fun.

Gabby Hartnett

I have been told that Gabby Hartnett is doing well in his years of retirement. It is a pleasure to know this. Those of us kids or teen-agers from St. Cyril's (the school has been renamed Mount Carmel) were proud we met him under the circumstances I have recounted here. It is good to know that he has been elected to the Hall of Fame. At the same time, I regret that Marty Callaghan did not make it.

When they came up as rookies, they were just damned decent young players. And I have yet to meet anyone who knows Gabby Hartnett, who does not speak well of him.

GABBY HARTNETT and Marty Callaghan, an outfielder, came up to the Chicago Cubs the same season, 1922. Gabby hailed from around the same area of Massachusetts as my high school football coach, Harry Curran, one-time halfback of Massachusetts Aggies and a teammate of Paddy Driscoll on the Chicago Cardinals. Harry brought Gabby and Marty out to meet us one day during football practice. They seemed interested in us, very genial and friendly. They hung around, watched us go through our routines, and went back to the lockers when we changed. Today, they seem to me to have been something like kids themselves, even though they were older. The next spring, our baseball coach left to barnstorm with a team which included some of the Black Sox players. Harry Curran took over, and Gabby and Marty, on one of their off days, came out all of the way to the South Side to see us practice. Gabby, like a visiting fireman, took his coat off and hit out flies to us for a long time. He liked it. Gabby enjoyed being with kids like us. He was making no personal appearance on request or orders. It was fun. And, also, he and Marty seemed like lonesome rookies in the big city. We used to kid a bit with them but were not only respectful but proud to think that they cared to be with us.

The two rookies also came to a couple of our school affairs. This meant a long late ride on the elevated train back to the North Side. After one affair, we sat around talking.

"You're getting slivers in your tail sittin' on the bench," Gabby kidded Marty.

Marty spoke of the slivers Gabby was accumulating. They went on in this fashion and we lapped it up.

One night about eleven-thirty, I boarded an elevated train at the Jackson Park elevated station at Sixty-third Street and Stony Island Avenue. There was Gabby, wearing a brown suit, and seated alone. His face broke into a smile, the warm, open smile which was to make him very popular with so many baseball fans for two decades. I felt that he was a friend, but I also became a little brash as an adolescent boy will.

"I think I'll come out and see you lose one of these days, Gabby."

"Any time you want to see a game, Jim, let me know. I'll leave passes."

I accepted his kind offer and felt that I had been recognized by an important person. Gabby left two passes for me, but at that time, 1923, I did not know that it is customary always to leave two. I took no one with me.

The school year was ending. We were having a senior prom, the first one in the history of our school, St. Cyril. All of us seniors were trying to sell tickets. One evening when I read the box score, I was happy to see that Gabby had hit a home run in Philadelphia. I wrote him a letter, congratulating him on his homer and asking if he and Marty would come to our senior prom. They did. When I arrived with my date at the Cooper Carlton, now the Del Prado, I saw Gabby and Marty, standing there alone, unrecognized. They seemed shy—almost as shy as I was. Gabby slipped me a folded ten dollar bill for the dance tickets. He and Marty hung around, not much noticed, but quite pleased to be watching us kids, and for having done me this favor.

Some years later, in 1936, I had come to know Heywood Broun, who wrote a column. Heywood now and then used to urge me to write on sports. Thanks to his suggestion, I covered the first Schmeling-Louis fight for *The Nation*. I thought of following up Heywood's suggestion further. The Chicago Cubs came to town. I phoned Gabby at the Hotel Commodore, where the Cubs stayed, reminded him of his rookie days and asked to see him for an interview. The next morning before going to the Giants ball park, he waited for me in the lobby of the Commodore. Again, he happened to be wearing a brown suit, and he was as genial as he had been in his first year as Cub catcher.

My idea had been to write an article titled, "Gabby Hartnett Looks at Life." I explained that I wanted to get his views and attitudes on matters other than baseball; I wanted

to get a sense of how he looked at life. Gabby shook his
head and said that he knew about baseball but not about
anything else. He didn't want to talk of other matters. I
couldn't frame any questions to get answers. He would
shake his head. I know how to interview people but this was
my one journalistic flop.

Then we talked about baseball for twenty or thirty minutes in the Commodore Lobby; I asked him about Fred Lindstrom, who had left the Dodgers earlier in the season. He
remarked that Lindstrom was still a good ball player. Then
he left for the Polo Grounds. I haven't seen him since, except from the stands when he was on the ball field. But I
followed his career. He was active for twenty years and
ended up with a lifetime average of .298. Gabby has long
since been recognized as having been a great catcher, and
he has been elected to the Hall of Fame. With the Cubs, he
came after a succession of outstanding receivers, Johnny
Kling, Jimmy Archer, Roger Bresnahan (at the end of his
playing career), Bill Killefer and Bob O'Farrell. Gabby had
it on his predecessors as a slugger, but he was—as I remember him—a good receiver and he had a good arm. In
1929, however, he had trouble with his throwing arm, and
was used only as a pinch hitter. He came back strong in 1930
and it took a long time for him to wear out. He caught on
the best Cub teams since the days of Frank Chance. As the
years caught up on him, however, he was slow of foot, and
hit some of the longest singles ever made.

Today, I understand, Gabby is the proprietor of a prosperous bowling alley in Chicago and is a good tournament
bowler himself.

At Cooperstown, you look at the plaques and note or recall the records of the players honored. But they are either
names, as is Willie Keeler, or else players whom you saw on
the field and about whose personality you do not have any
clear idea. But the personalities of players is part of base-

ball, and baseball is part of the social history of America. Here is a small memory portrait of a great catcher who was kind and pleasant to me and others of my age.

As for Marty Callaghan, he did not make it, either with the Cubs or with the Cincinnati Reds. His is just one of so many thousand names to be found in old box scores.

What I Think of the Dodgers

The Dodgers have been one of the class teams in baseball. After the long and daffy years, the Brooklyn Club put together a great aggregation. As I write this, the Dodgers are still up there and in the National League it is said that the club to beat is the Dodgers. Baseball fans will long remember them. They are better than some fans realize. Never has a team been more wrongly named. The Dodgers, since the end of the last war, have been anything but "Bums."

WHEN Dale Mitchell joined the Brooklyn Dodgers during the 1956 season, he is reported to have sat on the Dodger bench game after game, marvelling as he watched Gil Hodges play first base. He was not accustomed to seeing this position played the way Hodges does. Hodges came to the Dodgers as a catcher, but the club then had Bruce Edwards, who was quickly displaced by Roy Campanella. Hodges has also played third base and has been put in the outfield. However, he has never played one big-league inning in the position at which he started his career—short-stop. Tommy Holmes called this fact to my attention and added that with Hodges' hands and his ability as well as his power, he would today be definitely headed for the Hall of Fame had he been able to play at short, his original position. But of course, Pee Wee Reese was the Dodger short-stop, and he performed for years with such class that he was almost deceptive. Pee Wee was even better than he looked because of his grace and skill.

As a first baseman, Gil Hodges might never make the Hall of Fame. He must buck strong competition from the past. The game has known great fielding and hitting first base-men like George Sisler and Bill Terry, and power hitting first sackers such as Lou Gehrig, Jimmy Foxx and Hank Green-berg. In addition, there was Hal Chase who would long since have been in the Hall of Fame but for the charges of crook-edness which hang over his memory. But how many great shortstops—besides Honus Wagner—have there been who were also power hitters? Like Tommy Holmes, I believe Hodges could have been a great shortstop and that had he been, his position and reputation in the game today would even be much higher than it is.

Also I see in this hypothetical story about Gil Hodges, a symbol suggestive of the baseball fate of the Brooklyn Dodgers of the post-World War II era. They have dominated the National League almost as authoritatively as the Yankees have in the American League. Only once have they finished third. No National League club has won as many pennants and has been as strong a contender for additional ones in any eleven-year period as were the Dodgers from 1946 to 1956. They have been one of the great ball clubs of modern base-ball and with this, another remarkable fact about them, is their longevity, the core of the team has remained largely the same for that period. But they also have been almost completely over-shadowed by the New York Yankees who, in this same period, took them five out of six times in world series competition. The Dodgers have been a team of pros, of first-class ball players, some of them great.

I have written of my memories about the Chicago White Sox of my boyhood. Many fans have not seen that team play. The aura of tradition hangs over them just as it does for me in the case of, say, Wee Willie Keeler, Addie Joss or Rube Waddell. But millions have seen the Dodgers of post-World War II play, either on the field or the television screen. Familiarity does not only breed contempt, it sometimes induces under-evaluation. And when a great ball club has lost so regularly in world series play, this can be especially true.

I recall Joe Jackson, Eddie Collins, Buck Weaver, Ray Schalk, Eddie Cicotte on the field; I also remember Ty Cobb, Tris Speaker, Wahoo Sam Crawford, Honus Wagner, Nap Lajoie, Walter Johnson, Grover Cleveland Alexander, Rogers Hornsby, Joe Wood and Babe Ruth. But all of these players hang in my memory through the depths of time. The years have made their skill, ability, and greatness a tradition. Without necessarily comparing the Dodgers of our time with these players, I would stress that some of us are too close to the team and that we sometimes do not see it and many of its players as we might, and as other fans of the future will.

Along with others of my generation, I remember plays, players in games of thirty and forty years ago. Babe Ruth, coming in as a relief pitcher, and striking out Joe Jackson and Happy Felsch with the bases full. Happy Felsch ranging center field. Buck Weaver playing third base. Joe Jackson's shoestring catch in the first game of the 1917 world series. Ty Cobb running the bases. Tris Speaker, not in the field, but at the plate with his easy, level swing. The way Harry Hooper covered right field and went back for a long fly ball. The mastery of Eddie Cicotte in the box and the even greater mastery of Alexander. The perfection and grace of George Sisler's all-around play. Hal Chase pouncing on a bunt.

Memories like these, of specific plays and of the way stars
of the gradually dimming past, are more interesting to us
than the records and statistics.

The Dodgers are still too contemporary to us to be remembered similarly. In time, this may change. For the team that
Branch Rickey built has been one of baseball's great teams
and besides the dominance it has asserted in its own league,
it has left a major chapter in the history of the game as its
own baseball legacy.

The Dodgers as a ball club have suffered not only the
stings of Yankee defeat but from the reputation of their
predecessors. During the days of Wilbert Robinson, the
Brooklyn club got the reputation of being "Dem Bums."
When they travel, the local sports pages tell the news that
the Bums are in town. In the 1920's and 1930's, there were
times when Brooklyn clubs or players came close to playing
picnic rather than major-league baseball. The tricks pulled,
the stunts and errors and mental mistakes, all made good
copy. Thus the Brooklyn team is the Bums and there are fans
even in Brooklyn, who are disappointed because the modern
Dodgers do not play as some of their predecessors have.
The sentiment and the cliches about the Dodgers of the
daffy days have pulled fans through the turnstiles and created Dodger rooters all over the nation. A first-class team,
one of the great teams of baseball, has thus become, in part,
a phony legend. Yet those interested in the psychology of
baseball teams and of world series play will puzzle and spec-
ulate on the question— Why did the Yankees take the Dodgers so often?

And also plays, players and games will stand out from the
fogs of memory. Pee Wee Reese at shortstop will probably
become a baseball legend. Duke Snider in center field will
be recalled. His judgment of fly balls, some of his catches
will stick out as memorable moments of years in Ebbets Field.
Or Carl Furillo. In the past or the present, how many men

have played right field as well as he? And Newcombe over-powering the batter on days when he was right? And then Billy Cox, who handled third base with such class. Some fielders are a pleasure to watch. Cox was one such. It seems to me perhaps important to remind fans of the quality and all-around ability the Dodgers teams have displayed.

A few words about Jackie Robinson are in order. Robinson was a menacing, threatening ball player. Pitchers on op-posing teams have admitted that when he got on base, they became nervous. He was at least reminiscent of Ty Cobb on the base paths. He was daring, alert and demonstrably out to beat the other team. He took baseball as a challenge and in turn, the challenge he accepted was flung at the opposing teams like a gauntlet. He made baseball history and, also social history, as the first colored player to become a big-leaguer. He carried his race and the future of many other colored boys and young men on his shoulders. This appeared to become a principle to him, and perhaps even brought out a messianic touch in his personality. Robinson, a great athlete and ball player, was not merely a rugged competitor as some players are: he was a principle. All players hear boos. Jackie heard many boos. In Milwaukee, when he came to bat the boos were as sure to come and as inevitable as taxes. Often, he played with fire inside of him. He was the kind of athlete you always watched on the diamond. Ball players like Jackie are very singular. They remind you even of the Greek athletes who competed on Mount Olympus.

Robinson, on and off the diamond, is known as a pop-off. Somehow, I see him differently. An intelligent man, he could have succeeded in many walks of life. Baseball gave him the road for a career and offered him the challenge he needed. He is popularly known as a temperamental man who blows his top easily and at the suggestion of provocation. Yet there are other traits in him. He has a very gentle and quiet side, and the potential for attaining serenity of spirit.

Before a night game in Cincinnati, I sat at a hotel table with him, and interviewed him. He smiled gently and spoke softly.

"You know," he said, "I don't know how to tell a lie."

I believed him and I think this is the explanation of his reputation for popping off. He seems to be aggressive rather than hostile. In the club house, he would sometimes seem a bit removed. Before a game, he would take fielding practice and then sometimes sit alone on the bench, looking out on the field. I watched him and would wonder—what was he thinking? He loved baseball and gave it everything he had but, also, he seemed to be looking beyond the game. Sometimes in moments of rough club house talk, he would be quiet. He did not seem quite to like it or to need to indulge in those outbursts of unprintable conversation which is common, not merely in a club house, but in any all-male group, especially one which works together. At other times, he would joke and smile. But there was a part of himself which he kept within his own spirit. It seemed to be his pride. The Dodgers are a proud team, but also modest. Jackie Robinson was one of the proudest of the Dodgers.

Age was a standard joke among Jackie, Pee Wee Reese and Campanella. Campanella was teased about his age and jokingly told that he is older then he would admit. Possibly there was more than mere joking behind this passing raillery. But Campanella is as different from Robinson as two men can be. Mostly he is jolly and after a defeat he remains even tempered. His jolliness sometimes lightens the depression of defeat. As is known, Campanella was a kind of tramp ball player in the Negro League. In winters, he migrated to Latin America. He earned his living as a player by working the year around and was often paid by the number of games in which he participated. Since joining the Dodgers, he has been like a man sitting on top of the best of all possible worlds. A religious man, he seems to have the faith that things will right themselves in time, perhaps in God's time. It was hard for him coming up and the player in the Negro League did not live and travel in the style of the major-leaguer. But now, he is up, and he is determined to stay there as long as possible. He is the kind of player who will almost have to have his uniform taken off him when he quits. Even when injured, he will go out and catch, perhaps remembering his salad days. To get past him at the plate, you'll have to cut him down. Catching and hitting, he talks a lot, even to himself, and was once described as the kind of catcher who will knock you down if you come at him at home base but then will pick you up, help you and brush you off. His importance to the team has been quite obvious. It goes better when Campanella has a good year. Like Jackie Robinson, he seems a fair certainty for the Hall of Fame. The two of them have been key players in these years of Dodger dominance.

Opinions about Walt Alston as a manager vary widely. He does not have a big press box reputation as a skipper. Alston batted once in the big league and struck out. He came up through the Dodger organization and took over a team of first-class professionals, who could virtually play their own game. Alston is a quiet man, somewhat shy. His strategy is conservative, and he plays the averages and out of the book. He is serious and studious about baseball, and while not talkative, he will always answer a question about why he made various moves or decisions. He speaks a trifle haltingly, but to the point and, particularly as compared with men like Stengel and Durocher, his words are colorless. He gives the impression of being a man who thinks a great deal about baseball, who plans, calculates, and plays for points. He is reported to be a fine bridge player and, at times, you think that he manages as a good bridge player might. He is not intuitive as Stengel is. He has demonstrated that while quiet, he can exert his authority.

One should not write about the Dodgers without mentioning Jake Pitler. During the 1956 world series, I saw Jake at the Hotel Bossert, Dodger headquarters in Brooklyn.

"Hello Mike," Jake said to me.

We spoke a few minutes and Jake then realized his slip on my name. When I mentioned I was writing a book on baseball and would include something about the Dodgers, he looked at me and said:

"Something—write the whole book about us."

Jake is from another baseball era and loves to say:

"I played with Honus Wagner."

"Yes, Jake, I saw you play," I remarked the first time he told me this.

"Don't tell 'em how I hit," Jake laughed.

He came up through the Dodger organization to become first-base coach and he is happy about how well he has fared in the game. Most of those with whom Jake played are out of baseball and many have passed away. But Jake is still in the game and loves it. He is the object of much good natured raillery in the club house and a common joke is Jake's brown bag of practice baseballs. Under Jake's care, the baseballs seem almost like little chicks he is guarding. He is a ball hawkshaw rather than a ball hawk. Try and steel one of Jake's baseballs. Once his bag was, I believe, pilfered and hidden on him, but that should be marked down as an achievement as though Sandy Koufax were to hit a home run. Jake has a gruff voice, and is a lobby sitter, always ready to talk baseball or to reminisce about the old timers.

In streaks, Ed Roebuck is a good relief pitcher. A young fellow, he is proud to be a big-leaguer and feels that the major leagues, and the Dodgers, have given him his big opportunity. At a hotel table on a road trip, I sat with Carl Erskine and a couple of other players.

"What was your proudest moment in baseball?" Roebuck asked Erskine.

While Carl Erskine thought, Roebuck said:
"Mine was when I put on the Dodger uniform."
A moment later he said:
"Think of it, by becoming a Dodger, I can sit at a table with Carl Erskine."

Roebuck raised the question of pitching to Stan Musial. Roebuck said he wouldn't like to pitch to Musial in a clutch with men on bases. The best thing to do under such circumstances would be to give Musial an intentional pass.

"No," Carl Erskine said. "It's a challenge to you. If you can pitch to him and get him out you've met that challenge."

Erskine, the club's player representative, takes baseball to heart although he seems to be less temperamental than many pitchers. Even in the club house after a bad defeat, he is easy to talk to. Carl is modest, intelligent and friendly. He doesn't smoke or drink or even curse. But he is not a prudish man. After a defeat or a bad start when he is taken out of the box, he might shake his head slowly and say:

"Gee, I'm sorry."

Wish him luck before a game and he says:

"Thank you."

Sometimes players are not easy to interview but Erskine is quite accessible. He is a very polite man, he likes to read books on early American history, and Carl Erskine is, in a good sense of the word, a gentleman.

Cheerful and popular, Rube Walker is a good receiver but his base running is a common subject of conversation.

"That guy," said a Dodger coach, "isn't as slow on the bases as he looks: he's slower."

He's a cheerful, considerate fellow. If you go out to see the Dodgers and visit the club house or wander about the field during the practice session, Rube is one of the players you always want to see. He is a man with much simple good nature and geniality.

Pee Wee Reese has been much written of and he has a

well-earned popularity. Duke Snider has an even greater
potential than his record. He worries himself as a hitter but
even despite his famous sound-off at the Brooklyn fans
during the 1956 season, Snider is a congenial type of person.
And there is Clem Labine. He once planned to be a history
teacher but baseball provided him with a more lucrative
profession. Labine could be an intellectual and has more than
a baseball head on his shoulders. He is alert and of the type
who could make his way well in other fields than baseball.
As a starter he had difficulty finishing, and the many newspaper statements about his not finishing games seemed to
be getting under his skin. Then he blossomed as a relief
pitcher. He is like the scenery at Ebbets Field, walking out
of the bullpen in the late innings and sniffing out the visiting
team.

One Dodger whose determination to be a ball player is
like a personal saga is Don Zimmer. A small, scrappy kid
who sticks a big wad of tobacco in his mouth, he cannot be
knocked down. He is a fighting ball player of the type who
seems like a throwback to the earlier days of the game. Baseball to Zimmer seems to be a way of life. Perhaps his size
has something to do with his determination and scrappiness,
but in baseball he is proving Don Zimmer. Courage he has
but he is more than an example of courage. He is the sort of
boy who might have grown up in one of my old Chicago
neighborhoods, played in Washington Park or Fuller Park,
and have fought his way right up to the top. Obviously, all
players are in the game for the money. Baseball is a business
as well as a sport. But in the case of Zimmer I sense something
more. When he gets hold of a pitch and lays it out of the ball
park, it seems as though he is saying:

"See, that's me—Don Zimmer."

Baseball is like the seams on his personality.

Here then are some of the Dodgers as I see them. Jake Pitler's advice could be taken. A book could be written about

them. Perhaps the same is true of any ball club. But the Dodgers have been one of the outstanding teams of this era. Fans and devotees of the game are history-minded and for them, the Dodgers should be a source of great curiosity and interest. Not as "Dem Bums," but as a ball club of class, they have provided much of the baseball drama and excitement of the present modern era of the game. They are not a roistering, brawling club off the field. They are well-behaved and their colorfulness is mainly to be seen in their play. Often, that is just about as good as baseball can be played. But they have been sensitive about their world series defeats. Their great year, of course, was 1955. Losing out in 1954 had cut their pride like a knife. The following year they ran away with the National League. But even when they were so far in front that there was no pennant race, a defeat could turn the club house into a morgue. They wanted to prove themselves in every way, and especially against the Yankees.

One day in the clubhouse during the 1955 season, I heard Carl Furillo burst out to himself, cursing in an expression of determination to beat the Yankees. He was angry, angry to win and to erase all notions that the Dodgers were a club that folds up.

There is an ancient Gaelic poem which speaks of the Gael who went forth to battle and who always fell. Except for 1955, this has been the tale of the Dodgers in their subway world series. And ironically, the helmsman of four of their defeats is an old Dodger, Casey Stengel, whose career led him to play and later to manage the Dodgers in the daffiness days of Brooklyn baseball history.

A legend is told of Castle Ross on the Lakes of Killarney. It was the last castle to fall to Cromwell's troops. The more lightly armored Irish maneuvered the attacking English in the bogs. The English couldn't take Castle Ross. But there was an ancient prophecy which foretold that Castle Ross would never fall to foreign foe until it was attacked by water. And there was a catch in the prophecy. For the Lakes of Killarney empty into Dingle Bay which is too shallow for seagoing men of war. But Cromwell's general, on hearing of the prophecy, retreated to Dingle Bay, mounted cannon on flatbottomed boats and floated them up to within range of Castle Ross, which, incidentally, belonged to the chieftain, the O'Donoghue. One cannon shot was fired, and the O'Donoghue, believing that the ancient prophecy had been fulfilled, surrendered without firing a shot. The analogy here, like all analogies, is not literally exact. But the general of Webb and Topping floated his cannon over to the foreign land of Brooklyn on a warm October day of 1956. The shots were fired, and the Clan of O'Malley lost its Castle Ross of baseball, the 1955 prize it had won. It seems as though Yankee dominance over the Dodgers had been foretold by prophecy. And what then is the catch in the prophecy? Where is the Dingle Bay of Brooklyn world championship hopes? This is, to me, an enigma of baseball. For, and to repeat, the Yankees are not five out of six better than the Dodgers. Or should I merely say that as far as the Clan of O'Malley goes, Casey Stengel classifies as just a left-handed Cromwellian Irishman?

This is the way I see the Dodgers. I like them. I'd be happy to see them take any team in baseball except the White Sox. But just as Gil Hodges became a great ball player, but not as a shortstop, so the Dodgers became a great ball club but in one of the eras of the Yankee dominance. And in this fact, I see the truly dramatic story of modern baseball. When today turns into the mists of the past, this story will become one of the most interesting chapters in the long story of baseball. Briefly, the Dodgers have been one of baseball's great teams.

From Washington Park to the Big Leagues

Thinking of the baseball career of Fred Lindstrom, I am prompted to say that there, but for
the grace of superior ability went I, and, also,
many of us. The story of Lindstrom as a player
speaks to me, tells me much of baseball and its
environment. This is an American story.

After I had written this account, I read in a
newspaper that Fred Lindstrom, Jr., had been
signed by the Chicago White Sox. Possibly the
name, Lindstrom, will again become a prominent
one in the sports pages.

But Fred Lindstrom is much remembered here
in New York. And it is my hope that "From
Washington Park to the Big Leagues" will give
the reader some sense, at least, of the quality of
Fred Lindstrom as a man and as the naturally
endowed ball player that he was.

Of the thousands of boys who played baseball
in Washington Park and dreamed or hoped to be

259

*discovered and to rise to the rank of a big league
star, Fred Lindstrom, to my knowledge, was the
only one who succeeded. In Lindstrom and his
life story, there is a touch, and element of many
of these boys.*

ONE day in 1920, I was in the Jackson Park ball field trying out for my own high school team, St. Cyril, which
has since been renamed Mount Carmel. On the diamond at
the other end of the long field, two public high school teams,
Hyde Park High School and Tilden Tech, were playing a
league game. The crowd standing around and watching kept
growing as park stragglers and pedestrians came to the sidelines, and among the odd group of high school students and
miscellaneous men there was a growing and even electrified
excitement. Playing shortstop for Tilden Tech was a fifteen-
year-old boy who still wore knee pants and long black stockings. This kid was making sensational plays and the crowd
was swelling not so much to see the game itself as to watch
him. We stopped practice and also watched.

The kid's name, I learned, was Lindstrom.

In 1921, a sandlot or park team named the Duquesnes
used to play on Sunday afternoons in Washington Park. I
sometimes saw their games. They wore gray uniforms,
trimmed in blue. I took an especial interest in them because
I knew some of the players, and had even played ball with
them. A few were my own age but far better as players than
I; others were older boys. I remember some of those who
played on the Duquesnes, boys who like myself loved baseball. Some of them dreamed as I did of becoming big-league
stars. The centerfielder on the Duquesnes was a thin boy
named Johnny Kleutch who batted right-handed and threw
lefty. He was one of the boys in Washington Park who was
considered as a future big-leaguer. Johnny was several years

ahead of me at my first grammar school, Corpus Christi. He and the older boys used to play with an indoor ball in the small Corpus Christi school yard. I, a little fellow in the first grade, used to stare at them, wishing they would let me play. One day I ran into the field and caught a line drive hit in a scrub game. I wanted to show off. The bigger boys laughed at my interruption and praised me. Johnny Kleutch also played indoor ball in a vacant lot at Fifty-first and Calumet Avenue and later, baseball in the big Washington Park ball field. In 1918, when there was daylight savings time, men used to go out and play scrub games after dinner. Usually, it was easy pitching and I often played in these games with Johnny. This continued for a few years. Another chap who played in this group was named Cook; he was a brother-in-law of Buck Weaver.

On summer mornings in 1919, there was still another group who played chose up sides and played easy pitching. Johnny Kleutch played with this group also. There was also a big husky blond boy from Corpus Christi named Dick Hurney who came out on these mornings. He played first base.

In 1916, I used to play indoor ball on the Washington Park playground. There was an older group of boys also, some of them tough. But one of the group who was not tough and who never teased, picked on or shoved around the younger and smaller kids like myself, was Earl Brignall. He had a brother my own age named Claude who was a fancy kid ice skater. Earl played third base.

And one day in 1916 when I lived at Fifty-seventh Street and Indiana, a new boy moved next door to us. He was husky, quiet, dark-haired and told me that his name was Paul O'Dea. I was able to get him on ball teams with which I played. He batted left-handed, and threw right. He immediately stood out, and at the age of about thirteen, could hold his own in games with seventeen and eighteen-year-old fellows. Everyone who knew Paul thought that he would

make the big leagues. He never did. I do not know if he
ever tried. I lost touch with him and he has been dead for
many years. But he also played on the Duquesnes.

I mention these boys I knew not only because they played
with Fred Lindstrom on the Duquesnes, but also because
they inhabited a boy's baseball world similar to my own and
to that of Lindstrom. In various ways a boy's world today is
different from what it was in my own boyhood. Today, a
seventeen-year-old boy being signed by a big league team is
not at all unusual. In the 1920's, it was startling. In the days
of my boyhood, there were no little leagues, and we did not
have much equipment. So it was with Fred Lindstrom.

He played at Thirty-first Street and Canal Street on a team
called the Stanneck Juniors. The name came from the owner
of a clothing store in his neighborhood who helped to buy
the team uniforms, this was fairly exceptional for a team of
boys. Spiked shoes were a dream beyond most boys. Fred
remembers making his own ball. It was more dead than one
provided by an opposing team. He went first to a parochial
and then to a public school, and would sell bottles in order
to get a quarter with which he could get a seat in the left-
field bleachers in Comiskey Park. The first player he used
to watch as a hero was Ping Bodie. The next was Shoeless
Joe Jackson. He remembers seeing the game which Jimmy
Ring pitched against the White Sox in the 1919 series. This
was the fourth game and Ring was opposed by Eddie Cicotte. The Reds won 2 to 0, and in that game Cicotte inter-
cepted a throw from Joe Jackson, one of the disputed and
much written of plays of the fixed series. I sat in the same
section of the bleachers that day.

After Lindstrom had made the Tilden Tech team while
still a kid in short pants, he transferred to Loyola Academy,
a Jesuit school on the North Side of Chicago. He played on
the Loyola team, along with two of the Washington Park
boys I have mentioned, Johnny Kleutch and Dick Hurney.

Johnny, and the manager of the Duquesnes were the ones who convinced him to join the Duquesnes. The team's manager was a picturesque ex-Army sergeant from my old neighborhood whose younger brother went to school with me. The old buck sergeant and Johnny visited Fred and convinced him to join their team. He agreed, but in order to do so he had to put up five dollars towards his uniform. Fred's brother loaned him the five. Years later when Fred's brother had a spell of hard luck and was out of bucks, Fred spent $500 to make a policeman out of him. He did this because he remembered the loan of that five for the Duquesnes.

Fred does not vividly recall much of that Washington Park team. He remembers one game when they were playing a tough Irish bunch. A fight broke out. The opposition chased the Duquesnes boys and they took refuge in a shelter at the north end of the Washington Park ball field. There, they were protected by the park cops. I might add that the boys—or teen-agers if you will—of this team were not a rough bunch. They were quite different from many boys I knew on the South Side of Chicago. They were quiet boys, mostly, well-liked, and usually managed to keep out of trouble. Of those I knew on the team, I do not recall ever seeing one of them in a fist fight. Fred remembers John Kleutch, Dick Hurney, and Earl Brignall, but not Paul O'Dea. He also recalls a pitcher on the team, McGraw, who pitched for the Loyola team. He recalls the manager, whom I'll name Jackie. For Jackie never did give him his share of the team's winnings. When they played, the Duquesnes and the opposing team chipped in to make up a pot which the winner took.

This all provides a few background facts about the boyhood and teen-age baseball life of a Washington Park boy who became not only a big-league player but one who was highly regarded by John McGraw and whom many believe to have been a truly great ball player. A Chicago boy from the South Side, he could easily have served as the model for a character in a story I might have written. As far as baseball goes, he achieved what many, many South Side boys whom I knew dreamed of—he became a big-leaguer.

His high-school coach, Jake Werner, recommended him to the New York Giants. Werner was an old ball player who never made the big leagues. In 1923, Lindstrom and his father—a plumber—met the New York Giants scout, Dick Kinsella, in a Chicago hotel—I believe it was the Auditorium. Kinsella offered Lindstrom a contract at $300 a month.

"What, you say you will pay my boy $300 a month, just to play ball?" The elder Lindstrom asked in astonishment.

Kinsella thought that Fred's father was bargaining and added that the New York Giants would also buy the boy's shoes.

"If you pay my boy $300 a month to play ball, then I can buy his shoes."

Lindstrom was sent to Toledo in the American Association in 1923. A number of us on the South Side who knew of him had heard the story that both he and Johnny Kleutch had been signed but that Johnny had grown homesick and left Toledo. This story is still believed in Chicago but it is not true. Fred was the only one of the boys he played with who made it.

In 1924, the boy who had been the sensational kid playing with Tilden Tech in Jackson Park and who was an infielder with the Duquesnes was playing third base in the World Series for the New York Giants, and his manager was John McGraw. Lindstrom was almost the hero of the Series, but the Giants lost. The winning Washington hit was an easy grounder to Lindstrom, but it hit a pebble and bounced over his head. During the regular 1924 season, his first in the National League, he played in fifty-two games, at either second or third base, and hit .253. But late in the season, the Giants regular third-baseman, Heinie Groh, had an injured knee. Taking over at third, Lindstrom played well. He was going good so McGraw kept him in as a regular during the Series.

Speaking of his first season with the Giants, Lindstrom remarked:

"How little those fellows did to help us take their jobs."

By "us" he means the rookies brought up with him. In this group were Bill Terry and Hack Wilson.

The Giants veterans were, he said, a close knit group of tough and hardened baseball veterans. The rookies in 1924 were given no help by the veterans. At the spring training camp in Florida and also during the regular season, the young players were ignored by the regulars, High Pockets Kelly, Irish Meusel, Heinie Groh, Pancho Snyder, Frank Frisch and others of the team. The youngsters always had to keep to themselves.

Fred Lindstrom's years in baseball were during a time when the game was in transition. It was the Babe Ruth rather than Ty Cobb age. But the game was still shaped by the players of the earlier era, and theirs had been a pretty hard and fighting baseball background. Lindstrom compares it with the present, and insists that the practice of dusting off the batter or throwing bean balls is now nothing to what it was in the 1920's.

"We had some mean pitchers in our league."

He named several.

"They'd test you out and throw right at your head."

He also spoke of the dangers of being beaned. "It isn't dangerous when you are stepping into the ball and it's a fast one. But this is different when you duck back and a curve, instead of breaking, hits you behind the ear."

Fred also told me of an incident involving himself and Carl Mays. Mays, a submarine pitcher, was with the Red Sox and Yankees and then ended up in the National League, first with the Cincinnati Reds and then, the New York Giants. As is known, it was a pitch of Mays in 1920 which resulted in the

death of Ray Chapman, Cleveland short stop. At the time
Ty Cobb and other players were reported in the press as
wanting to drive Mays out of baseball.

"He didn't want any friends. When he came to our club,
he told us— 'Don't think I want friends.'

"One day, he was pitching against us and he didn't like the
way the young college player, Farrell, was riding him from
our bench. When I came in from the field, I sat next to Farrell, and Mays thought it was me. When I came up to
bat . . ."

Fred paused and ran his right hand in front of his fore-
head.

"Right across my cap."

He shook his head to indicate how close the pitch was and
also added how Mays, with his underhanded delivery, could
throw the ball right at the batter, and was particularly
dangerous.

Fred turned to the Reds' catcher after this close call and
the latter said:

"He thinks you're riding him. He doesn't like what you
are sayin' to him from the bench."

"Tell him it isn't me. It's one of the other players," Fred
said.

After the game, Mays saw Lindstrom and they shook
hands. Mays explained that he'd thought it had been Fred
who had been riding him from the bench.

In a few years, the Giants had a new team and Lindstrom
and Bill Terry were stars. Fred says it was not quite the same
with the new rookies as it had been with him. Ball players
were beginning to change. Also of these years, the 1920's, he
said, "It was a breeze. Those were wonderful years."

I compared a few notes with him on Hoboken, New Jersey,
a place to go and drink beer in the 20's, and he also talked
of restaurants. We were, I might add, sitting in the gymnasium at Northwestern University in Evanston. Fred is Ath-

letic Director and baseball coach there. A few of his boys
were playing catch or hitting in the batting cage.

I had heard that McGraw liked him, especially because he
would talk back. He said that he only did this when he
thought he was right. To this day, several of the sports writers
close to the situation believe that Fred's rebelliousness
turned McGraw against him. One remarks that McGraw
often used to have Lindstrom to his home, and many believed that Lindstrom was destined to be McGraw's successor. In 1932, the year McGraw retired, there was a revolt of
the players against the fading old man. Lindstrom, the bold-
est and most outspoken among them, defended himself
against McGraw's insults, and because of this he became the
spokesman for players who dared not talk back to McGraw.
Frank Graham, in his book *McGraw of the Giants,* mentions
a few instances of the rift between the two men. Another
sports writer tells me that he now wishes he had warned
Lindstrom to be more careful and less outspoken. From the
respectful way in which Fred now talks of McGraw, as well
as from the observation of sports writers who knew the
Giants in the twenties, McGraw must have seemed like a
second father to the young Lindstrom, one whom he re-
spected and opposed. The accounts of his rebelliousness
seem very much like that of a son against his father.

He was always liked by the sports writers because he always told them the truth. In this, he was like Rogers Hornsby
although he and Hornsby never seemed to have warmed up
to one another. When I spoke to Fred and mentioned the
name of Hornsby, he was non-committal. The sports writers
spoke warmly and well of Fred. Some of them emphasized
that he was quite intelligent.

As a ball player, Fred was a beauty. He began as a shortstop. He played second base, then third, and then the outfield. He had natural ability galore and even when he was a
boy, that ability was unmistakable. As I have indicated ear-

lier his reputation became almost legendary on the South Side of Chicago before he had been signed up. He was not a power hitter but rather a natural hitter. He had an easy, graceful swing, and he looked great even if he happened to strike out. With the Giants he moved his feet a lot when place hitting, but this was on McGraw's orders. He was fast and could throw. With Pie Traynor and Joe Dugan, he was rated the best third baseman of his time. However, when Fred suffered a leg injury, McGraw shifted him to the outfield and put a mediocre performer, Johnny Vergez, at third. Rarely have I seen a more naturally gifted ball player. He played with great stars—Youngs, Frisch, Terry, Hornsby, Ott, Roush—and he belongs in the same category as they—that of greatness.

In 1925, he was in 104 games, playing 2B, SS, 3B and hit .287. He hit over .300 every year from 1926 on through to 1931 when he went .300 in 78 games. But that year, he had a broken leg. In 1928, Fred hit .358 and in 1930 he went up to .379 in 148 games. No right-handed hitter in the modern history of the National League has hit that high except Rogers Hornsby.

If anything, baseball and success in the game came too easily to Fred Lindstrom. He was just too damned good to have to serve a long apprenticeship. He stepped into the shoes of one of the best third basemen in baseball, Heinie Groh, and he kept those shoes. He was a great ball player in the 1920's, a period fantastic in American life. Waite Hoyt is reported to have said that it is wonderful to be young and a Yankee. In the baseball world it must have been pretty wonderful to have been young and a Giant when you were as good a ball player as Lindstrom was.

But this was the boy's undoing. As is known, he hoped to become John McGraw's successor. Much has been written in books about Fred and the fact that Bill Terry became the manager of the New York Giants when McGraw retired. I asked Fred about it in the Northwestern gymnasium on a raw March day. He was then gray, fifty-one and in good condition but a little plump. His disappointment was years behind him and he was no longer in organized baseball as such.

"I was never the same after it," he said immediately. "It almost wrecked me."

He claimed then as now that he had been promised the position as New York Giants manager. Back in 1931, he was told to wait a year. He had had trouble enough with his injury, his broken leg. Also he was asked to take a cut of $1,000 in salary, but it was explained that as manager he would earn more.

I mention this because one of the versions of the story runs as follows. On a spring training trip, Fred, Terry, Travis Jackson and one or two other players were supposed to have been in a hotel room having a drink. Both Lindstrom and Terry were then supposed to have begun talking about what they would do when they became manager of the Giants. Thus, according to the story, Fred discovered that he was not alone in having been promised the manager's position.

Fred says this story is not true. In 1932, Bill Terry was holding out and refused to take a cut. According to Frank Graham, there was bitterness in the early stages of Terry's holdout. As I mentioned, Lindstrom had taken a cut but he had been told, "You'll be manager in 1932." He says that the managership had been promised him by Stoneham and Jim Tierney, Secretary of the Club. McGraw had failed to sign Terry. At the St. Francis Hotel in San Francisco, Terry, Tierney and Lindstrom were in a room and Terry agreed to sign but did not take the cut. When Lindstrom went downstairs, he says that he told McGraw that Terry would sign. McGraw acceded. Lindstrom suggested that Terry had better be signed immediately. They met Terry at the far end of the lobby and he signed. Then they celebrated the signing.

There was bad feeling between McGraw and Tierney.

Also, and although Fred did not mention this it is believed that Tierney was responsible for Fred losing out as McGraw's successor. Be this as it may, the question here is one of fact and now, years later, calls for no bitterness or anger. Fred expected to be manager in 1932, but in early June of that year, he says that Bill Terry called him into McGraw's office and showed him the fiery old manager's letter of resignation. Then Fred learned that Terry and not he was to be the manager. But in telling his version of the story, he made no charges against Terry nor did he say Terry had worked against him. All of his references to Terry were objective and friendly.

But this much is clear. There was behind the scenes maneuvering, and for some time McGraw's job was a matter of discussion, ambition, planning and jockeying. It all could be the material of a play in which emotions in conflict are at work, a play in which a baseball king is about to be dethroned because of age and illness. After all, McGraw was called "the Little Napoleon." The fading out of McGraw was a big event in baseball: it was one of those events which dateline the end of many things. It possessed the character of tragedy, and moved many of a generation. Something of the significance of the baseball end of John McGraw can be suggested by the letter Ring Lardner sent the old and retired manager. Donald Elder prints it in full in his biography, *Ring Lardner:*
I quote:

> Doctors Hospital
> New York City
> June 4, 1932

Dear John:
    This is just to say that I'm terribly sorry to hear of your resignation as manager and of the serious nature of the illness that caused it. Baseball hasn't

meant much to me since the introduction of the TNT ball that robbed the game of the features I used to like best—features that gave you and Bill Carrigan and Fielder Jones and other really intelligent managers a deserved advantage, and smart ball players like Cobb and Jim Sheckard a chance to do things.

You and Bill Gleason and Eddie Collins were among the few men left who personified what I enjoyed in "the national pastime." Moreover your retirement has ruined my hope of a resumption of amusing (to me) relations with Frank Belcher when, and if, I am ever physically and financially able to go into the Lambs clubhouse again. Two or three years ago, when the Giants lost a game or a series, I used to torture him by saying that it was due to bad management. When I had him on the verge of tears, I would "break down and confess" that I was kidding and that I really considered you the greatest of managers, and it was honestly pathetic to see him brighten up at my sudden change of front. If you ever had a loyal supporter, he was and is it.

Often I have wondered whether you ever enjoyed the feeling of security and comfort that must be a manager's when the reporters assigned to his club are "safe" and not pestiferous—a gang such as Chance and Jones and Jim Callahan were surrounded with for a few years in Chicago, and I don't say that just because I happen to be one of the gang. We had a rule, and lived up to it, that none of us would ever act as assistant managers, would be worthy of whatever confidence was reposed and would never ask, "Who's going to pitch tomorrow?" The result was mutually beneficial. We were kept

posted on whatever changes, deals and trades were
"in the air" and therefore knew what we were talking about when the trade or deal was put through
or called off. The managers referred to didn't wince
when they saw one of us approaching. They were
our friends and we were theirs. So far as I was concerned, Frank Chance knew that I was very close to
Schulte and lots of times when Schulte was not "be-
having," Chance would drop a hint to me, knowing
that I would warn Schulte, and I am positive I was
thus enabled to save Schulte money and Chance the
unpleasant task of fining and suspending him. . . . .

I do hope you get better soon and that eventually you get "back." I am lucky in that I have no
physical pain. My chief trouble is an increasing ha-
tred of work, and it happens that work is necessary.
Please remember me to Mrs. McGraw, or, as the in-
ternes would call her, Mrs. "McGror."

Sincerely,
Ring Lardner

To Fred, his own disappointment struck him as a betrayal.
"I must have been too immature to understand it," he told
me.

He could not understand this happening to him. In a sense,
he had been close to being a kind of glamour boy of baseball. Behind him were the gay 1920's, his years of success as
a great ball player and perhaps as something of a playboy.
At the end of that decade, there had been the 1930 season
in which he had hit .379. He was only 26 going on 27. Besides his success on the diamond, he had had fun, and had
met many types of people. Intelligent and living in a world
which seemed to have been made for him, he was no psy-
chologist. He appears then not to have been reflective. But

what successful and great ball player is at twenty-six? Today he is something of a reflective man.

And then in June, 1932, the breeze was over. He had a bad season in 1932, hitting only .274. He was traded to Pittsburgh and in 1933 hit .310. In 1934 with the Pirates he played in only 98 games and dropped to .290. And then at thirty he played with the Chicago Cubs. He was a hometown boy on a pennant-winning team. Playing at third and in the outfield in 90 games he hit .275. But he came alive late in the season when the Cubs put on a 21-game winning streak. In 1936, he was a Dodger. After a slow start, he seemed to be finding himself when he suddenly quit baseball. At the time, the Dodgers were a poor team, and it seemed apparent that the manager, Burleigh Grimes, could not last. Had Fred been patient and played out the season with Brooklyn, he well might have been Grimes' successor. This, at least, is the opinion of one of the writers who was then close to the Dodgers. However, Lindstrom clearly was broken by his disappointment. He quit, early in the season after appearing only in twenty-six games.

I mentioned above how writers recall him and his honesty with them. I spoke to Fred years later, and I sensed and felt this basic honesty of the man. Also, from the way he talked as a father and of what he said, almost in passing, of his mother. I believed that I could understand how his disappointment in not succeeding McGraw could have had a near shattering effect on him. In addition to his quick success, he appears to have lived in a world in which betrayals could not happen. And whatever all the facts may be, this disappointment struck him as betrayal. Perhaps his had been a dream world. It had been one in which things were easy and he had both realized and enjoyed his boyhood dreams. The story of Fred Lindstrom is one of when boyhood dreams come true. These dreams are one of the reasons why ball

parks are sometimes filled with spectators to this day. Fred
in this real life drama was admittedly shaken. And out of it
came an eventual development and growth.

There is a pathos about old-time ball players. In other sec-
tions of this diary I have given some impressions of old
timers. But Fred is now escaping some of this pathos, although privately he must have regrets. However, he has
found satisfactions, and enjoys his present connection with
baseball.

He spoke of his big disappointment further, and mentioned the late Mayor Frank Hague of Jersey City. Hague,
a friend of Lindstrom, told him that when political favors
were wanted, men went to Jersey City to get them, through
Hague of course. It was not sufficient to ask a favor, to get a
promise and to expect its fulfillment. After 1931, Hague explained to Lindstrom, Fred had gone home. He had been
given his promise and he expected to be manager. He had
not returned to New York in the winter and talked things
over as those wanting political help from Hague would do
in Jersey City. Nor had Lindstrom returned and politicked.
When something was wanted as much as Fred wanted to
become manager of the New York Giants it should have been
worked for. The final end of the drama then is that Fred has
developed and assimilated something of the kind of ruptur-
ing shock which he seemed totally unprepared to meet. It
hit him as though it had been a bean ball.

The first year after his retirement he felt a void when the
time for spring training came around. There were lonely
months. He tells the story of how, one day, he remarked to his
wife that he was going to the corner drugstore to use the telephone. She was surprised and asked why he didn't make his
call from home. Fred answered that he wanted to go and
check whether their telephone was in working order; he used
to get some thirty calls a day, and now no one phoned him. Although in his last years it was getting harder for him, he

missed the game. He had some property at Grayslake in Illinois and thought that he would be happy hunting and fishing. But inactivity was a relaxation, not a way of life. Then he worked in radio, managed Knoxville, and during the War, he was appointed Acting Postmaster in Evanston, Illinois, thanks to the intervention of the late Peter Carey, who had been sheriff of Cook County.

After the War, he secured his present position with Northwestern University. He likes it very much. It keeps him active, and he enjoys working with youth. Speaking of youths who want to play baseball, he always advises them to get an education first. Telling me of this, he spoke of old-time ball players. He mentioned Grover Cleveland Alexander, shaking his head regretfully. I asked him about batting against Alexander.

"He had that control. He'd fox you."

And he spoke of Hack Wilson with whom he broke in on the Giants. He had liked Wilson, and said that ball players generally had. But Wilson had drunk himself to death, as had Alexander.

I mentioned the story of how Andy High, now a Dodger scout, wanted to become a ball player. His father told him that he should first learn a trade. Andy did and then went into baseball. Lindstrom gives similar advice to boys. One of his sons, Chuck, has been signed by the White Sox. Lindstrom has pointed out to his son the advantages of an education even for baseball. Old ball players, he remarked, cannot get administrative posts in baseball now unless they have an education. This seems commonplace, but it has meaning to anyone who knows how crazy for baseball kids can get, or who has, say, seen them crowding to baseball schools in Florida, wanting only to play ball heedless of everything else. And it has meaning, if we think of the pathos of many old ball players. For as Fred learned, baseball is not a lifetime profession; it can only be played for a few short years, and with night baseball, the average span of a big league player's life is becoming even shorter.

Fred regards college coaching as a form of teaching. In his days he said that there was almost no teaching of baseball. And in explaining this and speaking of baseball coaching in college, he suddenly remarked on the verbal problems this involves. He paused now and again to find a word. He talked with clarity and used language well. He also remarked on his boys. They were being launched in life. This he feels is a job he has done well.

And hitting. He now thinks that much which is said of hitting is irrelevant and he does not pay attention to much of the talk about stance. Apparently he has changed his mind since his playing days.

"There are two principles of hitting. One is to see the ball meet the bat, if possible. The second is for your tail to move towards the ball. Look at Mel Ott . . ."

"And Heinie Groh," I said.

Groh had one of the most singular and peculiar stances of all hitters.

"But they all do these two things."

One of the pitchers who gave him much trouble was Tom Zachary. But he mentioned some others as rough, mean, tough pitchers, especially Burleigh Grimes and Dutch Ruether.

He is still in good shape and can run and hit with his college kids.

And this is part of his story, the story of an old ball player who was a boy like many boys I knew on that big South Side of Chicago. I hope this account of him will bring back to memory this graceful, gifted kid in a Giants uniform during the 1920's, an era which was unique in sports as it was in many other areas of American life.

Born in 1904 on the South Side of Chicago, James T. Farrell became an enthusiastic White Sox fan in his youth and remained an avid baseball fan until his death in 1979. Most remembered as a major voice in American realism and as the author of the Studs Lonigan trilogy, Farrell wrote extensively about baseball, incorporating the baseball- playing memories of his youth into his novels and composing essays that recaptured the legendary heroes of his boyhood and preserved his passionate love for the game.